1·95

£27. 50

State and Ideology in the Middle East and Pakistan

State and Ideology in the Middle East and Pakistan

Edited by
Fred Halliday
and
Hamza Alavi

MACMILLAN
EDUCATION

First published 1988

Published by
MACMILLAN EDUCATION LTD
Houndmills, Basingstoke, Hampshire RG21 2XS
and London
Companies and representatives
throughout the world

Printed in Hong Kong

British Library Cataloguing in Publication Data
State and ideology in the Middle East and
Pakistan.
1. Middle East—Social conditions
2. Ideology
I. Halliday, Fred   II. Alavi, Hamza
306′.42′0956   HN656.A8
ISBN 0–333–38307–9 (hardcover)
ISBN 0–333–38308–7 (paperback)

Contents

v

Acknowledgements

The editors and publishers are grateful to *MERIP Reports* for permission to reprint Hanna Batatu's 'Syria's Muslim Brethren' and the *Journal of International Affairs* for permission to print a revised version of Fred Halliday's 'The Iranian Revolution: Religious Populism and Uneven Development'.

Notes on the Contributors

Hamza Alavi is Professor in the Graduate School of International Studies, University of Denver. A former governor of the Bank of Pakistan, he has written studies on the theory of the post-colonial state, the military and bureaucracy in Pakistan, and peasant movements.

Marie-Christine Aulas has conducted research in Egypt and Lebanon, and is the author of several studies on contemporary society and politics in these countries. She is based in Paris and is a contributing editor to *MERIP Middle East Reports*.

Hanna Batatu is Professor of Arab Studies at Georgetown University. He is the author of *The Old Social Classes and the Revolutionary Movements of Iraq*.

Michael Gilsenan is Khalid bin Abdullah al Saud Professor for the Study of the Contemporary Arab World at Oxford University. He is the author of *Saint and Sufi in Modern Egypt* and *Recognizing Islam*.

Fred Halliday is Professor of International Relations at the London School of Economics. His books include *Arabia without Sultans, Iran: Dictatorship and Development* and, with Maxine Molyneux, *The Ethiopian Revolution*. He is a contributing editor to *MERIP Middle East Reports*.

Nikkie Keddie is Professor of History at the University of California, Los Angeles, and the author and editor of more than ten books on modern Iran and the Middle East. These include, *Religion and Rebellion in Iran: The Tobacco Protest of 1891–1892* and *Roots of Revolution: An Interpretive History of Modern Iran*.

Caglar Keyder taught at METU (Ankara) for several years. He has published books and articles on the economic history, agrarian conditions and political economy of Turkey. He now teaches in the Department of Sociology, State University of New York, Binghampton.

Teodor Shanin is Professor of Sociology at the University of Manchester. His books include *Peasants and Peasant Societies, The Awkward Class, Late Marx and the Russian Road, Russia as a 'Developing Society'*.

1 Introduction

FRED HALLIDAY AND HAMZA ALAVI

This is a book about ideologies and their relation to state power on the one hand and social classes on the other. It presents a comparative set of analyses of developing countries, covering Pakistan and the major states of the Middle East, and begins with a comparative survey of conditions under which Islamic political movements do, and do not, develop, before proceeding to a set of individual studies. Some of these chapters concern Arab countries (Syria, Egypt), others countries that are Muslim but not Arab (Iran, Pakistan and Turkey), and one focuses upon Israel. While written from distinct positions, and with a variety of concrete objects of analysis, the materials in this volume are convergent in their identification of key problems in the societies in question, and in the search for a theoretical framework through which a better understanding of them can be developed.

Study of this area is to-day conducted under the impact of two challenges. One is specific to, and produced within, the region itself, namely the rise of new contestant ideologies and movements and the apparent inability of the established state and authority systems to maintain their control over their respective populations. The 1979 revolution in Iran was the most remarkable of the challenges to state power in recent years, but the phenomenon of contestation and of ideological conflict is wider than Iran itself. It can be seen in Egypt, Lebanon, Turkey, and Pakistan. Much of the literature on these changes has, in our view, conceded too much to the autonomy of religious beliefs, abstracting social movements and changes in religious doctrine and interpretation from the broader social context within which they have occurred. It has treated 'Islam' in an essentialist way as a reified force that

1

denotes a common social phenomenon, and a common set of beliefs, one which transcends different societies and distinct historical epochs. This is, of course, the approach favoured by many Muslims, but it cannot, for analytic purposes, be the most appropriate way in which to treat these phenomena. A similarly essentialist and ahistorical view of 'Zionism' is also common amongst its proponents and, in contrary form, amongst its enemies.

The second challenge is theoretical. The prevailing and competitive theories of social and political change in the Third World represented by the poles of 'modernisation theory' and 'dependency theory', with many variants in between, have both been submitted to substantial empirical and theoretical critique since their crystallisation in the 1960s. Both can provide an explanation of recent events in the Third World – the rise to power of civil and military bureaucracies, and the Iranian revolution, to name but two: but they are not now as confidently espoused by their supporters as was earlier the case. In general, the theoretical field of development is in a state of some disarray, without even a professional consensus on such basic questions as the value of foreign aid or of appropriate agrarian policies, let alone an agreed historical explanation of why there exist such asymmetries of wealth and power in the contemporary world.[1] In the case of the Middle East, this general crisis of development theory has been compounded by the debate around 'orientalism', the thesis that Western writing has been distorting because it has been part of a hegemonic and exploitative project.[2]

There are no ready answers to these theoretical challenges, nor to the specific questions of interpretation posed by the histories and character of individual societies. We do, none the less, see this book as part of a broader reconceptualisation in the field of development, in an attempt to suggest approaches and examples that may be of relevance beyond the cases in question. A common theoretical framework for developing countries is, in our view, a valid intellectual goal, provided that it eschews both the more deterministic temptations of dependency theory, and a simplifying comparativism that suppresses the distinctive characters of developing countries. Such a theoretical approach, while rejecting modernisation theory, would not entail either an absolute abandonment of 'Western' social concepts, or automatic acceptance of conceptions suggested by the experience and writings of oppressed peoples themselves. Some of the easier escapes suggested by critics of 'orientalism' may themselves prove to be incarcerating, because they reflect national or other local values. An approach that identifies clearly structures of domination at both the national, and international, levels, and which rejects the oppressive implications of modernisation theory, may be of more relevance, both to a critique of dominant ideologies and to an understanding of social forces, and intellectual and political movements, resisting such domination.

Four general themes underlie the studies in this book and provide, in our view, a basis for developing a broader, comparative, theoretical framework. The first is recognition of the degree to which these societies have been incorporated into the international capitalist system, both politically and economically. As a result of their incorporation into the capitalist market, one long dominated by colonialism and its political system, the pre-existing, 'traditional', that is, pre-capitalist, social and economic systems of these countries have been replaced, by radically new systems and relations. The very distribution of territory of post-colonial states is a result of such a process, as is the manner in which these states were founded. One of these states, Israel, was established through a process of colonisation; others, such as Syria, Egypt and Pakistan, are the result of the formation of states on the basis of colonial legacies. The classes that ruled these countries were formed by colonialism. The political, economic and cultural tensions within these societies, and the conflicting alliances in which they find themselves, all reflect this continued and changing incorporation within a world system dominated by Western capitalism. While the ideologies of power and opposition found in these societies are, in the first instance, concerned with internal, domestic, conflict, the issue of external relations and of the role of external forces is always central and forms a vivid part of the world view that sustains such movements.

The second general theme is that of state formation, in the colonial and post-colonial periods. While states existed in pre-colonial societies, with identifiable territories and administrative apparatuses, controlling personnel and recognised powers, the state system as it exists today in these societies is a product of the colonial period, and of the reaction to it by indigenous social classes. This kind of post-colonial state has been evident in Pakistan as in Syria, and to a considerable degree, through the grafting on to it of previously distinct Zionist enterprises, in Israel. In countries such as Turkey and Iran that escaped colonial rule, new states systems were established in the post-First World War period by new military regimes and were encapsulated within world capitalism, even when they sought to emulate the imperial world and so preserve their domains. The territories allocated to those states by the colonial world have proved remarkably durable, the arbitrary and recent character of the divisions notwithstanding. Despite many calls for secession in the Third World, no breakup of a territorially continuous post-colonial state has taken place. The one case of a post-colonial secession that succeeded, Bangladesh, occurred precisely because the seceding area was geographically separated from its oppressor, Pakistan.

Within these post-colonial territories, new administrative entities have arisen, which have become the focus of contestation for power. The analyses that follow take up a series of questions relating to the internal dynamics of these states: the social groups that have sought power as a means of guaranteeing their interests in these states are remarkably similar, be they the military-bureaucratic establishment that heads the salariat in Pakistan, the military in Egypt, the urban educated in Turkey, the Zionist bureaucracy in Israel, and their counterpoint, those social forces that have developed in opposition to the state and have come to challenge it – with success, as in Iran, or in as yet unsuccessful but enduring hostility, as in Syria, and Egypt. A central concern of this book is analysis of the political projects of those with state power – be they industrialisation, national consolidation under certain forms of dominance, or secularisation – and the oppositions these hegemonic projects generate on social and ideological grounds.

One further observation may help to set these studies of state power in the context of current analysis of the Third World. While much of the literature of the past two decades has been, quite properly, concerned with the peasantry and rural change, the focus here will be on the urban social and political systems of the countries concerned. It is in the cities that the institutions of the new states have been situated, and where their employment effects have been the greatest. This is evident in the creation of a new educated salariat that is often the protagonist of nationalist and secular ideas, in the growth of urban working and semi-employed classes, and in the gradual erosion of pre-established trading groups. If the countryside has been the site of some of the most momentous conflicts of the modern Third World, and if rural conditions are, directly or indirectly, of immense importance for development in all societies, it is none the less in the cities that the decisive political consolidations and confrontations of many of these countries discussed here have been located. The cities are not only the locus of state power but, increasingly, of opposition to it.

Vital to the project of states, and to any legitimation of power within them, are ideologies, the third major theme of this study. We use ideology in a broad sense, to denote sets of beliefs concerning social and political issues, which are both explanatory and normative, that is, which purport to explain *why* the world is as it is, *how* it came to be so, and what the *goals* of political action should be. Amongst the core questions which such ideologies address are: what constitutes the community to which the individual belongs (for example, is it religious, ethnic, territorial, linguistic and in what combination of these?); what are its legitimate boundaries; who is entitled to hold power, and who should be opposed; and, of abiding interest, who is responsible for its ill-fortune and should be suppressed within the country? In advanced capitalist societies the importance of values as social bonds and political legitimisers and as constituents of any stable system of authority has long been recognised by thinkers as diverse as Weber and Gramsci. In developing societies, where the very name, language and identity of the community may be a recent creation, where no previously recognised territory or political system may have existed, ideologies have an enhanced role as the articulators of uncertainty and of contesting demands, both internally and internationally, as well as serving to instil acceptance of new and apparently arbitrary political entities.

Some of the studies are concerned with the ideologies of domination, that is with sets of beliefs designed to legitimise and support new forms of state and state power: Kemalism in Turkey, so-called 'Islamic ideology' in Pakistan, Pahlavism in Iran, Baathism in Syria, Nasserism in Egypt, Zionism in Israel. That these are all recently formed sets of beliefs is irrelevant to estimating their success and the reasons for it. What determined their success, or the lack of it, was the degree to which they articulated with social movements and the skill and tenacity of those holding state power. Some, such as Pahlavism, failed in the end to maintain themselves. Others have been more gradually eroded by the advance, and partial incorporation into the state, of oppositional ideologies – this has been true for Turkey and Egypt. Those in power have also changed by responding to events and emphasising different aspects of the, necessarily inchoate, ideological whole: Zionism in Israel and Islam in Pakistan have evolved in this way. Other studies in this book are concerned with oppositional ideologies: the individual case studies of Iran, Egypt and Syria discuss social groups excluded from power[3], while the introductory chapter by Nikki Keddie analyses the Islamic world as a whole.

This variation in the role of ideologies points to the fourth general theme of this book, namely the contingency of ideologies. Against the essentialism of Islam, Zionism or other belief systems, the studies here stress that ideologies are contingent in two senses – their dependency upon social support and conjunctures, even if they are not necessarily the expression of any one group or specific conjuncture, and their flexibility or ductility, their ability to change meanings and political character in different circumstances.[4] The tendency to see ideologies as dominant and virtually autonomous of other areas of social existence is by no means specific to the study of the Middle East, although, as already mentioned, it takes the particular form there of the hypostatisation of 'Islam'. The primacy and autonomy of ideologies, of 'discourses' and belief systems, have indeed become common currency in much theoretical writing across a wide range of social sciences during the past decade. This tendency has been in part a response to a previously dominant socio-economic reductionism in both political and ideological analysis. The solution to the problem may, however, not lie in allotting primacy to the ideological domain, but rather in producing a more accurate and systematic conceptualisation of the interaction of the ideological with the socio-economic, and of the manner in which the latter can shape and influence the former, as well as of the ways in which ideologies may have an independent role in society. The upsurge in Islamic militancy has appeared at first to strengthen those emphasising the ideological and the autonomy and pervasive power of belief systems. But the analysis of the causes of this upsurge, and of the way Islamic states have handled political power and economic policy, suggests that social contingency has rather more important a part than at first appears. It is precisely this kind of approach that informs the studies in this book. In the case of Pakistan, the call for a Muslim state reflected a secular project by Indian Muslims, Islamic ideology being invoked by those in power only after the state was created. Khomeini's theory of Islamic government contained a challenge for state power in Iran, as well as a means of legitimising the maintenance of power once this had been attained. The Islamic oppositions in Syria and Egypt express the aspirations of social groups that deny the legitimacy of established power, which is in the hands of comparatively secular power blocs.

The contingency of ideologies is also evident in the second sense, that of variation. What specific terms or symbols mean is a contingent matter in the sense that it is decided by specific situations and political forces. Ideologies are not *infinitely* flexible: they do exclude some possibilities, but they are sufficiently ductile to allow very different interpretations and uses. Ideologies claim that they provide a firm, unchanging, answer to the major issues in question, and that others are to be disqualified on the grounds that they are deviants or deformers of ideological essence: those that are not 'true Muslims', or 'true Zionists', or 'true Turks'. But ideologies supposedly based on long-established bodies of texts, such as contemporary radical Islam and, in part, Zionism, or newly confected ones such as Nasserism and Ba'thism, allow of multiple interpretations and ambiguities, and permit many entailments. The diversity of Islamic movements reflects a diversity of social forces all using the Islamic texts as their legitimation, just as the variety of 'Islamic' governments – Iran, Pakistan and Saudi Arabia – reflects the degree to which different rulers – clergy, military and a tribal oligarchy – can turn sacred writ to their own secular ends.

Most recent writing has been tempted to see ideological conflict in the states of the Middle East and Muslim Asia as one between an alien secularising and 'modernising' trend, and a more religious and conservative tendency opposed to such changes. The analysis of this book will approach the secular–religious conflict as an internal competition, articulated by predominantly urban social groups within the society in question, over what the appropriate response to an externally-initiated transformation process should be. In this perspective, the secular is as rooted in the societies in question and in their history as the religious, and the religious is as innovative and contemporary a development as the secular.

8   *Introduction*

Notes

1. For more general discussion of these themes see Hamza Alavi and
   Teodor Shanin (eds), *Introduction to the Sociology of 'Developing
   Societies'* (London: Macmillan, 1983) and Talal Asad and Roger
   Owen (eds), *Sociology of 'Developing Societies': The Middle East*,
   (London: Macmillan, 1983).
2. On 'orientalism' see Edward Said, *Orientalism* (London, 1978); the
   critique by Sadik al-Azm in *Khamsin*, no. 8, (1981); and Said's
   'Orientalism Reconsidered', *Race and Class* (Autumn 1985).
3. An excellent survey of oppositional ideologies in the Middle East is
   given in *Forbidden Agendas, Intolerance and Defiance in the Middle
   East*, articles from the journal *Khamsin*, edited by Jon Rotschild
   (London: al-Saqi, 1984).
4. An outstanding and pioneering analysis of the contingency of ideologies is Sami Zubeida, 'The Ideological Conditions for Khomeini's
   Doctrine of Government', *Economy and Society*, vol. II, no. 1
   (May 1982).

2 Ideology, Society and the State in Post-Colonial Muslim Societies

NIKKI R. KEDDIE

This essay will deal analytically with the relations between state, society and ideology in certain post-colonial Muslim societies. The emphasis will be comparative, with the aim of using comparison to shed light on each society and on the differences and similarities among them. For the purposes of this discussion 'post-colonial' is taken to begin with the Ataturk and Reza Shah regimes in Turkey and Iran, when important political and economic breaks were made with Western power, and to begin with the achievement of independence from colonialism in the other countries discussed. Hence there is a gap of twenty-five years or more between the two categories.

Islam and secularism: the first phase

As others have noted, without sufficient effect, 'Islam' is not a concept that should be reified, but like other religions, it has varied with time, place, social class, ethnicity, gender, and other variables. The varieties of Islamic trends before colonial conquest or influence differed from what developed after, and both differed from what developed after independence. Pre-colonial Islamic trends, at least outside Saudi Arabia, differed greatly from what is preached by Islamist movements today. As a gross generalisation,

9

pre-colonial Islam stressed law and practices led by an ulama who
were normally in general alliance with their governments to maintain the status quo. Contrary to some writers, there was major
differentiation between the sphere of the ulama and that of rulers.
Most of the time, Islam tended to be conservative rather than
militant or exclusivist. With Western influence or conquest in the
late nineteenth and early twentieth centuries there grew up schools
of Islamic reformism, associated chiefly with the Young Ottomans,
Jamal ad-Din 'al-Afghani', Muhammad Abduh, Rashid Rida and
the Salafiya movement, and Syed Ahmad Khan. These trends
tried to make Islam compatible with many Western scientific,
economic, and political concepts in order to strengthen Islamic
countries against the West, and adapt Islam to the needs of
modern bourgeois society. In addition, there were other modernist
movements that stressed national rather than Islamic identity –
radical Iranian nationalism stressed by the freethinking nineteenth-
century Mirza Aqa Khan Kermani and the twentieth-century
Ahmad Kasravi; pan-Turanianism in pre-Ataturk Turkey, and
Arab nationalism, which had a special appeal for Christians and
other minorities. The nationalist movements were more secular
than Islamic ones, although Arab nationalists usually paid obeis-
ance to Muhammad and Islam, partly as Arab phenomena.

If one looks at popular movements in the period before the end
of colonial rule, as defined above, it seems clear that for the bazaar
class or petty bourgeoisie, and for the masses of the population,
Islam, without a particularly reformist content, remained a focus
of identity and aspirations. The Iranian revolution of 1905–11 was
fought by its popular leaders in the name of Islam and got much of
its power from support by some of the ulama. On his way to power
in 1921–5 Reza Khan was careful to court ulama support. Similarly
Ataturk fought his popular war of liberation in the name of Islam,
which is frequently invoked in his early speeches. In Egypt the
popular nationalist Mustafa Kamil successfully invoked traditional
Islamic practices, including veiling and seclusion, in his attacks on
the British, while his modernist opponents appealed to a more
restricted bourgeois group.

One may roughly say that in both the colonial and post-colonial
periods Islam of a fairly traditional kind continued to appeal to the
masses, to those of the bourgeoisie who were tied to the traditional
economy, and to the ulama, while modernism, nationalism, and

secularism had their greatest appeal among classes tied to the modern economy and state – the bourgeoisie and landed classes tied to the West, the new army and bureaucracy. In both cases ideas suited interests.

The post-colonial states, whose leaders wished to centralise power and to build a stronger economy, were logically moved to weaken the classes most identified with Islam, especially the ulama, and to establish what is often called secularism, although state control over religion would be a more accurate designation. This was not exclusively a post-colonial trend: already in the nineteenth century those states most influenced by the West, notably the Ottoman centre, Tunisia, and Egypt, had taken steps to weaken the power of the ulama. With Ataturk and Reza Shah, however, the steps were much more dramatic. Ataturk abolished the caliphate, outlawed the use of the Arabic alphabet, ended the religious school system, gave women equal legal rights, encouraged unveiling, and so forth. These steps were emulated by Reza Shah somewhat less radically, though it was he and not Ataturk who actually outlawed veiling, in 1936.

Both rulers encouraged an ethnic nationalism which had its roots in the past but now took new forms and strength. While Iranian nationalism had started as a radical idea, praising the pre-Islamic religious socialist Mazdak, Reza Shah and his son favoured a monarchist version, stressing great pre-Islamic kings – Cyrus, Darius, and the Sasanians. Existing anti-Arab feeling was encouraged so that most educated Iranians came to feel that the inferior Arabs had caused Iran's backwardness by imposing their religion and ways. The break between the bourgeois-nationalist culture of the elite and the Islamic culture of the masses and bazaar classes increased with time. Radical nationalism *à la* Kasravi remained a trend among the educated classes.

Ataturk and his followers encouraged an ethnic nationalism which lost nothing in force from the fact that it was based on shaky intellectual foundations. Ataturk's Turks in Turkey had to adjust to the loss of empire and to the idea, new to most of them, that 'Turks' were not just unlettered countryfolk, but a nationality with a proud history. Not having pre-Islamic glories of an Iranian kind, Ataturk and his followers substituted pure inventions – such as the idea that the Anatolian Hittites were Turks, and that Turkish was the root of all human languages. The 'artificiality' of these ideas

did not bring discontent or instability. Turkey, in fact, has had
several advantages in maintaining itself in the modern world.
Among these are its long history of Western contact and internal
reform; the unique role of Ataturk as *gazi* (significantly, an Islamic
term) – the hero who beat the foreigner-infidel in the post-First
World War fighting; and the relative homogeneity of modern
Turkey and its overwhelming Turkish-speaking Muslim identity.
For all the recent rise of Islamic counter-movements, Turkey
remains the most secular of Muslim states, and none of its secular
law codes has yet been repealed.

None the less, the masses, especially in rural areas and among
recent urban migrants, continue to identify strongly with Islam,
regarding the Muslim marriage rather than the civil one as important, for example. While opposition has arisen from both the
Marxist left and from Islamic movements, the latter appear to
have a wider appeal, and Islamic politics have had a growing
influence, both in the opposition and in the government.

The state-backed ideologies of Ataturk and Reza Shah, including strong national identification, identification with the leader, a
downplaying of traditional Islam and its leaders, new freedoms for
women, and stress on self-strengthening, were highly appropriate
to their building of a modern, centralised national state, complete
with new armies, bureaucracies, school systems, and so forth.
They were also appropriate to the state or state-backed capitalism
which encouraged the growth of factory industry and the end of
capitulations (tariff privileges and extra-territoriality for Western
countries). The partial liberation of women allowed them to enter
parts of the modern labour market as teachers, nurses, secretaries
and in certain other positions. Although Reza Shah was more
authoritarian and less lettered than Ataturk, and hence less popular with intellectuals, he had much more intellectual and professional support than later Iranian writers usually claim. While his
Iranian nationalist ideology was more 'natural' than Ataturk's
Turkish one, being based on several prior Iranian dynasties, it
was ultimately less successful among the people as a whole than
Ataturk's 'artificial' ideology, mainly because Iran was more backward and less integrated than Turkey and because Reza Shah
lacked Ataturk's past as a national hero. The Iranian ulama also
retained under Reza Shah powers that the Turkish ulama lost
under Ataturk or even before – the economic power given by their

direct collection of *zakat* and *khums* taxes (a Shi'a feature), more control over *vaqf* property and income, and more retention of Islamic schools and religious powers. Hence, the Iranian ulama, long more powerful than the ulama elsewhere in the Middle East, remained in a position to stage a comeback after Reza Shah was forced by Britain and Russia to abdicate in 1941.

The official ideologies of Reza Shah and Ataturk contained features already found in the Muslim modernists (rationalised and partly secularised Islam) and in early nationalists (stress on the national past and the superiority of one's own nation), but like other state or governmental ideologies they did not simply adopt intellectual systems from pre-existing intellectuals. Rather, those features of earlier systems of thought that were appropriate to the goals of the state were chosen, whether consciously or unconsciously. Both Islamic modernism and nationalism in fact borrowed heavily from Western liberal and nationalist thought systems. Modernism found new values in the Islamic past, just as less liberal Muslims are doing today. In the case of nationalism such values were found in the national past, and it was natural not to acknowledge a debt to the West, as each nation tried to convince itself of its own superiority.

What defines ideology

An important, and insufficiently studied, aspect of ideology is the question 'Who is the Enemy?' against whom a given ideology is chiefly directed. In a classic study of medieval Islamic ideologies, Claude Cahen has noted that the same intellectual movement may have had opposite social meanings according to who was the powerful enemy the movement opposed – and opposite-seeming ideological trends may similarly have allied social roles in relation to rulers with objectively similar roles but different ideologies.[1] In the post-war Muslim world the strength among intellectuals of Islamist ideologies is often in inverse proportion to its strength in ruling groups opposed by most intellectuals. Notably in Pakistan today, even though Islamic terminology is *de rigueur*, there are very few intellectuals with a really Islamist outlook, and this is largely because of the unpopularity of a government that calls itself Islamic. On the other hand, in Egypt, Tunisia, and pre-revolutionary

Iran Islamism is or was on the upswing, largely because the government opposed by intellectuals and others was or is largely secular, and also seen as subservient to the secular West.

The papers in this book mostly stress another important aspect of ideology, its class basis, which is crucial, but which does not in itself allow us to predict or understand what ideology will be followed by a given class at a given time and place. The petty-bourgeoisie, for example, is notorious for switching ideologies, yet these switches are not random, but reflect given situations. The petty bourgeoisie as well as what Alavi calls the'salariat' and also the big bourgeoisie tended to rally round nationalist, secularising, national unity ideologies when these were seen as the most effective way to overcome weak monarchies dependent on the West and backed by old land-owning and clerical classes, and to set up strong nation-states. This was the case in Pahlavi Iran, Ataturk's Turkey, and Nasser's Egypt. All three brought in significant reforms from the top, promoted private and/or state capitalism, and brought landlords and religious institutions under state control. As noted above, it is state control of religion rather than separation of church and state that constitutes what is often misleadingly called the 'secularism' of these regimes. Although Nasser's rule is with reason considered more radical and socialist than were Ataturk and the Pahlavis, the difference is smaller than rhetoric would suggest. The land reforms of the late Shah were as extensive as Nasser's, while Nasser's nationalisations did not result in permanent dispossession of the local bourgeoisie. What ties the Ataturk, Pahlavi, and Nasserist ideologies and movements together is their stress on national unity, on reform, on centralised bureaucratic controls, and on opposition to a prior weak monarchy that was complaisant to foreigners. The importance of overcoming weakness and foreign control while playing down internal class differences that might lead to internal strife brought forth totalistic and radical-sounding ideologies. The Islam faced by the three regimes, at least at the beginning of their rule and even later, found its representatives in an ulama who had ties to traditional ways and to traditional landlords (ulama were often large landlords themselves, or guardians of large landed *waqf* properties). A regime that wanted, as all three did, to expand secular education and a modern unified judicial system, and to introduce other modern institutions, would naturally want to control the ulama as much as possible. Nasser's ideology differs from the secular nationalism of Ataturk and the Pahlavis in stressing Arab unity, and even larger Islamic and African spheres, but as time went on Nasser had to fall back increasingly on Egyptian national conditions and interests.

The rise of Islamist movements in the Middle East, beginning especially in the 1960s and growing in the 1970s and 1980s, is not at all a traditional phenomenon or a return to the medieval, as some think, but is largely a reaction of dissatisfied groups and classes to the areas of failure of secular nationalism. As secular nationalism may be seen as a response to weak foreign-backed old regimes on the part especially of several educated classes, so Islamism is largely a reaction to successor nationalist regimes, like the three mentioned above. As Alavi's paper suggests, this is true even in Pakistan, whose founders were secularists, as was Zulfiqar Ali Bhutto, against whose secularising populist regime an Islamist movement broke out. In the case of Pakistan Islam has a special role as the *raison d'être* of the state and the only apparent glue holding together ethnic groups, but the country is, none the less, less unique than it may seem.

Reasons for the variable strength of Islamism

The term 'Islamism', which apparently originated in both Arabic and French in North Africa, and has begun to be used in English, is used in place of the inaccurate and resented 'fundamentalism' and the overly vague 'Islamic Revival' and the like. Although some dislike 'Islamism', it has the great practical value of being the term most acceptable to Muslims. 'Islamism' refers to twentieth-century movements for political Islam, usually aiming overtly or covertly at an Islamic state that would enforce at least some Islamic laws and customs, including those related to dress, sex segregation, and some economic measures and Qur'anic punishments. Outsiders and even insiders often have the impression of a trend sweeping the entire Muslim world, but my own extensive travels from Indonesia to Senegal in the summer of 1983 through late 1986 (three long summers plus all of 1985) do not support the view of Islamism as a major force everywhere. I here recount some of my experiences, impressions, and readings, all of which suggest that Islamism tends to be strong in certain specific circumstances, and weak in others.

To begin with, Islamism is not strong in states which are *really* largely traditional and have not experienced a major Western cultural impact, though such states are increasingly rare as Westernisation impinges almost everywhere. The people in such states may still follow a number of Islamic laws, but militant mass movements calling for an Islamic state and the end of Western influence are relatively small. The prime example of such a state in my travels was the Yemen Arab Republic (North Yemen), as of 1983, though Islamism has developed considerably since then. In North Yemen republicans overthrew a traditionalist Imam (leader of the Zaida Fiver Shi'a line) in 1962, and still had to fight for several years with Nasser's help against the Saudi-backed monarchists. The Imam of Yemen had tried to keep out Western influences, and though he was not wholly successful, he was largely so. Yemeni emigration to Saudi Arabia, the US, and elsewhere has brought in large remittances, so that Japanese cars, trucks, VCRs, video cameras, and so forth, are plentiful, but major elements of law and custom remain traditional and are considered Islamic. Law is a codified sharia; most women veil; and many are secluded in the home. Even within 'tradition' there are changes, as unveiled village women have been made to veil by their religious leaders once modern roads brought in strangers, and many urban women sport the top-to-toe black skirt, cape and face veil that used to be reserved by the Imam's family. Its rapid spread after the Imam's overthrow led it to be called 'the banner of the revolution'. The spread of such veiling differs from Islamism's conscious 're-turn to Islam'. The most 'modern' female costume, worn by students and some professional women, is called the *balto* (a word of Franco-Russo-Egyptian derivation). This is a long, unbelted raincoat worn over blue jeans, topped by a headscarf. When I was in Yemen, students were turning to this 'modern' dress, not to the veil. Yemen (as of 1983) had neither the large, alienated, educated class, nor the extensive break with traditional culture that would encourage a major Islamist movement, although elements of socio-economic change and the forced return of emigrant workers as a result of declines in oil production and world-wide recession may be bringing in a significant alienated class. It is not certain that under Yemeni conditions such a class would turn to Islamism, but could. Eye-witness reports in 1986 say that the Muslim Brethren have grown, encouraged by Egyptian teachers and intellectuals.

The profile of countries with strong Islamist movements nearly always includes the following. The country should have had one or more nationalist governments which tried to unify the country by relying more on national than Islamic ideology. It should have experienced rapid economic development and dislocations, which have brought rapid urbanisation and visibly differential treatment for the urban poor and the urban rich. Although not all such countries have oil income, virtually all have profited from oil economies at least at second hand, and oil income has hastened the urbanisation and income gaps, corruption, and visible wealth for the few that have made many responsive to the Islamists' call for equity, simplicity, and honesty. In addition, countries ripe for Islamism have experienced a longer and more radical break with an Islamically-orientated past government and society than is true of a country like Yemen. Most have experienced a heavy Western impact and control and Western and secularly orientated governments.

The above characteristics are derived from reading and observation, though naturally to generalise meaningfully one must be able to see which of the multiplicity of trends within each country would be likely to encourage Islamism. Since the generalisations were derived from experience, however, it is not surprising that they fit experience. Iran, for example, is a prime case of a country where the rulers tried to suppress Islamic and customary ways and laws, where a huge oil income allowed rapid economic change and over-rapid urbanisation, and where Western influence was acutely felt. Also, on the ideological level, Islamism was encouraged by the fact that the late Shah and his father actively suppressed Islamic ways and were thoroughly identified with Western, non-Islamic powers. Egypt is another country ripe for Islamist trends and movements, which have been growing. Although not an oil economy, Egypt in recent decades has been almost a *'rentier* state', living not on the production and export of goods, but on the export of workers and professionals, primarily to oil countries, and on foreign aid. Sadat was seen by many Egyptians in much the same way as the late Shah was by many Iranians – as an American-supported collaborator with Israel whose economic policies

benefited old and new elites while bypassing the needy. Mubarak
has tried to steer a more Arab-orientated course, but it is unclear if
this will help him solve Egypt's overwhelming economic problems,
especially in a period of worldwide oil slump and economic difficulties

The influence of moderate or radical Islamism in Egyptian cities
is striking to a visitor who had not been there between 1964 and
1985. While in 1964 very few women showed concern for Islamic
dress, now most do, although covering-up takes numerous forms.
It ranges from the top-to-toe gloved outfits of Islamist students, to
the modified look of calf-length skirts and long-sleeved, high-
necked blouses, with scarves worn tied behind the hair which is the
minimum costume. Even foreign residents often adopt the latter
dress as it generally keeps one from being hassled or annoyed.
Many women in Egypt and elsewhere defend Islamic dress by
saying that it keeps male co-workers from seeing and perceiving
them as sex-objects, which may be true, but I have yet to hear any
of them say that young men should be socialised not to harass girls
and women, even if they are not in 'Islamic dress'.

More dramatic has been the continuation of extremist Muslim
movements, some of which are discussed in Gilles Kepel's recent
book.[2] And even more threatening to some has been what many
call 'the unholy alliance' between recently permitted opposition
groups and parties – specifically the hitherto secular Wafd Party
and the Muslim Brethren, today the least militant of Egypt's
Islamist groups. A prominent scholar and member of Egypt's
Human Rights organisation assured me that the Muslim Brethren,
having seen how Human Rights groups defended them when they
were persecuted, are now convinced believers in human rights,
free speech, and the like. One may be permitted some scepticism,
as human rights are generally popular with persons who follow
totalistic ideologies when they are out of power, but are almost
never supported by them when in power.

Tunisia is a country with some features favouring Islamism,
especially the rule since 1956 of President Bourguiba and his
followers, who have enforced a secular, nationalist, and pro-
Western orientation. Some of the burden of flight from the countryside has been absorbed by emigration, usually conditional on
work, to places like Libya and France. With those countries now
making Tunisians leave, Tunisia faces new economic difficulties. A

series of riots and risings in recent years, aimed against a rise in bread prices or having more political goals, suggests that ferment may be as great in Tunisia as in Egypt. In this situation there have been various moves back from secularism somewhat reminiscent of the last years before Iran's Islamic Revolution. Like Egypt and pre-revolutionary Iran, Tunisia has several Islamically-orientated groups. The mildest is a small group of intellectuals, known as progressive Islamists, who put out a journal called *15/21* (fifteenth Muslim, twenty-first Christian century), oppose militant political activity, and favour an Islamic dialogue with Western and Christian thinkers. The most militant group is part of an international clandestine organisation, the Islamic Liberation Party, and its members have been arrested and blamed for assassinations of prominent figures. In between, and the most important, is the Islamic Tendency Movement, MTI, led by men with some Islamic training who have also had a Western-style education. Recently the MTI has stressed its moderate and democratic side in the hope, abortive thus far, of gaining a permit to publish legally and to be a political party. MTI leaders were arrested and jailed for a time, but then freed. Their published programme contains nothing illegal, and, as in Egypt, there are some secular Tunisian oppositionists who take the programme at face value and wish to work with the MTI. However, the vagueness of their leader's discourse when he describes the second, Islamic, phase that follows the democratic phase; the militance of the student followers of MTI who won control of the University of Tunis student union; and a secret document that has been published outlining their clandestine goals and tactics, indicate that democracy is just a way-station for the MTI.[3]

MTI leaders are clever in questioning government policies without putting forth Islamic alternatives that might be controversial. They call for a referendum to review Tunisia's reformist Personal Status Code, but do not say what they want in its place. Thus a male MTI leader could tell me that women have more rights than men under the code, while a young woman lawyer in the MTI said review was needed because the code is patriarchal and favours men!

As in many countries, Islamism of the MTI variety has an appeal for many young women. Meeting together they get mutual support and also learn how to argue articulately. They, like Islamist women elsewhere, wear a recognisable 'uniform'. In Tunisia they wear long dresses in plain colours, usually belted, and a large scarf, tied in front. They consider that this uniform shows that they are Islamic activists and also not open to sexual advances. Some girls actually gain freedom by becoming Islamists: they were formerly never allowed to go out alone, but now can go to mosques or meetings. Also, they can reject marriage partners chosen by their parents on the grounds that they are not sufficiently Islamic. These advantages also apply to many Islamist women outside Tunisia. It seems that Islamism can present a cultural alternative that many men and women do not find in school or in the official discourse, both of which are highly Western and secular. In this way Tunisia somewhat resembles pre-revolutionary Iran. Secular or feminist-orientated Tunisians have a discourse hardly distinguishable from Westerners, and know much more about Foucault or de Beauvoir than they do about Islamic thought, which in general is barely taught in the schools. This creates a gap between the Frenchified group with good secondary or higher education and the masses; in one way the gap is even greater in Tunisia than in Iran, as the educated group may speak French by preference, and often cannot deliver a talk in Arabic, while the masses generally know only Tunisian Arabic.

In both Tunisia and Egypt, it is important to remember that the Islamists are not the only opponents of the regime, and various secular groups and parties exist at different points of the left-right scale. Nevertheless, the Islamists can have a great appeal in an age of cultural and economic crisis, and so they should be taken seriously.

In my travels I spent brief periods in two countries where Islamism has a special point of appeal greater than in Tunisia and Egypt – namely, Nigeria (northern), and Malaysia. Both countries fit the 'Islamist' profile of oil-producing countries that have undergone rapid economic and social change and migration to cities, and both have also experienced nationalist governments. It appears to me that the main reason why Islamism is important in these countries is that in both Muslims make up a plurality (or a small majority in Nigeria) who have not been able thus far to impose their will as much as they wish on the large minority populations. In both countries the Muslim plurality is also relatively economically backward, and would like more economic favours to enable them to get ahead of the other communities. In Malaysia the two principal non-Muslim communities are the larger Chinese one and the smaller Indian one, and it has been noted that a Muslim immigrant from Indonesia will immediately be regarded as a native, while a fifth-generation Chinese will not. Although Malaysia's current government has favoured the mainly Muslim Malay community by a variety of economic concessions, this has not satisfied all of them. Early on the Muslims adopted a formula that would give them a fictitious majority; if they had called themselves Muslims, or even Malay-speakers, it would have been clear that they were not in a majority, so the term 'Bumiputra' ('sons of the soil') was adopted, which lumped together with its Malay-Muslim majority, 'natives' of island Malaysia who were neither Muslim nor Malay. The leading Islamist party, PAS, wishes to enforce the sharia in all Malaysia, which could hardly be more felicitous than it was in Sudan. When I was in Malaysia in 1984 PAS had referred to the ruling Muslims as unbelievers, and there was talk of a debate between PAS and the ruling party, though each side demanded different terms for a debate. There were also PAS-supported risings in 'backward' areas. The government was pleased to have brought some Islamic leaders into its fold, especially – as a minister – the leader of the Muslim Youth Movement, Anwar Ibrahim. This made it hard for PAS to monopolise Islamist sentiment. Government moves to incorporate Islamist leaders, and policies like Islamic banking and home loans, helped reduce PAS's appeal.

Women in Islamist dress were numerous in Malaysia in 1984, but the dress was a world away from that found in Iran. It was a form-fitting sarong and long-sleeved top, both generally in bright colors, and a kind of light cowl headdress, often fastened by jewellery. My Iranian ayatollah informants who noted that the whole point of Islamic dress was for women not to be noticed would not have been pleased, and one Malay specialist called it the dress of 'sexy nuns'. When I spoke to a women's group at one university I found a clear generation gap; scarcely any of the teachers or other middle-aged women wore Islamist dress, while all students did. The older women said that students were coerced by peer pressure into dressing and behaving in an Islamist way.

Malaysia has features that have reduced the appeal of oppositional Islamism, as demonstrated by the defeat of PAS in the 1986 elections. Besides the incorporation into the government of

Islamist leaders and policies (which may, however, have increased the Chinese opposition vote), the government is almost unique in allowing Islamists to have a legal party and contest elections. This made PAS pronouncements *appear* strong, but also allowed the government to gauge the opposition and counter its appeal. Malaysia is significant in showing the oppositional Islamists can be reduced. It is possible that legalising Islamist parties in some other countries might decrease, not increase, their appeal, although only if accompanied by policies to meet mass grievances.

The main comparative point is that Malaysia, like Nigeria, not only meets the general criteria of a country favouring Islamism, but has the added feature that the Islamist path is seen by many Muslims as a way to overcome their backwardness *vis-à-vis* other communities, and to forge ahead economically and politically. As elsewhere, questions about the rights and status of minorities are generally met with vague remarks about Islamic tolerance and the flourishing of minorities under Islamic rule.

Nigeria, like Malaysia, has had Muslim rulers for decades, but as in Malaysia, this is insufficient to satisfy Islamists. Nigeria with its population of about 95 million, about half Muslim, is by far the most populous state in Africa, with by far the most Muslims. Discussion of Nigerian Islamism is difficult, as there is not a single Islamist group, and Westerners often mix up a radical heretical group that was involved in urban risings in the early 1980s; radical Islamist and Khomeinist mainly student groups; and the old Muslim elite, including lawyers and judges, who have been calling for a return to sharia law. To an extent the last two are related, but the last one is in some measure more conservative and traditionalist than Islamist. Under the British protectorate, the sharia did have a larger role in Northern Nigeria, and so those who call for the application of the sharia are not far-out utopians necessarily – they may actually be calling for a return to a system under which they flourished more than they do now. What is newly powerful in the Islamist *Yan Izala* group is its 'Wahabi' attacks on the Sufi orders.[4] Also new is the movement to extend the sharia to the South, which is strongly resisted by southern non-Muslims.

Student radical Islam is another matter, and as in many countries Nigerian Islamists are strongest at the universities. Although Khomeini's Iran is the only popular model for many Islamists everywhere, the two places I travelled where Khoemini seemed most popular (not counting the Shi'a of Pakistan who have a sectarian identification with him but are not planning a Khomeinist revolt) were Northern Nigeria and Malaysia. One might guess that Khomeini's popularity increases with the square of the distance from Iran, but this, though it has some merit as an idea, would not account for his apparently lesser popularity in the more distant Senegal and Indonesia. Rather, I would guess that the same factor of economically and educationally backward communities that want to impose an Islamic state so as to put dominant economic and political power in Muslim hands operates in both. Among Nigerian radicals only Khomeini, I was told more than once, is considered a truly Islamic ruler, largely because of his radical Islamic rhetoric and programme and his revolutionary path to power. Islamist students were very angry at a talk I gave at a northern university in which I tried to show that Khomeini's Islamic revolution was not replicable elsewhere, as it was heavily based on the power and independence of Iran's Shi'i ulama, even though other Islamic revolutionary paths might be possible. Not only was I openly accused of being a CIA agent sent in to talk them out of revolution, but I was told that since they had not heard of Shi'ism until a few years ago, it must be an American invention to split the Muslims. (Such a reaction is not exclusive to Nigerian students – some of my Tunisian students in Paris in 1977 were suspicious of my mention of Arab Shi'a.)

In Northern Nigeria I had the privilege of being an observer at a three-day conference of Muslim women. This was one of many experiences that indicated that self-consciously Muslim women's groups and the behaviour they advocate are far from being the wholly negative phenomenon that Westerners often think. For in this gathering educated women Muslim leaders insisted that the large audience, mostly of college students, should insist on such rights as the right to be educated, the right to work and to carry out respectable activities outside the home. In an area where many women are secluded in the home and rarely can go out, this insistence was clearly one that would better the position of women. So too were rights in the family, where a pro-woman view of Islamic injunctions was presented. On the other hand, the leaders stressed that Muslim women should not join inter-faith organisations or follow their programme.

If Islamism is strong in Nigeria and Malaysia, it should be

realised that anti-Islamism is also very strong. The secular Muslims of these countries appreciate what tensions would be brought in along with Islamic laws and practices, especially if they were imposed by non-Muslims. So many Muslims and all non-Muslims oppose the Islamist programme, but economic and other difficulties may none the less increase Islamist strength. In Nigeria there have been controversial government moves early in 1986 to join an international Islamic organisation, which may have been aimed partly at appeasing Islamists, but alarmed secularists and non-Muslims.

Last, I shall deal with countries where Islamism is apparently not strong, even though, unlike North Yemen, they have moved far from traditional ways. One of these is Senegal, where the weakness of Islamism may be tied to the peculiar interaction of Islam and politics. Instead of having a single class of ulama, as in most Muslim countries, Senegal is still dominated by Islamic orders, especially the large and nearly equally strong Tijaniya and Muridiya (a local twentieth-century order). These orders offer support to politicians in return for patronage and favours, and they are rivals to one another. One might almost say that for many loyalty to Islam in the abstract is replaced by loyalty to an order, and that each order vies for influence. In this situation one has vertical, not horizontal, religious groups and identification, and it would be hard for an all-Islamic movement to get far. The Catholic ex-president, Leopold Senghor, was sometimes ridiculed by Westerners for giving so much attention and patronage to Islamic orders, but in so doing he helped to perpetuate divisions among Muslims and to forestall Islamic unity against Christians and animists; his Muslim successor does the same. Among the highly educated there are movements for greater Islamic orthodoxy and all-Islamic identity, but as yet no major radical Islamist movements. In addition, Senegal has seen less rapid socio-economic change than Islamist-profile countries. A small Islamist current has, however, developed in recent years.

Another non-Islamist area visited was West Sumatra, in Indonesia. Although there have been Islamist trends in Indonesia, I found almost none in West Sumatra, except one from a student of the Technical University of Bandung, Java, which is the centre of student Islamism. (In all countries that I know of, scientific and technical students are the most Islamist – this was dramatically true in Iran and also in Tunisia.) To look only at West Sumatra, an area I know: here is an area which does not have the profile of an Islamist region; it has had very little industry, its cities are not overcrowded with migrants, and living standards are relatively egalitarian (this may be true of Indonesia in general). Most women wear either Western or Indonesian dress and do not cover their hair. In addition, West Sumatra is a matrilineal society, and although its inhabitants are very strict about prayer and the other '5 pillars' of Islam, they would not want to change their matrilineal landholding and inheritance system in order to conform to Islamic law. However, the crucial point is probably the lack of rapid economic change and inequalities.

The figures for Islamist trends versus non-Islamist trends in the countries discussed thus far are four with such trends being important: Egypt, Tunisia, Malaysia, and Nigeria; and three where they are less important or unimportant: Sumatra, Yemen, Senegal. With my last two countries the majority turns in favour of those with weak Islamism, though if one considers Yemen to be border-line as of 1986, it is a draw.

In my brief observation I would say that true Islamism is weak in Syria. The government appears to be generally successful in defending the rights of minorities, which include not only its own Alawi group, but various Christians, Jews, Druze and Shi'a. If it is true, as it appears to be, that many Sunnis identify with the Sunni Muslim Brethren, this does not mean that most of them would like to enforce a Sunni Islamic state. Rather, they would like to see the Sunni majority favoured in politics and economics. In Syria there seems to be considerable appreciation of the problems that may come from stressing sectarian identity, or giving one religious group the chance to enforce religious law. Hence I would doubt that true Islamism is growing in Syria, which also does not seem to have the socio-economic profile of a state that encourages the growth of Islamism. This is said tentatively, as Westerners say that the two questions not to discuss in Syria are religion and politics, and it is difficult to do so in a brief visit. Nor must one forget the brutal suppression of a Muslim Brethren-sponsored rising in Hama.

More dramatic is my final instance, the case of Pakistan, which many Westerners, at least until the April 1986 return and huge rallies of Benazir Bhutto, assumed was a supporter of Islamism. Visiting Pakistan in the autumn of 1985 and in 1986, I was struck that in conversations with a wide range of intellectuals, including members of Islamic organisations, I found only one man who defended the Zia Government. I met him on my last day in 1985, in Karachi, and that night had dinner with a senior literary figure and his sons and told them about it. They pressed me to say who it was who had defended the government, but I prudently decided not to say; one son burst out laughing and said, 'You see what Pakistan is like; she has to protect the identity of someone because he favours our government!'

One may say, with the examples of Zia, Numeiry in Sudan, and probably ultimately Khomeini and his followers, that there is nothing like having a government that calls itself Islamic to discredit Islamism. Zia's government has done this in various ways. For the popular masses he has not brought significant economic or social improvements, and education, health, and social welfare remain at abysmally low levels, despite overall economic growth.

In addition, his policies have offended several key groups, who have generally mounted a more militant and effective opposition than have their counterparts elsewhere in the Islamic world. Pakistan has the most effective and militant women's movement of any Muslim country I know. It originated as a coalition of women's groups, mostly professional, in response to Zia's proposed Islamisation laws that would reduce the status of women. The most important such law fought by the new coalition organisation, the Women's Action Forum, was the law of evidence, which made the testimony of one man equal to that of two women. Women on peaceful marches protesting against this law were beaten and jailed, but that did not stop them. Although the law went through, there seems no doubt that continued protests by women and their male allies slowed down much of the rest of Zia's Islamisation programme. For example, the proposal for separate higher education for women has not got off the ground. The ruling that women television broadcasters must cover their hair brought the resignation of one prominent woman, while the others now wear filmy chiffon scarves over the back of their hair (of Hollywood 1930s glamour style), show the rest of their hair, and wear make-up and jewellery. (Indeed, there are very few women in Islamist dress in Pakistan; those who veil and cover their hair are in a minority and are generally popular class or tribal women in traditional dress.) Women's continued activism was almost certainly largely responsible for making Zia set up an activist 'Women's Division' in his government, and also create a Commission on Women, whose 1985 report, under appropriate Qur'anic quotations, was almost entirely egalitarian. It remains unpublished and, like the reports of many US Government commissions, unacted upon.

Zia's regime has had what may turn out to be a long-term benefit; as discourse must be Islamic, it has forced many women and other activists to study Islam, and to learn Qur'anic and legal precedents for their programmes. This means that secular or semi-secular oppositionists are not nearly as alienated from the masses and the Islamic petty bourgeoisie as was the case in Iran. It does *not* mean that, like the Iranian Ali Shariati and some contemporary Egyptian intellectuals, Pakistan's intellectuals are compromising on such issues as equal rights for women; rather they are finding Islamic precedents for this. In delivering an endowed lecture at Radcliffe College in 1985, Benazir Bhutto insisted that the Qu'ran was egalitarian for women. This brought negative letters from several Westerners and Muslims, but Benazir was only following the general pattern of Pakistani oppositionists, which is aimed at defending equality and making that defence more acceptable by tying it to Islam. This is the *modus operandi* of the Women's Action Forum, and it seems worse than useless to question its sincerity or its accuracy in depicting what was meant by the Qu'ran in the seventh century.

Another group offended by Zia's Islamisation have been the Shi'a (which in Pakistan and most countries means the larger, Twelver Shi'a – the Isma'ilis are apolitical in accord with the instructions of their imam, the Aga Khan). Every country that has tried Islamisation has found that by enforcing one branch of Islamic Law it offends Muslim minorities – this includes the minority Sunnis in Iran and the minority Shi'a in Saudi Arabia.[5] In Pakistan the Shi'a, like the women's organisations, became more activist as a result of Zia's policies. The first object of Shi'a opposition was Zia's ruling that *zakat* be collected by a 2½ per cent tax on bank accounts. The Shi'a pointed out that their zakat tax did not go to the government, but to religious leaders, *mujtahids*. They had strong enough demonstrations that the government was forced to rule that anyone who signed an affidavit that the zakat law was against his or her *fiqh* was exempt from it. The saying in Pakistan was that Zia had done more than anyone to create Shi'a,

as a number of Sunnis (in a situation where there are no for-
malities for conversion to Shi'ism) declared themselves Shi'a to
escape the tax. In the autumn of 1985 when I visited Pakistan, Zia
was still trying to extend Muslim law (meeting Hanafi Sunni law),
and the Shi'a were still objecting that Shi'a law differed on numerous points, and if Sunni law were to be applied to Sunnis, then
Shi'a law should be applied to Shi'a. Some of the Shi'a lawyers
engaged in finding all the differences between schools that they
could were really aiming at killing the whole idea of promoting
Islamic law: 'Scratch a Shi'a and Find a Secularist' was an apt
expression I heard more than once, and one that would apply to
most minorities, Muslim and non-Muslim, in the Islamic world.

While middle-class and wealthy Shi'a tended to be secularists,
for many this does not preclude admiration for Khomeini as a
great anti-imperialist Shi'a. Popular-class Shi'a mostly admired
Khomeini, whose name and picture were found in homes in the
remotest areas. This should not, I think, be taken as a sign of
widespread militant Islamism so much as of admiration of a Shi'i
hero who had put Shi'ism on the map and made it more prideful to
identify as a Shi'a. There are, however, pro-Khomeini militant
Islamists in Pakistan.

The Pakistani Shi's Westernised middle class had an attitude
towards Shi'ism radically different from the Iranian Shi'i Westernised middle class. I asked several educated Pakistani Shi'a what
they identified Shi'ism with, both as children and now, and overwhelmingly they spoke of the justice, egalitarianism, and self-
sacrifice of Ali and Husain, which they identified with their current
democratic (and in one case left socialist) values. When I asked the
same question of educated Iranians, they identified Shi'ism with
mourning, self-flagellation, fanaticism, and the like. This may be
mostly the difference between a minority and a majority community, but is also a general situation that educated Muslim
Pakistanis refuse to see Zia's Islam as true Islam, and often study
Islam quite deeply to find precedents for a different kind of Islam.

Zia's encouragement of a rigid Sunni Islam has alienated Sunnis
and also helped produce Sunni – Shi'a tensions expressed in
murderous rioting in the Punjab in Moharram (September) 1986.

Another group in Pakistan who have been militantly active
against Zia are lawyers' associations, who in many marches, publi-
cations, and demonstrations have taken the place of the banned

political parties. Their members have also been beaten and jailed, but they have kept up activity. Much of the press has also been increasingly oppositional as Zia's absolute controls were weakened, and in late 1985 important newspapers like Karachi's *Dawn* and Islamabad's *The Muslim* were largely oppositional, as was the serious popular magazine *The Herald*, whose editors are mostly women. Finally, the political parties continued to exist, and even to be constantly referred to in the press as the '(banned) Pakistan People's Party', and so forth. The latter party, the populist party of Zulfiqar Ali Bhutto, who was overthrown by Zia in 1977 and executed in 1979, remains the most popular party in the heterogeneous opposition coalition called the Movement for the Restoration of Democracy. Benazir Bhutto is the PPP's chief leader, and her huge rallies are an indication of her and the Party's support. The popularity of a young, non-Islamist, Western-educated woman as the heir apparent of the opposition is one indication of how little popular support Islamism now has.

Although nobody can predict the future, it seems that Islamism at present is not as strong worldwide as is sometimes suggested. It is weak at two ends of the spectrum – places like Senegal, Syria, and Sumatra, which do not fit the Islamist socio-economic and political-cultural profile suggested above, and in countries that have had bad experiences with Islamism, like Sudan and Pakistan. It is quite strong in countries that do fit the profile, like Egypt and Tunisia, and in a very few countries where a Muslim plurality or slight majority wants to increase its economic and legal power, like Nigeria and Malaysia, although its popularity has now dropped significantly in Malaysia. Naturally there are specific local situations and traditions that influence and modify the large generalisations made above, but since such general comparisons are rarely made and can be illuminating, it seems worth while to hazard them. Some countries may still have to live through the experience of Islamist government (which has several models – Pakistan is not like Iran) before becoming disillusioned with its excesses, while in others like Sudan and Pakistan, it is or may be on its way out. The frequent Western (or Islamist) picture of a constant growth of Islamism nearly everywhere in recent years is an over-simplification that can be rectified by local and comparative studies of the Islamist phenomenon.

A final point concerns the image of Khomeini and the Iranian

Revolution. Although both have dropped in popularity since the early Muslim enthusiasms of 1979, they still represent the *only* Islamic government taken seriously as such abroad, and still evoke various degrees of admiration among educated and urban groups. Their admirers are not Islamists, however, but include many who see Khomeini as the first Muslim revolutionary who has effectively stood up to the West, especially the US, while keeping equally independent of the USSR. This independence plus Khomeini's reputation for simplicity, probity, and egalitarianism, give him an appeal beyond Islamist circles, even among many who dislike some things about the Islamic republic.

Notes

1. Claude Cahen, 'La changeante portée sociale de quelques doctrines religieuses', *L'Elaboration de l'Islam* (Paris: Presses Universitaires de France, 1961).
2. Gilles Kepel, *Le Prophete et Pharaon: Les mouvements islamistes dans l'Egypte moderne* (Paris: La Decouverte, 1984); English editions (under the title *The Prophet and the Pharoah*) have been published by al-Saqi Books, London, and University of California Press, Berkeley (1985).
3. 'The Islamist Movement in Tunisia', forthcoming, *The Maghreb Review*, special issue honoring Albert Hourani, and the sources and interviews therein. The MTI internal document and useful articles are in *Sou'al* (Paris), V (April, 1985), issue 'Islamisme aujourd'hui'.
4. See especially Peter B. Clarke and Ian Linden, *Islam in Modern Nigeria* (Mainz: Grünewald, 1984).
5. See the Introduction and relevant chapters of Juan R. I. Cole and Nikki R. Keddie (eds.), *Shi'ism and Social Protest* (New Haven: Yale University Press, 1986).

3 The Iranian Revolution: Uneven Development and Religious Populism

FRED HALLIDAY

Introduction[1]

The Iranian Revolution has been one of the epic events of post-war history, involving remarkable levels of political mobilisation, international crisis, and political brutality. Contrary to the expectations of many, the apparently stable regime of the Shah was overthrown in 1978–9 and a new post-revolutionary system successfully established and maintained. Yet beyond its importance for the history of modern Iran and of the world as a whole, the revolution has posed analytic questions of considerable complexity, both for those who seek to relate it to the overall course of modern Iranian history, and for those who want to compare it to other modern revolutions. If the Iranian upheaval deserves the name 'revolution', defined in terms of levels of mass mobilisation, destruction of an existing political and social order, and the establishment of a distinctly new order, then it would seem to be an unusual variant of this type of social event, a development as atypical as it was unexpected.

It is, however, worth remembering that all revolutions exhibit characteristics that are unexpected, that they can upset the schemata of social analysis as much as they overthrow established

31

systems of power. The French Revolution challenged many of the rationalist assumptions of the Enlightenment. Antonio Gramsci, himself a Communist leader in Italy, called the Russian Revolution 'the revolt against *Das Kapital*' because of the manner in which it appeared to defy the economic determinism that had underlain much previous Marxist thinking. The Iranian Revolution was certainly an original event, but it is advisable to be more than a little cautious about specifying precisely where this originality lies.

A tentative discussion of this revolution's originality can serve two functions: to prevent facile assimilation of the Iranian case into preconceived schemata of Iranian history or the sociology of revolutions; and at the same time to rescue it from the claim that the Iranian Revolution is a wholly original process, a *sui generis* revolution to which available concepts of historical analysis and rational explanation cannot be applied. A proper emphasis upon the novelty of the Iranian Revolution can be balanced by some comparative caution, by suggesting that not all that has occurred in Iran is unique or as resistant to external comprehension as many would suggest. Such an endeavour is always limited and the sociology of revolutions is an area of considerable theoretical contention.

Analysis must confine itself to the fall of the *ancien regime* and its immediate aftermath, but the novelty of the Iranian Revolution can be said to reside, in the first instance, in the role played within it by religion and in particular by what is loosely termed 'religious fundamentalism'. For the first time in modern history (that is, since 1789), a revolution has taken place in which the dominant ideology, forms of organisation, leading personnel, and proclaimed goal have all been religious in appearance and inspiration. This in itself would mark off the Iranian from other revolutions of the modern era. Given the manner in which Islam seeks to legislate for many areas of social activity, this religious imprint has involved an attempt to transform the law, culture, polity, and social practices of Iran to conform with a model supposedly elaborated in the seventh century AD.

Moreover, other features of the ideology of the Iranian Revolution may be obscured by the religious emphasis, but these in fact derive from it and can also serve to distinguish the Iranian case. The first is that the Iranian rejects ideas of historical progress:

Ayatollah Khomeini explicitly proposes a return to an earlier model of social and political practice and a rejection of almost all that the modern world stands for. Such historical and ideological throwbacks have been seen in other revolutions and nationalist movements – the past provides convenient legitimation for many. But the Iranian case is far more than this, because such a regression is the basis of the whole revolutionary programme. In the proper sense of the word, the Iranian revolution is therefore a comprehensively *reactionary* revolution, restoring to the term its original, astronomical, meaning of a *return* to a previous order. A second consequence follows from this: while economic and material factors and aspirations played a part in the Iranian revolution, the leaders were reluctant to recognise this and have tended to reject the idea of material improvement. Khomeini has tried to lower the material aspirations of the population according to his ideal of generalised austerity, in which Western consumer goods are rejected, and in which the faithful can live in a state most conducive to religious devotion.[2] Khomeini on one occasion declared that the goal of revolution was not to provide the people with cheap melons. On another, he told President Bani-Sadr that the American embargo during the hostages crisis would not be detrimental to the population: 'In the time of the Prophet, they ate only one date a day.' Thirdly, while the Iranian Revolution has articulated nationalist themes of assertion and rejection, it was undertaken in the name of universalistic religion and laid comparatively little stress on Iran as a national entity. Its universalism was more pronounced than that of France or Russia. This was evident both in the cultural shift accompanying the revolution, where many features of the indigenous Iranian culture were rejected along with the values of the West, and in the projection of Iran as the first part of an insurgent Muslim community to overthrow its oppressors.[3]

A fourth ideological peculiarity followed from this, namely the rejection of history. Far from vaunting the heroes and strugglers of earlier generations, as other revolutionary and nationalist movements have tended to do, Khomeini appeared to regard almost all the earlier leaders of Iranian oppositions, secular and religious, as obstacles to his legitimacy which derived from the Islamic leaders of the seventh century, the Prophet Muhammad, and the founders of Shi'ite Islam.[4] This religious legitimacy accounts for the fifth ideological feature of the Iranian revolution, namely the fact that while a mass uprising, it cannot be considered a democratic revolution even in theory.[5] Khomeini's writings and the constitution of the Islamic Republic made clear that ultimate power rests with the divinely-inspired religious authority, the *faqih*, who can override all elected bodies and can dictate his views to the faithful. Khomeini has tended to suggest that this is not a problem since the faithful and the *faqih* will not be in contradiction; but were such an unexpected event to occur then he is in no doubt that it is the *faqih* who has superiority. The Iranian Revolution therefore rejects historical progress, material improvement, national assertion, historical legitimation, and democratic sovereignty – five themes which, however violated in practice, have been at least formally invoked by modern revolutions from 1789 onward.

Yet this fundamentalist religious character is not, even in its appearance, as all-encompassing as might be assumed. First, Khomeini's ideas are fundamentalist in their claim to derive everything from sacred texts, but they are not fundamentalist or traditional if these terms are meant to imply that Khomeini's views are inherited from the past. Both the ideas themselves, and, even more so, the political and social effect they have, are novel ones, dependent upon modern social conditions and modern political debates upon which they draw, without attribution.[6] Second, it is possible to pose the same questions which arise when any set of radical ideas finds a mass following and makes an impact on history. Which social groups supported these ideas, and for what reasons? What were the determining factors in the history of the country concerned which enabled the movement to gather force at the time it did? Why was it possible for this opposition to defeat the established state? What kinds of social and political change have accompanied its triumph? The Islamic revolutionaries have their own answers to these questions which usually involve divine agency. Others may be hesitant about accepting these answers, even while they view them with interest for what they tell us about the intentions and ideology of those who directed the revolution itself. Different responses may, therefore, be suggested.

Abstracting for a moment from its religious character, the Iranian Revolution appears more familiar. It was made by a wide-ranging alliance of social groups, drawing its support from dissident sections of the civil service and trading communities, and from much of the poor urban population. They were mobilised against a dictatorial political regime by a charismatic leader and by an ideology of revolutionary legitimacy.[7] In other words, the Iranian Revolution developed in the context in which populist movements have arisen in many other Third World societies. Even the religious character of the revolution is, in historical perspective, not so unique. History is replete with instances of rebel movements challenging temporal rulers in the name of God, and of clerical leaders organising such movements. The aspiration to create a sanctified order on earth runs through much of the history of medieval Europe and the Middle East and through that of nineteenth-century China. Newly-urbanised populations in other countries have been known to turn to religion as a means of responding to the tensions of their new environment. In Iran itself, the *mullahs* have been at the forefront of other protests in modern times, specifically the 1891 Tobacco Protest and the Constitutional Revolution of 1906–8.[8] What is unique about the role of religion in the Iranian Revolution is that it became prominent in the latter half of the 1970s and, even more so, that it succeeded in over-throwing the established regime.

However, the originality of the Iranian Revolution lies not only in its religious character. If Iran's upheaval was unique in the prominence occupied by this 'traditional' feature, it was equally so for the opposite reason: the 'modern' character of the event. If the Iranian Revolution was the first contemporary instance to be religious in orientation, it was also the first ever 'modern' revolution. This 'modernity' is evident in four respects. First of all, the revolution took place in a society far more socio-economically developed, in major respects, than was Russia in 1917 or China in 1949. Half of the population lived in urban areas, per capita income was over $2000 and, however unevenly this was distributed, it meant that most Iranians living in the cities were materially better off than a decade before. It was not the *sans-culottes* who made the revolution, but people who had benefited materially from a process of a rapid capitalist modernisation.[9] Second, in contrast to all other Third World revolutions, the Iranian Revolution took place in the cities. Many of those who participated in it may have been peasants (that is, of rural origin), but it was an urban event, produced by the conditions of the major cities in the 1970s. The contrast with China, Vietnam, and Cuba is evident. Thirdly, and again in contrast to other Third World revolutions, the Iranian upheaval was carried out by political confrontation, not by armed conflict. Thousands of people died in the last months of the Shah's regime, but they were mainly unarmed demonstrators, not guerrillas. Only in the last days of the Shah's regime was armed confrontation the dominant form of resistance: the preceding months were dominated by the street demonstration and the political general strike, forms of opposition associated with schemata of revolution in the most advanced capitalist countries.[10] Finally, the fall of the *ancien regime* happened without it having been weakened in any external confrontation, which is normally believed to be necessary for the removal of authoritarian regimes. Neither defeat in war nor serious international economic pressure assisted the advance of the Islamic revolutionaries, and they themselves received no significant help from abroad.

From the perspective of twentieth-century revolutions, these 'modern' features are as original as the Islamic character of the Iranian case. *It can therefore be said that the originality of the Iranian Revolution resides neither in its 'traditional', nor in its 'modern' character but in the interaction of the two.*[11] It is this combination which accounts for both the success and the peculiarity of the Iranian Revolution in its initial stages, but it may also be the increasing disassociation of the two which has complicated the establishment of a post-revolutionary order.

The course of the Revolution

The events that led directly to the fall of the Shah spanned a period of little more than one year. Mohammad Reza Pahlavi had been on the throne since 1941 and had been an autocratic ruler since 1953 when, with the assistance of the United States and Britain, a military *coup* had overthrown the nationalist government of Mohammad Mosaddeq. Since that time, there had been only sporadic open opposition to the regime, with the exception of the period 1960–3, when nationalist politicians and a section of the clergy led by Ayatollah Khomeini had protested at the Shah's control of political life and the reforms he was instituting. After over a decade of apparent calm, marked only by minor urban guerilla activities, the opposition became more active in 1977, circulating critical statements and holding protest meetings. In January 1978

street protests began, organised by religious students in the city of
Qom protesting at a newspaper article which insulted the exiled
Khomeini. For the next few months there were successive protests
and strikes in the main urban centres of Iran, in which the local
clergy usually played an important organising role, and in which
the bazaars, the historical centres of trade and finance, gave
support by going on strike.

The regime did not appear to be in mortal danger, however,
until September 1978 when, at the end of the fasting month of
Ramadan, the traditional religious processions rallied over 1 million people in Tehran for what became political protests. The
imposition of martial law, on 8 September, followed by the shooting of demonstrators, only temporarily stemmed the protest movement, and in October a wave of strikes began. Although at first
organised for economic demands, or as protests at press censor-
ship, these strikes set in motion a process which led to a nation-
wide political general strike in late November and December. The
first victims were the oil fields. This blocked off Iran's export
earnings and deprived the armed forces of diesel fuel. On 5
November, under pressure from a restive military leadership, the
Shah appointed a military government. But it lacked political
cohesion and was in any case unable to end the strikes. It was
forced to permit a new round of street demonstrations in early
December to mark the traditional Shi'ite festival of Ashura, at
which the demand was made more clearly than ever before that
the Shah must depart. By this time, Khomeini had become not
only a symbol of opposition but also an increasingly active leader;
from his base in Paris he insisted on no compromise with the Shah
or those in any way associated with him.

On 15 January 1979 the Shah left Iran, leaving behind a de-
moralised and divided army, and a government headed by former
opposition leader Shahpour Bakhtiar. A committed secularist and
a courageous individual, Bakhtiar overestimated both his own
political resources and the loyalty of the army. He also underesti-
mated the degree to which he had discredited himself by being
seen to accept his office from the Shah. Khomeini refused to
negotiate with the Bakhtiar government and, after returning to
Iran on 1 February, he pronounced Mehdi Bazargan head of a
rival government. For ten days Iran had two governments; but on
10 and 11 February, following pro-Khomeini mutinies in the

garrisons of Tehran, groups of armed civilians seized control of government buildings and military camps. The army command declared itself neutral in the conflict between Khomeini and Bakhtiar; the latter and his associates, together with remnants of the royalist court, either fled or were arrested.

The new Bazargan government then proceeded to institutionalise the post-revolutionary regime. On 30 March a referendum proclaimed Iran to be an Islamic Republic. In November 1979 a new Islamic constitution was similarly passed by referendum, and Khomeini was officially accepted as the *faqih* or supreme judicial authority with extensive powers. In January 1980 Abol-Hassan Bani-Sadr was elected president and, following the election of a *majlis* or parliament, dominated by the Islamic Republican Party, it selected as prime minister Mohammad Ali Rajai, an opponent of Bani-Sadr. These institutional developments were, however, over-shadowed by other processes and crises: the virtually undisputed dominance of Khomeini as leader of the new republic weakened any other political forces and encouraged factionalism among those eager for his support; meanwhile, the deterioration of the social and economic structures of the country, combined with increasingly antagonistic international relations, impeded effective attempts to create a new and viable post-revolutionary order.[12]

Beyond those unique characteristics that comprised its paradoxical traditional/modern originality there are many remarkable features of this revolution. One was its suddenness: despite the underground opposition of the 1960s and 1970s, and despite the socio-economic tensions associated with the uneven and rapid economic expansion, the years prior to the revolution were not marked by major political or social unrest. Neither was the upheaval preceded by a significant economic crisis, such as a recession affecting substantial parts of the population. Nor did this crisis develop inside Iran as a result of conflict with other states: the frequently observed pattern of revolution following war or comparable international challenges to the power of a state was not evident in Iran. Few people, whether observers or participants, were conscious even six months before the Shah fell that the regime was in serious trouble, and even the pronouncements of the Ayatollah Khomeini indicated a progression in his confidence, as he made more militant demands in response to the course of events in Iran itself. Yet the revolution was not a chance event: it defeated not a decayed autocracy but what had appeared as one of the stronger and more decisive Third World states, one, moreover, that enjoyed considerable support from abroad. Although it is necessary, in the light of subsequent events, to revise the picture of the Shah's regime as one at the zenith of its power, it would be a mistake to underestimate the combined force of the revolutionary pressures which were necessary to overthrow the established Iranian state. In a condensed and preliminary form, there are five central areas in which the causes of the revolution may be discerned.

Rapid and uneven economic development

In the two decades prior to the revolution Iran had undergone substantial socio-economic transformation and had made considerable advances in becoming an industrialised capitalist society.[13] Yet Iran had, in previous decades, undergone relatively little transformation, and the accelerated changes of the 1960s and 1970s both produced exceptional tensions within the society, and sustained certain pre-capitalist or pre-industrial sectors that were to facilitate the upsurge of 1978.

The main reason why the revolution occurred was that conflicts generated in capitalist development intersected with resilient institutions and popular attitudes which resisted the transformation process.

The impetus for economic expansion came from Iran's oil industry, the revenues of which rose from $45 million in 1950 to $1.1 billion in 1970 and, following the multiplication of prices by OPEC, to $20.5 billion in 1976. By the late 1970s, per capita income in Iran was over $2000, industrial output was growing at over 15 per cent a year, and up to half the population was living in the towns. Urban Iran appeared to be enjoying widespread prosperity, virtually no social groups in the cities suffered a net fall in income. But the very process of transformation, mistermed 'modernisation', was itself contradictory.

This oil-fuelled growth generated its own problems. First, the availability of oil revenues subsidised many areas of the economy and so enabled them to remain uncompetitive and unproductive. Oil assisted economic changes, but it also subsidised inefficient sectors, fostered a large service sector and state apparatus, and gave the Iranian government the illusion that it could dispense with the disciplines that developing societies without oil had to respect. Although much of the change was real, there was also much that was illusory. Even in its own terms, however, the oil boom could not last, and the period 1977–8 saw a relative slowing down: GNP stagnated in these years; inflation increased, particularly in rents; certain commodities grew scarce; and power cuts occurred, angering urban-dwellers. There was no widespread hardship, but the slowing down had political effects, as entrepreneurs lost confidence, and as the government enforced price controls on merchants to combat inflation. The decision of the cost-cutting Amuzegar government to suspend state subsidies to the clergy in 1977 must also have had its consequences.

More important for the mass of urban poor, however, were the inequalities and tensions associated with the boom itself; while the gap between rural and urban incomes began growing in the late 1960s, there were also increasingly pronounced inequalities in the urban areas themselves. By the mid-1970s it was calculated that the top 10 per cent of the population accounted for 40 per cent of expenditure; in addition, the urban poor suffered from the housing shortage, with the result that some had to spend up to 70 per cent of their income on rents. The population of some cities doubled in a decade: the migrants may have had higher incomes in the cities, but they lost the support systems of village society. To make matters worse, there was widespread corruption, involving members of the royal family. On top of the unevenness of the expansion, there was the unevenness of the transformation itself; that is, the fact that together with the industrialisation and partial modernisation, the transition was not taking effect. In agriculture the land reforms of the 1960s produced a cash-crop sector tied to the urban economy, but far more of the land was cultivated in family-sized units relatively isolated from the rest of the economy. The towns had a long tradition of commercial and religious institutions grouped around the bazaars which, in the face of the changes from above, adapted to them but retained their independence and their hostility to the Shah's state. There was a high degree of industrialisation, with two and a half million people employed in manufacturing of some kind – a very high figure by Third World standards, representing about a quarter of the total labour force.

Yet, the great majority of these were in small artisanal units, retaining the production processes and cultural values of an earlier epoch.

Comparable dichotomies could be observed in the fields of distribution and finance; despite the emergence of a modern banking system and of modern retail outlets, a substantial degree of the financial and commercial activity remained under the control of the bazaar, which had in the past controlled these sectors. The bazaar merchants resented their relative demotion by banks and new retail systems; yet their absolute position improved greatly with the expansion of economic activity in the country, so that the two-thirds of retail trade they retained enabled them to lend to those whom the banks regarded as unacceptable. It was the bazaar that had traditionally financed the religious institutions – the mosques, shrines, and religious schools.[14] This was, then, a sector that combined considerable influence in the country with a deep antagonism to the economic structures and to the regime that was trying to reduce the area in which the bazaar merchants could manoeuvre. It was one component of an explosive triangular partnership that also incorporated the clergy and the urban poor, the latter retaining the values of the pre-industrial society. The transformation of Iranian society therefore preserved and even promoted institutions of economic and social activity that acquired new potential for opposition within the altered context created by this transformation.

The political weakness of the monarchy

The Shah's personality helped weaken not only the army but also the state. The role of the individual in history is not only as instigator and agent, but also as a weak link in a system of political power. This factor alone cannot explain the Iranian Revolution, any more than the characters of Louis XVI and Nicholas II can explain the fall of the Bourbons and Romanovs. But the Shah's grandiose distance from the realities of Iran helped introduce those development programmes which created the socio-economic context of the revolution; his ignorance of conditions in the country, together with his tendency to withdraw into silent meditation and his paralysis of will, were ill-suited to his coping with the crisis of 1978.[15] He seems to have known from about 1974 that he had cancer, and this may account both for the recklessness of some of his projects and for the fatalism he displayed in his final months of power. If such speculation is possible, one could argue that no monarch could have saved the regime in the last few months of its existence, but that an autocrat of a different stamp might have been able to prolong its existence or take effective corrective measures early in 1978. Whatever importance this personal factor has, it certainly seems to have contributed to the unexpectedly rapid disintegration of the regime.

In certain respects, the Pahlavi regime never enjoyed widespread legitimacy. Both the Shah and his father had come to power through military *coups*, and both ruled through political dictatorship. By the time of his fall, the Shah had had many thousands imprisoned and tortured. Khomeini's designation of the Shah and his father as 'usurpers' therefore struck a chord in Iranian political life, although the precise interpretation of this term may have varied, depending on whether it was alternative secular forces that were seen as having been displaced (the 1906 Constitution, or Mosaddeq) or rather the legitimate leading role of the clergy. Both Pahlavis were also seen as illegitimate because of their reliance on foreign support. Certainly, the attempts by the Shah to generate intermediate institutions of legitimation in the post-1960 period were a failure; the *Majlis* and the parties in it were phantoms, and neither Pahlavism, as a national ideology stressing the pre-Islamic past, nor authoritarian concepts of *far-mandari* or 'commandism' were widely accepted. Yet the quality of the Shah's political illegitimacy was not constant: the dictatorship of the 1950s, and the prospects of economic improvement of the 1960s and early 1970s seem to have produced at least some tacit acceptance. But the ironic consequence of the greater boom of the mid-1970s was that it undermined this tacit acceptance by highlighting the inequalities and the corruption inherent in the regime. Nor was this just a matter of concern to the urban poor and the bazaar merchants: it exposed one of the fatal weaknesses of the regime, namely, the alienation of large sectors of the middle class. Despite the fact that these people benefited from the regime, and could have had little expectation of improvement without the Shah, they failed actively to support his government. Nor can this alienation be attributed solely to the fact that the regime was a dictatorship which denied the rich and educated a voice in affairs of government, reflecting the specific fissures produced in the favouritism of the court and the distribution of oil wealth. In this respect, Iran differed from Franco's Spain and Pinochet's Chile: while the material improvement offered to the middle class was also far greater, the separation of those in power from the middle class was far greater in the case of Iran. The result was that the Shah failed to mobilise an active social constituency in his period of success and was thus left isolated throughout the course of the revolution.

This fissure helps explain another important feature of the revolution, the demoralisation of the army. One cause of this was the form that the confrontations of the revolution took. Huge unarmed crowds assembled, backed by the disconcerting and potentially hegemonic ideology of Islam. This was a threat any army would have had difficulty resisting in the absence of an occasion to take the offensive. The army, with its corrupt top officer corps and mass of conscripts beneath, was also liable to such political demoralisation. Khomeini himself devoted considerable attention to this issue, making appeals that would be most likely to undermine the army while seeking to avoid bloody confrontations. Another important factor was the conduct of the Shah himself; he failed to give strong leadership in the final months. When he left the country in January 1979 the army leadership was divided. The crisis of the final days was settled because, in the face of Khomeini's movement, the top army leadership signed a secret agreement with the opposition.[16] Yet beyond all these factors lies the fact that the army was, from the beginning, isolated in Iranian society: it was the instrument of the Shah. It had never fought a successful war and lacked any martial legitimacy. The gap between the majority of the middle class and the regime meant that in Iran, in contrast to other countries where armies have seized power to pre-empt revolutions, the military lacked the political and social support which an active political constituency can provide.

The broad coalition of opposition forces

Skocpol's study of the French, Russian and Chinese revolutions forcefully contests the idea that revolutions are purposive activities in which a group of people consciously organise to overthrow a regime.[17] It points out that revolutions arise in situations of structural crisis for the society in question, and that those who initiate revolutions are not necessarily those who ultimately wield power in the post-revolutionary order. All revolutions produce groups who say the cause has been 'betrayed'. In Iran, the liberals and guerrillas who were openly contesting the regime in 1976 and 1977 were displaced in January 1978 by the clerical and bazaar forces; indeed, even within the Islamic forces the leadership gradually passed from cautious clergy like Sharriat-Madari and from reformist Muslim militants like Bazargan and Bani-Sadr to the more fundamentalist clergy of the Khomeini-Beheshti variety. At the same time, the revolution was not carried out by a political party. One of the proudest claims of the Islamic militant was: 'Our greatest strength is our lack of organisation.'[18]

The broad and rapidly congealed coalition of forces that overthrew the Shah was strong precisely because of its diverse and spontaneous character; it was also one of the causes of the factionalism and paralysis of the post-revolution period. On the other hand, political organisation did play its part in the Iranian Revolution. The secular political parties were small and played only a secondary or even marginal role in the events of 1978–9; even when they participated they were forced to join the dominant Islamic trends. Far more important were the organisation of the clergy themselves which, based on each locality of the city and with centres in the mosques and shrines, were able to use religious networks to mobilise the population. These religious networks may have been decentralised and, initially, not designed for political purposes, but they acquired a leading organisational role in the crisis of 1978 and had, by the latter half of the year, acquired in Khomeini a determined and appealing leader. Behind the clergy there also lay the underground Fedayin-i Islam grouping, a militant sect founded in the 1950s. There is reason to doubt if Khomeini himself was a member, but some of the leading clerical figures were, and they had been determined for over two decades to wrest power from the Shah. The case of the Iranian Revolution demonstrates the possibility of purposive action in a revolutionary situation: it was the clergy who directed the struggle throughout.

The social forces that responded to the movement varied: in the first clashes of 1978 the main components were theology students and bazaar merchants, but these groups, far more in touch with the population than the secular parties, were able to call on the urban poor who formed the foot-soldiers of the major demonstrations in the latter part of the year. Parallel to these protests the students and parties continued their actions, and in the final weeks of the regime it appears that significant numbers of middle-class people also joined in the demonstrations. The slogan raised in the final weeks was simple enough: 'Independence, Freedom, Islamic Republic'. The one commanding aim was to oust the Shah: many who doubted the suitability of Khomeini none the less supported the movement in the hope that it could achieve the desired aim. Among the secular and middle-class forces many hoped that once the Shah had gone they could deflect the movement away from its clerical patrons. This enabled such people to support the movement with appropriate optimism, but it represented an underestimation of the strength of the religious forces.

The resulting relationship between social classes and political leadership was an example of the combination of traditional and modern forces in the Iranian revolution. The revolution mobilised large numbers of people representing various social groups. Without a mobilisation of such numbers and the arousing of insurrectionary consciousness in these social groups, the revolution would not have succeeded. The strikes that paralysed the country from October 1978 on became a great and unified exertion of social power by different classes in pursuit of a defined political goal. Yet these classes acted in the name of, and under the leadership of, an Islamic force that denied the relevance of class forces and class goals. The post-revolutionary period showed that the workers and merchants, despite the power they had demonstrated in the revolution, were unable to wield their power independently of the religious authorities, let alone in opposition to them. Subsequent accounts would argue either one side of this process or the other – that this was an Islamic revolution brought about by the exertions of an undifferentiated body of believers, or that the revolution was a proletarian upheaval later betrayed and crushed by a usurping and counter-revolutionary clergy. Neither of these appears to be sufficient. The strength, as well as much of the tragedy, of the Iranian Revolution lay in the manner in which both aspects were combined.

The mobilising role of the Islamic religion

In the Iranian Revolution the Islamic element is a reflection of several factors which, together, produced the unique result of a twentieth-century state run by the clergy along lines derived from the Koran and Islamic law, and in which the major influence is in the hands of a personage who is constitutionally designated as the interpreter of holy texts. One negative factor played its part in giving prominence to Islam as an ideology of opposition, namely, the destruction by the Shah and his father of the *secular* opposition forces that had mobilised protest movements in earlier decades.[19] Even the guerrilla groups, the *Fedayin* and *Mojahidin*, were at a low ebb by the mid-1970s. The result was that, as in other societies where secular forms of protest are blocked off, religion in Iran became a symbol and an organising centre for a protest that might otherwise have taken a more conventional secular form. Had Mosaddeq not been kept inside Iran and subsequently died, he might have developed some of the allure of the Ayatollah Khomeini.

This 'vacuum' theory is not, however, sufficient. Several other factors have to be taken into account. First, in all its forms Islam claims to be able to legislate for the whole of human activity. In Islam there is no formal distinction between church and state. The very concept of the secular is theoretically excluded, and all social ideas must be legitimated by derivation from the holy texts. In terms of political theory this assertion finds its expression in the attempt to define an 'Islamic' concept of government. In social activity, Islam prescribes modes of behaviour for everyday life and human relations. Like Judaism and Hinduism (though not Christianity), it has concepts of clean and unclean and stipulates ritual activities for each day. As a result, the call for an Islamic society or Islamic policy is far more deeply rooted in the basic doctrine of Islam and in the historical consciousness of Muslim societies than comparable Christian claims. Islamic countries have in practice often exhibited a wide gap between the religious and secular domains, but this has not altered the theoretical overlap of the two upon which Islamic thinkers can draw.

A second factor is the ideological ductility of Islam in general, and in Shi'ite Islam in particular.[20] While considerable energy is expended by believers and non-believers alike in arguing which political principles can be derived from Islam, both the evidence of interpretation and the fluid formulations of the Qur'an itself suggest that Islamic theory allows a wide range of derivations. These latter depend on the external circumstances of the time, and the concerns of individual interpreters. The doctrine does not enjoin a specific course of action but it does provide themes that can justify such courses. One possible line of interpretation is what one may term the *demotic* (as opposed to *democratic*). Islam does not have a religious hierarchy and the position of its clergy depends to a considerable extent upon popular assent. At the same time some of the themes of Islam can serve the cause of popular mobilisation: emphasis on the common concerns of the community of believers, opposition to tyrants, and support for struggle.[21] The very plainness of Islamic prayer meetings, in contrast to the ceremonials of Christianity, confirms this *demotic* tendency. Because all such policies claim to be derived from the word of God and are interpreted by those with authority, they are not at all democratic, but can still serve the purposes of political mobilisation.

In Shi'ite Islam there are further dimensions of this demotic and undemocratic potential. In Sunni Islam the *caliph* or his equivalent is the head of state. The *caliphs* were direct descendants of the Prophet and since they embodied temporal and religious power, in theory at least, there was no problem of deciding how legitimate government was to be ensured. Born of a division in the early Islamic movement, Shi'ism holds that the twelfth Imam went into hiding and it believes in the occultation or *gheiba* of God's representative on earth, the Imam. It also lays great stress on the sufferings of Shi'ites at the hands of unjust rulers, and upon the cult of the Shi'ite martyrs, Ali and his sons, Hassan and Hussein. Both these factors combine to the permit the idea that Shi'ism is an ideology which rejects temporal order, a permanent dissidence *vis-à-vis* both orthodox Sunni Islam and established state authorities. Other interpretations are, of course, possible. Conservatism and political quietism are just as reconcilable with Shi'ism: it is neither inherently radical or compliant. For over a century after Iran become an officially Shi'ite State in 1502 the clergy was properly integrated into the state structure. Shi'ism in sixteenth-century Iran served the function of Protestantism in Elizabethan England – as a state religion designed to distinguish the monarch's realm from other states, in Iran's case Ottoman Turkey. But this arrangement broke down in the eighteenth century and from then on there has tended to be opposition between state and *ulema*, a clash that reached its height at the turn of the twentieth century.[22]

Within the many variant and contingent consequences of the original Shi'ite theory, two have had particular political pertinence – one institutional, the other ideological. The institutional

consequence concerns the financial bases of the clergy: in Sunni
Islam, where the state is legitimate, the faithful pay their *zakat* and
a further levy known as the *khoms* (fifth) is paid directly to the
clergy. This means that the clergy are independent of the state in a
manner unique in the Muslim world, and that the populace is able
to make the religious personnel responsive to their demands. In
Iran in the 1960s and 1970s there existed a religious establishment
of several thousand mosques and shrines, several tens of thousands of *mollahs*, and a network of *madrases* (religious schools).
Mainly funded by *bazaaris*, these were independent of the Shah's
control.[23] Ideologically, this link with the people meant that the
clergy had little room for improvisation or change. Reflecting the
concerns of a conservative constituency, the Iranian *mollahs* were
far less concerned to face the intellectual challenges of the modern
world than their more autonomous counterparts in the Arab Sunni
countries.[24] One of the central Shi'ite debates concerned the status
of authority in the period of the *gheiba*: while one school accepted
temporal authority or advised a process of patient dissimulation or
taqiye, others advocated a political role for the clergy and derived
this course of action from certain Qur'anic principles. It was this
latter option that Khomeini was to embrace. In popular Shi'ism,
there also lay ideological themes that could be used for political
advantage. One was the theme of martyrdom and sacrifice, celebrated every year in the passion plays commemorating the death
of the Shi'ite leader Hussein in the seventh century. The other was
the belief in a future golden age, a time when the Twelfth Imam
would come and create a just society upon earth. If the former was
conducive to extremes of political militancy in a revolutionary
period, the latter provided a theological goal that enabled many to
hope that an Islamic Revolution would indeed create a new and
better society on earth. By failing to specify the characteristics of
such a society, Khomeini maintained the support of a wide range
of social groups, all of whom could believe in his perfect society.

Revolutions require organisation and ideology, and both were
provided in some measure by Iranian Shi'ism in its traditional
form. But revolutions also require leaders, and in Ayatollah
Ruhollah Khomeini the Islamic movement found such a person.
Khomeini had a history and a personality appropriate to his role.
He had opposed the Shah in the early 1960s and had been exiled in
1964. He was known to be honest and courageous; he spoke in

clear, uncompromising, and often cruel tone. He also exhibited shrewd political judgement; he saw that his greatest asset was to have nothing to do with the Shah's regime, and he kept his intentions for the future regime as vague as possible in order to maximise political support. He also found the proper moment to strike – mobilising his supporters for the final push in late 1978, skilfully weakening the army, and returning to seize decisive control of the Iranian state.

Khomeini was in many respects the epitome of a charismatic leader. He came to the fore during a time of rapid social change and tension, and appeared to be exempt from the sinful and compromising world around him. He also appropriated the religious title of Imam, which suggested that his role was analogous to that of the returning Twelfth Imam. One reason for his assuming this title was that is circumvented the problem of his not being the senior ayatollah. But it also invested him with a religious authority which suggested he had God-given powers. There are certainly many who seem to have believed not that he was the Twelfth Imam, but that he would none the less introduce a just society as promised in the Shi'ite dramas.[25] He himself never claimed to have the specific attributes of the Imam in Shi'ite doctrine – the ability to transmit the word of God as conveyed by angels, the power to effect miracles, and the quality of being *ma'sum* (immune from sin). But the position of *faqih*, or supreme interpreter of the law, where both interpretation and law are invested with religious authority, certainly raised him well above other mortals and members of the Shi'ite clergy. Assuming this religious legitimacy had been established *before* the revolution, the very success of this venture appeared to strengthen his authority and the aura of God-given power he sought to cultivate.[26]

It is in this context that the thought of Khomeini became particularly influential. Khomeini belonged to that minority faction within Iranian Islam who held to the activist interpretation of the Shi'ite dilemma: he criticised monarchy and thought the clergy should play a leading role. Yet even his thought developed in response to the potential effect it might have. His early writings of the 1940s were critical of monarchy, but did not condemn it outright. Even in the 1960s he accepted the 1906 Constitution. His lectures on Islamic government, published in 1971, reject monarchy and advocate the concept of *velayat-i-faqih* (*velayat* means government or legal authority, and *faqih* is the standard Islamic term for someone who interprets the law). The concept of the *faqih* as elaborated by Khomeini is therefore a forthright attempt to solve the Shi'ite problem of legitimacy. In 1978, however, he went further and openly rejected the 1906 Constitution. Instead he developed the concept of Islamic Republic, his idea of the society Muslims should try to recreate.

For all its invocation of the past, however, the concept of the Islamic Republic is like many of Khomeini's other ideas: a skilful fusion of Qur'anic and modern themes with the Shi'ite hope of a just society to be created by the returning Imam. He divides societies into two categories of people – the *mostazafin* and *mostakbarin* (literally those made weak and those made big) – two Qur'anic terms which are used in the populist sense of 'oppressed' and 'oppressor'.[27] His attacks on *fesad* or corruption certainly have a Qur'anic moralism about them: the main charge on which many of the Shah's supporters are executed is of 'spreading corruption upon the earth'.[28] Yet the term corruption would, in the eyes of many poorer Iranians, include more secular derelictions as well. Even Khomeini's relation to nationalism is ambiguous because in the first period of his rule he virtually never mentioned the word *Iran* at all, laying stress instead on Islam and on the need to recreate the Islamic 'Universal State'. Yet much of his diatribe against the West and Western values had an unmistakeably nationalist ring, and followed what some secular Iranian intellectuals had been saying for a long time.[29] It picked up on the influence of Franz Fanon that had been mediated to Iran via the thought of Ali Shariati, the lay Muslim philosopher whose writings had a great impact upon the younger generation.[30] The war with Iraq that began in September 1980 forced Khomeini to lay greater explicit stress on nationalist themes: just as Stalin was forced by the German invasion of 1941 to evoke the greatness of Mother Russia, so Khomeini turned to mobilising support in the name of Iranian patriotism. Even the *faqih* and the role of the Imam epitomise standard populist leadership themes.[31]

Where Khomeini has not accommodated secular forces is in what may be termed his attitude toward modernity: in contrast to some earlier Islamic thinkers such as al-Afghani, who did emphasise the need for Islam to come to terms with science and democracy, and who openly acknowledged the ductility of Islamic thinking, Khomeini has re-asserted the hostility of Islam to modern ideas and the need to re-establish authoritative doctrinal purity in all matters.[32] Yet even this misleading traditionalism is, as we have seen, not a product of some purely doctrinal derivation, but an accommodation to the popular mood in Iran itself and of the way in which the clergy is sensitive to this. Indeed, both the political strength of the Islamic movement in Iran and the particular theological interpretations that emerged in the 1970s were made possible only by the new socio-economic conjuncture in which the clergy found themselves. In sum, the transformation of Iran, with the unevenness and transitional features already discussed, provided the context for the fusion of a discontented urban coalition with the opposition current within the clergy. What might otherwise have been a more recognisable populism, a movement of the oppressed against the oppressor and in search of a perfect society, was shaped and was given that organisation and ideological confidence with which to prevail by the clerical forces led by Khomeini.

The ambivalent international context

At first glance international factors seemed to play an atypically minor part in the course of the revolution itself. The Iranian state had not been weakened by any foreign military defeat or comparable external challenge to its prestige and capacity to govern.[33] Neither the opposition movement nor the Shah enjoyed active foreign support in the final months of the contest. Indeed the absence of any financial or other material backing for the opposition, and the failure of the United States more actively to intervene on the Shah's behalf, are among the most striking characteristics of the whole process.

The Iranian Revolution was in a very definite sense an international event. It had deeply unsettling effects on the West Asian region, both westward, where it appeared to challenge the rulers of Iraq and the Arabian Peninsula, and stimulate Shi'ites in Lebanon, and eastward, where it encouraged the Islamic forces fighting the revolutionary Afghan government which came to power in April 1978. After the revolution, Iran extricated itself from the alliance system that the United States had created in the region and became embroiled in two major international conflicts: the fifteen-month dispute over the American hostages, and the war with Iraq that began in September 1980. The Iran crisis of

1946 was (together with Poland) one of the two issues which started the Cold War. The rejection thirty-five years later of the Yalta arrangements by the populations of the two countries introduced a major element of international uncertainty in the 1980s.

Yet the revolution was international in another overt sense, namely in the manner in which Iranians perceived it. Despite the revolutionary universalism posed by Islam, it was felt as a nationalist movement against the political, economic, and cultural influences of the West, and of the United States in particular. This perception was reinforced by one of the most enduring features of Iranian political culture, the belief that political events are determined by a foreign hand. This is as true of the Shah and his supporters, who blamed the revolution on a Western conspiracy to 'bring' Khomeini to power, as it was of Khomeini and the forces associated with him, who regarded the Shah as *sag-i Carter* ('Carter's dog'), and who continued after the Shah's departure to uncover foreign conspiracies at every turn of events. There was a considerable degree of foreign influence in Iran prior to the revolution, and in this sense the perspective of the revolutionaries had justification; but the real interference was far less than was supposed and pointed to the prevalence of that collective paranoia which is such a strong feature of Iranian political life. It fosters such a debilitating atmosphere of helplessness that, far from enabling Iranians to emancipate themselves from foreign domination, it all too often incapacitates them. Although such conspiracy theories are common in many societies, their particular virulence in Iran owes much to the pattern of foreign policy domination in earlier decades: never a formal colony of any European power, Iran did not therefore pass through the clear break with foreign authority that independence involves. Moreover the patterns of semi-colonial control used by Britain, Tsarist Russia and later the US – influencing ministers, fostering dissension in the provinces, suborning the military – were precisely those most likely to engender a conspiracy mentality among Iranians.[34] Once this was coupled with the intense exposure to foreign influences at the everyday level in the 1960s and 1970s, and to the fact that the Shah himself *had* been brought back by American covert assistance in 1953, it was less surprising that a simplified picture of foreign control should persist and should substitute for more accurate, but intellectually more demanding, analyses.

Essentially, foreign forces shaped the revolution in at least three respects. First, the whole context in which the upheaval occurred was one of socio-economic transformations under which Iran was increasingly integrated into the world market and exposed to the economic, social and cultural influences of the West. The rate of Iran's oil output – over 6 million barrels a day – was dictated not by a rational calculation of what revenues Iran could most effectively absorb but by the demands of other countries for greater supply. The political and military build-up of the Shah's regime was made as a result of strategic decisions made in Washington. The cultural gap between the Westernised middle class and the class of new migrants in the major towns was one of the underlying tensions that helped ignite the revolution. Above all, oil revenue was important as external revenue, introducing revenue into the society without any comparable transformation of its socio-economic and productive structures.[35] Unregulated oil revenues progressively dislocated the regime from its social context and thereby rendered Iran more vulnerable to a sudden upsurge from below.[36]

A second international factor was the Shah's reliance on foreign support in 1953 and his visible friendship with the United States, together with his quiet but overt sympathy for Israel. This support certainly facilitated his control of Iran in the 1950s and 1960s but in the longer run, like the oil revenues, it undermined his internal bases of support and encouraged the belief that he could dispense with a loyal domestic following. For this reason, the United States was unable to intervene to save him. The pattern of such interventions, from Vietnam to Iran in 1953 shows that an action of this kind requires certain internal conditions to succeed, and such conditions – a sympathetic middle class or a motivated, repressive army – were absent by the time the full dimensions of the crisis had become clear.

The third aspect was US policy in the 1977–9 period. Certainly, it would be a mistake wholly to exclude those factors to which the Shah himself draws attention – the Carter human rights policy and the confusions of US policy-making in the final weeks.[37] Yet, these were not the determinant factors. Those issues upon which US critics focused attention – human rights violations and the high level of arms sales – were not those most prominent in the complaints of Khomeini and his followers; the subsequent vicissitudes of Islamic justice do not suggest that a desire for due process or improved prison conditions was paramount in the minds of those who flocked to the Ashura demonstrations. What can be said is that the Carter policy on human rights reinforced the internal process of political decompression in Iran in 1977 that the problems of the 1974–6 boom had created, and through which certain liberal politicians were able to begin some public activity. It was this example of secular forces that contributed to the feeling among the *bazaaris* and *mollahs* that they too could now be somewhat bolder.

The events of 1978–9 themselves show little signs of having been influenced by US policy. Until early November 1978 the American government did not see that Iran was undergoing a revolution and by that time no course of action, except the dispatch of substantial numbers of troops, would have staved off defeat. The constraints upon the latter were internal to US society – the post-Vietnam reluctance to engage in foreign wars – and also in Iran's strategic position. Such an action, as Brezhnev warned in November 1978, would have run the risk of Soviet intervention in accordance with the Soviet interpretation of their 1921 treaty with Iran. The overriding reason why such a course of action was impossible, however, was the crumbling of the Shah's own regime and of his own determination. There remains the question of whether, in the final days, the United States could have achieved some compromise between Khomeini and the army commanders which would have stemmed the full tide of insurrection that followed.[38] This too is an unlikely scenario since there was little incentive for Khomeini to accept it, and once in power, Khomeini in fact did not respect the agreement on immunity of top commanders which he had signed in early February. Therefore, despite the fact that the revolution was affected by both the realities and the myths of Iran's international context, the actual course of events took place on a stage from which, for a variety of reasons, foreign states were for the most part excluded.

Conclusions

Three general conclusions seem relevant to the over-all issue of religion and politics, and of how exemplary the Iranian Revolution may be of other upheavals in the contemporary world.

*(1)   The unique combination of 'modern' and 'traditional' in
the Iranian Revolution had both institutional and ideological
features*

The modernity of the revolution was above all accounted for by
the transformation of Iranian society in the 1960s and 1970s, the
rapid urbanisation and industrialisation, and the demographic and
social tensions this produced. Without this transformation, the
Islamic movement could have arisen again, as it had in the 1890s,
1900s, and early 1960s, but it would have been much less likely to
succeed. The destruction of the imperial regime and the neutralisation of its foreign support were made possible by the great force
with which the urban movement erupted, a force derivative of this
transformation. Even in ideological terms, the movement reflected
the world environment, both in the themes it invoked and in the
manner in which the enemy was viewed. At the same time, the
movement drew on traditional forces which had survived and even
flourished in the years of transformation. In the cities, the bazaars
(and the link of bazaar and mosque) gave the opposition a rallying
point and an organisational backbone. The clergy provided an
ideology of resistance and the principles for an alternative society.
The political culture of the mass of the urban population continued
to be characterised by religious beliefs and an acceptance of the
role of the clergy in political life.

*(2)   The Iranian Revolution was, only to some extent, a religious
revolution: the values, personnel, goals were all defined in
religious terms, and the society which has subsequently been
created is one which its creators argue is modelled on the Koran
and the Islamic law*

Undoubtedly, religious beliefs and the specific interests of the
clergy made indispensable contributions to this revolution. Yet the
image of an 'Islamic Revolution' is too simple. First of all, the
concept of religion is itself variable: in Islam it encompassed far
more than in Christianity, where the principle of a division between church and state has existed for some centuries. The doctrine of Islam does not admit the secular: though a separation of
secular and religious has come to prevail over the centuries, it has
been far easier for those who wish to re-assert the comprehensive

claims of Islam over all areas of social and political life to do so. Second, the factors enabling the clergy to challenge and overthrow the Shah were eminently secular ones. Thus the Iranian Revolution has more in common with other societies than the specifically religious dimension will permit. Material living conditions, opposition to royal dictatorship, and hostility to foreign influence all played important roles in preparing the Shah's downfall. Third, even the very ideology and programme of the revolutionaries contained many themes common to other revolutionary situations: re-establishment of national independence, expropriation of the rich, punishment of the guilty and corrupt, and redistribution of wealth. The decisive manner in which Khomeini's forces took control of the state and consolidated their hold by the creation of a set of new revolutionary institutions was eminently intelligible to anyone aware of what is involved in the establishment of a new state power.

(3)   The paradoxical unity of the 'modern' and the 'traditional' in the Iranian Revolution accounted for the success of the Shah's opponents, but this unity did not long survive the monarch's fall

The history of post-revolutionary Iran is to a considerable extent that of a growing dislocation of these two components. The attempt to create a clergy-dominated or hierocratic society, based on allegedly seventh-century principles, in the last quarter of the twentieth century has encountered many problems that permit no easy resolution. The impact of the revolution and its aftermath on the economy has been to lower living standards throughout nearly all of the urban society and to provoke considerable unemployment and inflation. The defiance of all outside powers and the call for the spread of Islamic revolution has led the regime into a full-scale war with Iraq, with enormous loss of life and considerable disruption to the economy. The imposition of a new form of centralised rule, dominated by the clergy, has generated widespread opposition from political forces who supported the overthrow of the Shah, but who do not support the establishment of an Islamic Republic, ruled by the *faqih*. These three dimensions of reality – the economic, the international, and the political – therefore present external limits to the plan of creating an Islamic Republic.

The Iranian Revolution achieved great levels of mobilisation and political impact in the struggle against the Shah and in the immediate post-revolutionary aftermath. Once difficulties arose, and the broad united front that had toppled the Shah broke up, Khomeini was able to establish a regime built in his own image and successfully to crush the various opposition forces he faced. The success of the Iranian Revolution lay not, therefore, only in the destruction of an old regime, but in the successful establishment of a new one, different in many significant respects from that which it had replaced. If it shared more than it admitted with the Pahlavis, it was none the less built on very different systems of power, social support, and values. Yet, while this regime survived its first few years, it remained unclear whether its long-run stability was assured.

The hopes raised by the Iranian Revolution were extremely high, and it is not the only revolution to have disappointed its original supporters, let alone to have failed to create a perfect society on this earth. The post-revolutionary history of Iran has not only showed the limitations of the solutions offered by the Islamic clergy, but also forced Khomeini to stress an archaism inherent in this thought: the appeals to blood and sacrifice, the persecution of enemies and former allies, the brutal imposition of discriminatory Islamic codes of behaviour for women, the callous neglect of human life in the war with Iraq, and the incitement to persecute sexual and religious deviants. All these and more are the themes and policies to which the Imam resorted in order to implement his programme.

Through the revolution Iran became the site of a competition between the theological and the material, the clerical and the secular. The first round certainly went to the theological and the clerical. But how far these forces could sustain their advance in the face of material problems and an inability to meet many of the basic needs of the population remained an open question.

Notes and references

1. An earlier version of this chapter was published in the *Journal of International Affairs*, vol. 36, no. 2, Fall/Winter 1982/3. I am grateful to Hamza Alavi and Nikki Keddie for their most helpful comments during the revision. The revised analysis was completed before the publication of Said Arjomand's pioneering article 'Iran's Islamic Revolution in comparative Perspective' (*World Politics*, April 1986) which touches upon many of the points raised here. Despite its too

easy dismissal of class factors in the revolution (pp. 400–2), and its
espousal of the fallacious continuity between millennarian and secular
revolutionary thinkers (p. 411), Arjomand's article is a major contribution to understanding of the Iranian revolution.

2. Karl Griewank, *Der neuzeitliche Revolutionsbegriff* (Weimar, 1955),
   ch. 1.
3. Thus Radio Ahvaz, broadcasting in Arabic on 1 September 1980:
   'This awaiting universal Islamic state will demolish all tyrannical
   thrones built on the corpses of the oppressed. The sword of justice
   will claim all charlatans, agents, and traitors.' See my 'Iranian Foreign
   Policy Since 1979: Internationalism and Nationalism in the Islamic
   Revolution', in Juan Cole and Nikki Keddie (eds), *Shi'ism and Social
   Protest* (London, 1986).
4. One exception is the nineteenth-century Shi'ite writer Mullah Ahmad
   Naraqi, an exponent of the *Usuli* school which did emphasise the
   powers of juridical authorities in Islam. But Naraqi did not extend
   this to include full political power, as Khomeini was later to do (Said
   Amir Arjomand, 'The State and Khomeini's Islamic Order', *Iranian
   Studies*, vol. XIII, nos. 1–4 (1980), p. 154). What is striking is that
   Khomeini does not invoke the precedent of those conservative writers
   who opposed the secular constitution of 1906. Indeed, while he
   exhibited an initial tolerance of the 1906 Constitution, he seems later
   to have regarded the whole period of the Constitutional Revolution as
   an embarrassment.
5. This point has been well made by Mohammad Ja'far and Azar Tabari,
   'Iran: and the Struggle for Socialism', *Khamsin*, 8, 1981.
6. Sami Zubeida, 'The ideological conditions for Khomeini's doctrine of
   government', *Economy and Society*, vol. II, no. 2 (May 1982).
7. Ervand Abrahamian, *Iran Between Two Revolutions*, (Princeton,
   1982), pp. 530–537.
8. For a guide to the earlier role of the clergy in Iran see Nikki Keddie,
   Iran: Religion, Politics and Society, (London, 1980) and her *Religion
   and Rebellion in Iran: The Iranian Tobacco Protest of 1891–92* (London, 1966). Strictly speaking Islam does not have a clergy in the sense
   of an ordained body of men. But in this text I have used the term
   'clergy' interchangeably with the word *ulema*, literally 'those who
   know', the standard Arabic Muslim term, and the word *mullah*, the
   word normally applied to Shi'ite clergy in Iran. Iranians themselves
   tend not to use the word *mullah*, but to talk of the *akhund*, a slightly
   derogatory term for an ordinary clergyman, or of the *ruhaniyat*, the
   body of religious personnel. Higher-ranking clerics are called *mujtahids*,
   meaning that they have the authority of *ijtihad*, independent judgement on holy matters, whilst the highest ranking are called *ayatollah*,
   literally 'sign of God'. For a general discussion of Iranian terms for
   the clergy see Roy Mottahedeh, *The Mantle of the Prophet* (London,
   1986), pp. 231–2. Given the absence of any established hierarchy, the
   designation *ayatollah* is a result of promotion and reputation within
   the Islamic institutions. Prior to the revolution it was a term confined
   to a small number of clergyman, of whom Khomeini was neither the

senior nor the most learned. The term *Imam*, applied to Khomeini, represents a verbal inflation, but is an honorary title and, at least officially, does not indicate any claim to his being one of the line of Twelve Imams of the Shi'ites believe are the true followers of Mohammad.

9. We do not yet have the detailed information necessary to establish who were 'the faces in the crowd' that made the Iranian Revolution, that is, a precise evaluation of the social forces behind the revolution. While it appears, from the very size and superficial appearance of the demonstrators, that members of all social groups participated, it is much less clear what the proportions were. Some initial indications are given in Farhad Kazemi, *Poverty and Revolution in Iran* (London, 1980). He suggests that it was second-generation migrant industrial workers, not the poorest inhabitants of shanty towns, who participated most in the revolutionary protests. The poorest sections were still outside the social networks that would have drawn them into the demonstrations of late 1978. For an important, earlier study of this issue see Ervand Abrahamian, 'The Crowd in Iranian Politics, 1905–53, in Haleh Afshar (ed.), *Iran: A Revolution in Turmoil* (London 1985).

10. The demonstrations in the last months of the Shah's regime, involving up to 2 million people in Tehran, and several million more in provincial towns, were the largest protest demonstrations in human history. States have mobilised larger numbers in supportive marches – as in China's Tien An Men Square – but such crowds have never before been seen in an oppositional context.

11. The terms 'modern' and 'traditional' have been subject to considerable criticism. Their use here does not denote acceptance of a more general picture of social development as being conceivable in terms of a unilinear progression from one to the other. They are used here in a more figurative sense, to distinguish characteristics of Iranian society associated with its past from those resulting from the changes of the last decade.

12. No full account of the revolution has yet been written, but surveys are included in Abrahamian, and in Nikki Keddie, *Roots of Revolution* (New Haven, 1981). Also of interest are Robert Graham, *Iran: The Illusion of Power*, Second Edition (London, 1979), Mohammed Heikal, *The Return of the Ayatollah*, (New York, 1981), and L. P. Elwell-Sutton, "The Iranian Revolution: Triumph or Tragedy", in Hossein Amirsadeghi, ed., *The Security of the Persian Gulf* (New York, 1981). The best eyewitness account is Paul Balta and Claudine Rulleau, *L'Iran Insurgé* (Paris, 1979). On post-revolutionary developments the outstanding study is Shaul Bakhash, *The Reign of the Ayatollahs*, London 1984. Bakhtiar's own account is given in his *Ma Fidelite*, Paris, 1982. See also my interview with him in *MERIP Reports*, no. 104, March-April 1982.

13. Graham provides invaluable analysis of many aspects of the economic change; see also my *Iran: Dictatorship and Development* (London, 1979), and the references contained therein. On rural conditions, see

Eric Hooglund, *Land and Revolution in Iran, 1960–1980* (Austin, 1982). A general economic overview is given by M. H. Pesaran, 'Economic Development and Revolutionary Upheavals in Iran', in Haleh Afshar (ed.), *Iran: A Revolution in Turmoil*.

14. The merchants of the Tehran bazaar were particularly incensed in 1976 when the municipal authorities proposed to build a new urban highway that would have passed through the middle of the bazaar area.

15. American Ambassador William Sullivan complained bitterly of the Shah's indecisiveness, a characteristic foreign observers had noted during the crisis of the early 1950s. One British journalist who met the Shah in September reported that the monarch flatly refused to believe there were any slums in Tehran, a fact evident to the most casual observer. Some pertinent observations are given in Fereidun Hoveida, *The Fall of the Shah*, (London, 1980).

16. The army chief of staff, General Qarabaghi, was allowed to retire to his home and later went into exile. More mysterious was General Fardust, the former chief of the Shah's private intelligence service, who reportedly became head of SAVAMA, a new state security organization.

17. Theda Skocpol, *State and Social Revolution* (London, 1979), pp. 14–18. Skocpol's own reflections on the Iranian revolution are in 'Rentier State and Shi'a Islam in the Iranian Revolution' in *Theory and Society*, May 1982. She points to the sociological weakness of rentier states and the mobilising potential of Shi'a Islam as special factors enabling the Iranian revolution.

18. Ibrahim Yazdi, Foreign Minister of the Islamic Republic, in interview with the author, Tehran, August 1979.

19. An important comparative perspective on the 1979 revolution is given by the Mosaddeq period when secular nationalism and a mass Communist movement predominated: see Richard Cottam, *Nationalism in Iran* (Pittsburgh, 1964). The clergy at that time gave some support to Mosaddeq, but turned against him in 1952 and did not oppose the 1953 *coup*. Khomeini never mentions Mosaddeq's name in a positive light and argues that his fall was a result of his abandonment of Islam.

20. For discussion of this issue see Said Amir Arjomand, 'Shi'ite Islam and Revolution in Iran', *Government and Opposition*, vol. 16, no. 3 (Summer 1981), Edward Mortimer, *Faith and Power* (London, 1982), ch. 9, and Hamid Algar, 'The Oppositional Role of the Ulama in Twentieth Century Iran', in Nikki Keddie (ed.), *Scholars, Saints and Sufis*, (Berkeley, 1972). Also indispensable is the work of Akhavi, cited in n. 22 below.

21. Muslim radicals find confirmation in certain verses of the Koran which are supposed to reinforce their orientation: for example, 'We willed that those who are being oppressed would become the leaders and the rightful inheritors of the world' (*Sura Qesas*, 5); 'Very soon the oppressors will know how they are going to be punished' (*Sura XVIII*, V, 227). The word used for 'oppression', *dhulm*, is the conventional Islamic word for tyranny.

22. An extremely shrewd and careful discussion of these points is contained in Shahrough Akhavi *Religion and Politics in Contemporary Iran* (Albany, New York, 1980). Akhavi demonstrates the contingency of Islamic thought and hence the availability of a wide range of equally valid 'interpretations'. On Islam as a state religion under the Safavis, see I. B. Petrushevsky, *Islam in Iran* (London, 1985), ch. XIII.

23. A careful study of the organisation and curricula of the Qom *madrases* in the mid-1970s is given by Michael Fischer in *Iran: From Religious Dispute to Revolution* (Cambridge, Massachusetts, 1980).

24. Akhavi, *Religion and Politics*, pp. 126–7. He quotes one reforming *mollah* who denounced *avam zadigi*, the effects of mass mindlessness, and said it was better to be affected by 'floods, earthquakes, snakes, and scorpions' than to be subject to the will of the masses on matters of reform.

25. Some of the theorists of Islamic revolution have developed a concept of a just or unitary society, based on the Islamic concept of *touhid*, or unity of God and man. These writers include the lay theoretician Ali Shariati and former President Abol Hassan Bani-Sadr. But it does not seem that Khomeini ever accepted this concept, and he laid much greater stress on the need to implement the rules of Islamic jurisprudence.

26. In the post-revolutionary period Khomeini was officially described by three titles: Imam, Leader of the Revolution, and Founder of the Islamic Republic. These three sources of his legitimacy represented religious authority, the aura of success, and the programme he sought to implement. His frequent designation as 'Imam of the Islamic Nation', where 'nation' is a translation of the word *umma*, illustrates the ambiguous character of constituency he was meant to represent – Iran, or a wider Islamic world.

27. Khomeini's main writings are contained in *Islam and Revolution*, translated and annotated by Hamid Algar (Berkeley, 1981).

28. The charge of being a *mofsid fi'l arz* ('spreader of corruption on earth') is one common charge in such cases. The other is that of being *mohareb be khoda* ('declaring war on God'). If concepts of legitimacy are essential in mobilising populist coalitions, so too are concepts of denying legitimacy to the other side. Khomeini's favourite term for the Shah was *Taghut*, a term usually derived from an Arabic root meaning to tyrannise. In fact, *Taghut* has a different root, meaning idol or a false god. In later terminology Khomeini was referred to as the *Bot shekan*, the 'Idol Smasher', with the Shah as the first idol to be broken, Carter the second, Bani Sadr the third, and it was hoped, Iraqi leader Saddam Hussein the fourth. *Bot* is a Persian language equivalent of *Taghut*.

29. In particular, the writer Al-i Ahmad, whose work *Gharbzadegi* ('intoxication with the West'), was very popular among university students in the 1970s. Although the son of a *mollah*, Al-i Ahmad himself was rather anti-clerical in his writings. For an account of his ideas see Mottahedeh, pp. 287–315.

30. On Shariati see Fischer, *Iran*, Keddie, *Roots of Revolution*, and Mangol Bayat-Phillip 'Shiism in Contemporary Iranian Politics: The Case of Ali Shariati', in Elie Kedourie and Sylvia Haim, (eds), *Towards a Modern Iran* (London, 1980). Shariati too was quite anti-clerical, and is regarded by most religious authorities as an unlettered upstart. His writings fall into the mainstream of Third World cultural and nationalist writings of the 1970s. He died in London, in 1977. See his *On the Sociology of Islam* (Berkeley, 1979).

31. One exceptional element in Khomeini's populism is his use of irate paternalism, as he threatens to chastise and punish his followers. This is of course partly a note of Qur'anic punitiveness which will be familiar to his audience, but contrasts with the rhetoric of other secular populists. In a speech in August 1979 he declared: 'When we broke down the corrupt regime and destroyed this very corrupt dam; had we acted in a revolutionary manner from the beginning, had we closed down this hired press, these corrupt magazines, these corrupt parties and punished their leaders, had we erected scaffoldings for the hanging in all the major squares, and had we chopped off all the corrupters and the corrupted, we would not have had these troubles today'. But he goes on: 'I beg forgiveness from almighty God and my dear people.'

32. See Keddie, *Religion and Rebellion*, pp. 27–8, where the Muslim reformer Malkam Khan discusses how to justify modern principles in Qur'anic terms.

33. Skocpol, pp. 19–24, outlines a theory of the international dimension of revolutions on which I have drawn here.

34. For the earlier decades of the century see the classic E. Brown, *The Persian Revolution* (London, 1909); for the early 1950s see Kermit Roosevelt, *Countercoup* (New York, 1980), a vivid account of the American and British roles in preparing the 1953 *coup* that re-installed the Shah.

35. Hossein Mahdavy, 'Patterns and Problems of Economic Development in Rentier States: the Case of Iran', in M. A. Cook (ed.), *Studies in the Economic History of the Middle East* (London, 1970) and Homa Katouzian, *The Political Economy of Modern Iran, 1926–1979* (London, 1981).

36. Skocpol stresses the growing autonomy of the state as another central feature of the revolutions she describes. While in my view she over-states the disassociation of ruling class and state apparatus, she none the less indicates a feature of revolutionary situations which contributes to explaining why, at a particular time, an existing state is overthrown. See n. 16 for her application of this thesis to Iran.

37. In his post revolutionary memoirs, the Shah seeks to ignore the growing crisis in his country and focuses uniquely on the role of the US mission to Iran in the last days of his reign: *The Shah's Story* (London, 1980).

38. William Sullivan argues that some accommodation with Khomeini might have been possible in early 1979, but that this was excluded by

an unrealistic 'hard line' being pursued by Brezezinski, the President's National Security Adviser: in 'Dateline Iran: the Road Not Taken', *Foreign Policy*, Washington, no. 40 (Fall 1980) and his *Mission to Iran* (New York, 1981). The best accounts of US Iranian relations are in Barry Rubin, *Paved with Good Intentions: The American Experience in Iran* (New York: 1980) and Gary Sick, *All Fall Down, America's Tragic Encounter with Iran*, London 1985. See also my discussion of variant US accounts in MERIP Reports no. 140, May–June 1986.

4 Pakistan and Islam: Ethnicity and Ideology

HAMZA ALAVI

There is a pervasive belief, held more widely outside Pakistan than in the country, that Pakistan, with Israel and Iran, is one of three confessional states in the world; that, like Israel, its very origin was to fulfil a religious ideal, to create an Islamic state and Islamic society for Muslims of India. That has been the slogan of the Jamaat-e-Islami, the fundamentalist extreme right-wing party, since Pakistan was created. Interestingly enough it was not their slogan before the creation of Pakistan, for they had opposed the Pakistan movement. The regime of General Zia has declared likewise, that Pakistan was created to establish an Islamic state for Muslims of India. Lacking a popular mandate the military regime has sought its claim to legitimacy, if not its purpose, in divine ordinance.

When, after seizing power, the Zia regime discovered that it was totally lacking in authority (its power base being the army itself) it took refuge in divine providence and it was soon claimed that the Almighty has communicated with the General in a dream; that he had experienced *ilham*, a state of grace in which a divine message entered his heart, charging him with the task of creating an Islamic state and Islamic society in Pakistan. Such a claim to the seat of power is more in line with medieval claims of the divine right of kingship rather than any desire to submit to the will of the people who might be given the opportunity to affirm such a purpose through a free and genuine expression of the popular will. To justify and reinforce this claim, it is loudly proclaimed with the full force of Pakistan's captive media that Islamic ideology was indeed at the heart of the Pakistan movement, the *raison d'être* of the new state, an ideal that more than thirty years after the foundation of the state, it had been left to General Zia to realise.

The idea that the Pakistan movement was motivated by Islamic ideology is, as will soon be quite apparent, a misconception. An alternative explanation of the Pakistan movement is that it was a movement of 'feudal' landlords of the Muslim majority provinces of India, especially the Punjab and Sindh and, to a lesser extent, Bengal. This has been argued by Indian Nationalist and also Communist Party historians before 1942 and after 1946. They suggest further that this movement was instigated and fostered by the British who wished to divide the nationalist movement. This theory too is misconceived and slurs over many facts and aspects of a complex history.[1]

A third view, which was adopted by the Communist Party between 1942 and 1946, held that the Pakistan movement was a movement of the (weak) Muslim national bourgeoisie and there-fore a legitimate anti-imperialist movement, deserving of com-munist support, in line with the stand taken by Lenin at the Second Congress of the Communist International in 1921.[2] This view has been reiterated by Soviet scholars, notably in the influential work by Yuri Gankovsky and Gordon-Polonskaya on the history of Pakistan,[3] who produce the names of a few prominent Gujerati Muslims from a business community background who were associ-ated peripherally with the early Muslim League, to support their argument. That view is also mistaken. The predominantly Guje-rati Muslim trading communities of India, barring one or two individuals, took little part in the Muslim movement, which was dominated above all by Muslim professionals and the *salariat* (see below) of northern India, especially of the UP (United Provinces, later Uttar Pradesh), Bihar and Punjab. The Gujeratis were isolated from them linguistically and culturally as well as politically and had no objective class interests of their own that the Muslim movement could then serve. There were a few individuals, es-pecially professionals, drawn from Gujerati business communities – notably Mr Jinnah himself, a rich and successful lawyer son of a not too successful trader – who did play a part in the Muslim movement. But from this we cannot infer class involvement.

Muslim state and Islamic state

The irony of the argument that Pakistan was founded on religious ideology lies in the fact that every group and organisation in the Subcontinent of India that was specifically religious, was hostile to Jinnah and the Muslim League and had strongly opposed the Pakistan movement. Foremost amongst them was the *Jamiat-ul-Ulama-e-Hind*, the leading organisation of the so-called 'Deobandi ulama, whom we might categorise as Islamic Traditionalists. A great deal of effort was devoted by the Muslim League leadership to win them over. Eventually they succeeded in that, but only partially, on the eve of the Partition, through the defection of a section of the ulama, led by Maulana Shabbir Ahmad Usmani, who formed the Jamiat-ul-Ulama-e-Islam. The Islamic Fundamentalist Jamaat-e-Islami, led by Maulana Maududi, was no less opposed to the Pakistan movement, although since the Partition they have gone to great lengths to conceal or explain away their earlier stance. Again, the Nationalist Muslims who were in the Indian National Congress not only included secular-minded figures like Rafi Ahmad Kidwai, but also, and especially, Muslims educated in the classical tradition who were deeply religious, such as their leader Abul Kalam Azad who was steeped in Muslim classical and religious learning.

This was in marked contrast to the modernist education and style of life and aspirations of the Muslim League leadership. A claim that the creation of Pakistan was a fulfilment of millenarian religious aspirations of Indian Muslims would therefore stand in contradiction to the alienation of the principal bearers of the religion of Islam in India from the Pakistan movement and, contrariwise, the explicit commitment of the leaders of the movement to secular politics. These apparently contradictory aspects of the history of Pakistan are overlooked by scholars who are mesmerised by the spectre of militant fundamentalist Islam arisen throughout the 'Muslim world'.[4] In Pakistan itself, history has been systematically rewritten and ideologists of the regimes in power have spared few efforts to present the Pakistan movement as a fundamentalist religious movement.

My contention is that the Pakistan movement was neither a millenarian ideological movement devoted to the realisation of an Islamic state nor was it a movement of feudal landlords nor yet again a movement of an emergent Muslim national bourgeoisie. It is true that by 1946 the Muslim League reached an accommodation with the landed magnates who ruled over Sindh and Punjab, on their terms, in order to gain a semblance of authority in those Muslim majority provinces by virtue of their agreement to take on the Muslim League label (the implications of that will be examined below). It will be argued that the central driving force behind the Muslim movement was a class that has a distinct place in colonised societies whose role needs to be recognised more fully and explicitly. I have labelled this class the *salariat*, the urban, educated classes who qualify for employment in the colonial state. With them were associated the new professionals who emerged in the context of the colonial transformation of Indian society, the lawyers, journalists and urban intellectuals generally, who share many of the problems and aspirations of the salariat.

In a nutshell, the argument of this paper is that the Pakistan movement was a movement of Muslims rather than of Islam; a movement in which diverse Muslim ethnic groups from different regions, representing different social strata and interests, were allied in pursuit of quite material objectives. At the centre of that movement was a coalition of the emerging Muslim salariats of different regions of India, a coalition that was to break down as soon as Pakistan was created and the Muslim movement had outlived its purpose. Moreover, Muslim nationalism was at its weakest in the Muslim majority provinces, having little appeal to the rural classes. Even for those who were drawn into the movement, there was no automatic or permanent translation of the attribute of Muslim by faith or Muslim by descent into an enduring conception of an ethnically undifferentiated *Muslim* nation. On the contrary, the central axis of Pakistan's political history has revolved around strident affirmations of regional and linguistic ethnic identities that have refused to be set aside, delegitimised and dissolved by slogans of Islamic ideology or claims of *Muslim* nationhood raised on behalf of the dominant ethnic groups.

The unity of the movement that ultimately resulted in the creation of Pakistan was a precarious one. Jinnah's political genius lay precisely in his ability to orchestrate a loose, volatile and unpredictable coalition of forces. He is generally pictured as a man with a firm and total grip over the groups that he was leading. But that is a myth, made plausible by his powerful and commanding

personality. In reality his hold over the various groups was quite
tenuous and he had to take them on their own terms. He merely
stood at the centre of a political process around which diverse
regional groups revolved, over whom he had little control.

By the late 1940s, Jinnah and the All India Muslim League
provided the predominantly rural landowning groups, who ruled
in the Muslim majority provinces, with a now necessary and urgent
voice at the centre of Indian politics, in the dialogue with the
Indian National Congress and the colonial masters, at a time when
Independence was in prospect. They were prepared to make use of
him and the All India Muslim League for that purpose. That
supported the illusion of a unified Muslim nation in India. But it
was a marriage of convenience, for the provincial magnates, on
whom Jinnah depended for support and his own legitimacy, were
not prepared to surrender to him or the Muslim League their local
autonomy. It was they rather than the central leadership of the
Muslim League who were in a position to dictate the terms of the
alliance. Nevertheless the idea of a Muslim nation gained temporary currency and Jinnah became the embodiment of that conception. The Pakistan movement, in that sense and to that extent,
became a national movement, on the basis of the 'Two Nation
Theory' that Jinnah propounded, affirming that Muslims of India
were a separate nation from Hindus. But, in so far as their politics
entailed the establishment of 'Pakistan', however they might have
conceived it (and that was not at the time very clear to anyone),
their objective was the creation of a 'Muslim state', as a nation
state; they did not seek an 'Islamic state', as a theocratic conception.

The Muslim salariat and Muslim ethnicity

There was one particular social group for whom, more than any
other, the conception of 'Muslim' nationhood (and not religious
ideology) was particularly meaningful. That class was the product
of the colonial transformation of Indian social structure in the
nineteenth century and it comprised those who had received an
education that would equip them for employment in the expanding
colonial state apparatus as scribes and functionaries, the men (for
few women were so employed) whose instrument of production
was the pen. For the want of a better term I have referred to them
as the 'salariat'. The term 'middle class' is too wide and 'petty

bourgeoisie' has connotations, especially in Marxist political discourse, that would not refer to this class.

The 'salariat' is an 'auxiliary class' whose class role can be fully understood only in terms of its relation (through its role in the state apparatus) to 'fundamental classes', the economically dominant classes – namely the still dominant metropolitan bourgeoisie, the nascent indigenous bourgeosie and the powerful landowning classes – as well as the subordinate classes, the proletariat and the peasantry. Given a particular configuration of class forces in the state and society the political role of the salariat entails class alliances, by virtue of class commitments of its members either through class origins or through class affiliation. An example of this is its willingness to serve the anti-national purposes of the colonial state and, after the Partition, the United States' interests in the region, (through military alliances) at the cost of the nation that they purport to serve.

The salariat looms large in colonial societies where the production base and the bulk of the population is rural and agricultural. In the absence of a significant number of people clustered around urban industrial activities, and leaving aside a small number of people engaged in petty trading or in the relatively tiny sector of export trade and finance, the urban society revolves mainly around functionaries of the state, and the educated look primarily to the government for employment and advancement. The salariat itself is not undifferentiated in terms of location and functions of its members within the state apparatus and access to power. Its upper echelons, the bureaucratic and military oligarchies, play a role that is qualitatively different from that of its lower-level petty functionaries. Their relative weight in the political process *vis-à-vis* elected political representatives, is the greater the lower the level of development of the society in question. It is very prominent in many societies of Africa, for example, as it is in Pakistan. It is less prominent in post-colonial India which has experienced relatively higher levels of economic and political development, though even there it has not failed to make its mark. The salariat not only serves the economically dominant classes in the colonial and the post-colonial state but it also has its own specific interests by virtue of its particular structural location and its powers, privileges and opportunities for corruption as the 'governing class' in the post-colonial state, by virtue of its direct grip over the state apparatus in the absence of institutional structures of democratic political control.

This is a striking feature of the political scene of Pakistan.[5]

It was the Indian salariat and professional classes who were at the core of the Indian nationalist movement in its early stages during the late nineteenth century, demanding a rightful place for Indians in the state apparatus, for 'Indianisation' of the services and the creation of popular institutions of representative government through which they could have a share in the excercise of power, or at least some measure of control over the state in the name of 'self-government'.[6] It was only later that the Indian bourgeoisie threw its weight behind the nationalist movement and Indian nationalism mobilised wider sections of the Indian people.

Jinnah's 'Two Nations' theory expressed the ideology of the weaker Muslim salariat *vis-à-vis* the dominant high caste Hindu salariat groups. The Muslim salariat was central to the Pakistan movement. But as a class the salariat itself has a propensity to be easily fractured into different ethnic groups which vie with each other for preference and privilege. Such groups are not defined and determined, once for all, by cultural, linguistic, religious or regional criteria. There is, rather, a process of definition and redefinition of ethnic identity in changing political contexts, on the basis of perceptions of the distribution of privilege and politically viable options, as they are brought into focus from one stage to the next. Thus in Pakistan Muslim ethnic identity, once it had fulfilled its purpose for the salariats of Bengal, Sindh, Sarhad and Baluchistan, gave way to the respective regional ethnic identities. The newly affirmed identities are not, of course, constituted out of nothing. They draw on deeply embedded cultural, linguistic or regionally significant symbols around which they can mobilise popular support, symbols that can generate a powerful political charge.

The conception of a unified 'Muslim Nation' of South Asia did not outlast the day of independence and the creation of Pakistan. The inter-regional coalition of the 'Muslim' salariat broke up in the new state, for a new equation of the distribution of privilege and deprivation between them became visible. The Punjabis (who were temporarily joined by an elite group from *muhajirs*, Urdu-speaking migrants from India) were preponderant in the bureaucracy and the army and were quickly perceived as the privileged and dominant group, whereas the other ethnic salariat groups had less than their fair share of access to education, jobs and power.

TABLE 4.1 English literates over 20 years of age: Muslims and non-Muslims (1931)

	UP	*Punjab*	*Bengal*	*Sind*
Population				
Total	48.4m	28.5m	51m	3.9m
Muslims	7.2m	14.9m	27.8m	2.8m
% of total	14.9	52.3	54.5	71.8
Literates in English of 20 years and over				
Total	266 000	185 000	722 435	33 850
Muslims	49 400	58 800	175 600	4 900
% of total	18.6	31.8	24.3	14.5

Source: Census of India, 1931: Compiled from relevant Provincial Volumes.
Note: The 1931 Census data are used because the 1941 Census, the last pre-partition Census, is notoriously unreliable.

Overnight the 'Muslim' identity, behind which they had all rallied together in the Pakistan movement, was laid aside by the regional groups and new ethnic identities were affirmed – Bengali, Sindhi, Pathan and Baluch. It must be added though that the Pathan position has been a little ambiguous after Zia's military *coup d'état*, in view of the relatively strong representation of Pathans in the army. Again, we find a replication of the Indian example, for now the slogan of *akhand Bharat* was echoed in Pakistan by a new slogan of the indivisibility of the Muslim Nation that was proclaimed on behalf of the dominant Punjabis. A person could not legitimately declare himself or herself to be Bengali or Sindhi or Pathan or Baluch, because he or she was a Muslim, and Islam was a religion of equality and brotherhood and would recognise no divisions amongst the people of the faith. It is in that context that Islamic ideology was first placed at the centre of political debate, only after Pakistan was created, to oppose regional ethnic movements.

The Muslim salariat was not evenly distributed in size and influence in different parts of India and its future fragmentation was written into the pattern of its uneven development. If we take the numbers of persons of over 20 years of age who were literate in English as an index of their size, we get the picture shown in Table 4.1.

Muslim ethnicity therefore was only one stage in a process of ethnic definition and redefinition. It represented a temporary alliance of various regional groups. Its original thrust came from the Muslim salariat of the UP, where it was especially privileged rather than otherwise but where it was fast losing ground. Elsewhere the Muslim salariat was less developed than the Hindu salariat, so that the interests of the Muslim salariats could be counterposed to those of Hindus.

The Muslim salariat of the Punjab was the largest in absolute size amongst Muslims (with the exception of Bengal) though its relative share of the Punjab salariat was lower than that of Hindus. This was the principal grievance that fuelled the Muslim movement there. Later, after the creation of Pakistan, the Punjabi salariat, by virtue of its much greater size and development, came to occupy a dominant position in the army and the bureaucracy and thereby in Pakistan society and the state. Those of them who were on the other side of the boundary at the time of the Partition came over to Pakistan, thus consolidating their preponderance in the country.

The Urdu speaking salariat of the Gangetic Plain, that is UP and Bihar, was the next largest. In contrast to the Punjabis, with the exodus of Muslims from India only a proportion of them came over to Pakistan and their relative weight was therefore much reduced. Historically the share of Muslims in the overall salariat in the UP was greater than their share of the UP population, but their relative position declined sharply in the nineteenth century. Their share of jobs in the highest ranks of colonial service that were then open to Indians, declined from 64 per cent in 1857 to about 35 per cent by 1913, a dramatic decline.[7] They developed, as a result, a deep sense of grievance and insecurity, notwithstanding the fact that they were still a privileged minority, for their share of population was only about 13 per cent. This perceived threat to their (privileged) position probably explains the fact that the initial and major thrust of Muslim nationalism in India came from the UP and Bihar.

The Bengali Muslim salariat was the largest in terms of absolute size as compared to Muslims of other provinces. But its share of government jobs was proportionately much smaller than that of the Bengali Hindus; in sharp contrast to the Muslims of the UP, Bengali Muslims were always an underprivileged majority and they were poorly represented in government service, especially in the bureaucracy and the army. This grievance was to be the driving force behind Bengali nationalism in Pakistan that led eventually to the liberation of Bangladesh. Sindh figures show how small the Muslim salariat was in that province. These figures, low as they are, give a somewhat inflated picture of the insignificant share of ethnic Sindhi Muslims in salariat positions, as they include the considerable numbers of non-Sindhi Muslims who were employed in Sindh.

After Pakistan was created the slogan of Islam was adopted by the dominant component of the salariat in Pakistan, the Punjabis and, for a time, the Urdu-speaking Muhajirs, who feared the challenge of regional ethnic movements. It was invoked at first only nominally. In so far as it was included in the vocabulary of political debates in Pakistan during the first thirty years, only a few symbolic concessions were made to men of religion to make the argument look convincing. It was no more than a political argument that was used by the dominant Punjabis against the assertion of the new regional and linguistic ethnic identities of Bengalis, Sindhis, Pathans and Baluch. The ruling bureaucratic-military oligarchy, which has dominated Pakistan since its inception, had no intention, thereby, of allowing mullahs and Islamic ideologues to encroach on their monopoly of power and privilege.[8]

It was only after the seizure of power by the Zia regime that Islamic ideology was invoked in a rather more strident manner for a new purpose, the legitimation of state power itself for a politically bankrupt regime that lacked legitimate authority. It has had to go much further in affirming, symbolically, its commitments to Islam than any previous regime. But the issue of Punjabi dominance (Urdu-speaking migrants from India who had shared that position with them gradually fell behind) has not thereby been displaced by politics of Islamic Ideology, for it was recognised by oppositional groups that this is only a cover for continued Punjabi domination. Politics of ethnicity and religious ideology therefore remain closely intertwined and the various disaffected regional groups are unimpressed by the dramaturgy of religious fervour.

The formation of the structure of Muslim society in India

In view of the relatively low development of the Muslim salariat in general and its uneven development regionally, the question has often been asked why Muslims did not take more to education or to trade or commerce, that is, to middle-class occupations. Was this due to some peculiarities of their religion or culture or was it due to the idea that is sometimes put forward that Muslims, as the erstwhile rulers of India, were hostile to the colonial rulers and their institutions and that, in turn, they were systematically discriminated against? Speculation along these lines is most favoured by Muslim nationalist historians.[9] But the question is better inverted and we may well ask why in pre-colonial India the urban middle classes who were engaged in government service or trade did not convert to Islam. This had much to do with the route through which Islam came into the Indian subcontinent.

There are clear patterns of conversions to Islam by different social strata in different regions, which have been little noticed, let alone explained, although the patterns themselves are not difficult to see. There are two distinct and contrasting patterns, each related to the route by which Islam came to a particular region. One route of the advent of Islam was with the Muslim conquerors – though this did not mean that Islam was therefore spread by the sword; quite the contrary. The other route was by the sea, through contact with Arab seafarers and traders who for centuries dominated the Arabian sea. These two routes of the penetration of Islam into India had quite different effects on the class distribution and regional patterns of Islamisation. It is the resulting distribution of Muslims between different communities and regions that has constituted the context in which the later ethnic movements, that we are concerned with here, were to arise.

A paradox of the advent of Islam with Muslim rule was that at the heartland of the Muslim empires of India, in the Gangetic Plain, conversions to Islam were minimal. On the other hand, they were maximal in the two peripheries of the empire, namely the Indus Plain (now Pakistan) and Bengal. We have no answers yet to the question why that was so, though we would suspect that there are social structural explanations to be found. The peripheries were perennially given to heresy against the Brahminical orthodoxy that ruled at the heartland of empire.

Before Islam, Buddhism flourished in the two peripheral regions. Even after the advent of Islam, it was a dissident version of Islam that took root there rather than the orthodox puritanical version of Islam that was established in the UP, where great

seminaries of Muslim religious learning flourished. The Islam of
the periphery was influenced instead by Sufism and was ruled over
by pirs who claimed miraculous powers and made profitable business out of the credulity of their followers. It was also infused with
a large dose of syncretism, much condemned by the UP-based
ulama. By contrast in the UP the influence of pirs and Sufism was
minimal.

The divergence in patterns of religious belief between the
Gangetic Plain and the two peripheries is paralleled by di-
vergences in many other aspects of their respective social life. A
study by Marriott, for example, plots the scale of rigidity and
fluidity in caste ranking and ritual between different regions of
India. He found greater fluidity in these the further west one
moved away from the Brahminical heartland of the Gangetic Plain
towards Punjab and Sindh. Marriott found such differences also
among Hindu communities of these regions.[10] My own work in the
Punjab shows likewise that there is no social institution operating
there that can seriously be treated as caste. Even in the matter of
structures of kinship there are differences, for patrilateral-parallel
cousin marriage (that is, preferential marriage to father's brother's
daughter or structural equivalent) is the rule in the Indus Plain
whereas, as one moves east, to East Punjab and Western UP, the
so-called 'Muslim' structure of kinship gives way to *gotra* exogamy
practised by jat and rajput Muslim peasants. Parallel to the regional differences in religious ideology there were also regional
differences in social structure, which raises questions about the
nature of the connections between the two.

If we consider the pattern of conversion to Islam along another
axis, we find that there is a fairly clear class pattern of Islamisation associated with the advent of Muslim rulers. Muslim rule
installed expatriate Muslims brought from Arabia, Iran, Turkey
and Afghanistan as feudal lords at the foundations of their empires
and many Hindu, especially Rajput, chiefs converted to Islam.
Their dependant peasants 'converted' *en masse* likewise. Islam was
established thereby as a predominantly rural religion. It made
much less headway in towns and cities.

The relatively low level of conversions to Islam among urban
classes suggests absence of coercion by Muslim rulers, who were
quite happy to be served by Hindu officials. In the UP Kashmiri
Brahmins and Kayasthas are the two main Hindu castes who have

traditionally worked for the state both before and after the colonial conquest. The UP and Punjab diverge from this general rule, for there far more Muslims found themselves in the salariat than elsewhere, as descendents of those associated with the courts at Delhi, Agra, Lucknow and Lahore found their way into salaried state service. When Pakistan was created men from Punjab and the UP, where the Muslim salariat was the most developed, dominated the bureaucratic-military oligarchy. Over the years, Punjabis have acquired complete ascendency in Pakistan.

In contrast to the UP and Punjab, Muslims had little share of urban middle-class occupations in Sind and Bengal or in Baluchistan and the Sarhad. In Sindh, under Muslim rule, government service was virtually the exclusive prerogative of Amils, a Hindu community. The number of ethnic Sindhi Muslims in government service was minute. Trade in Sindh was traditionally in the hands of another Hindu community called Bhaibands, though during the latter half of the nineteenth century there was an influx of Muslim and non-Muslim trading communities mainly from Gujerat (including Kathwiawar and Cutch) into Sindh. Bengal was no different, for the size of the Muslim salariat there was small and suffered much from discriminatory colonial policies. Aparna Basu notes that 'In lists of qualified candidates drawn up by the Council of Education in Bengal in the years after 1846, Muslim names are conspicuous by their absence.'[11] Politics of Muslims in Bengal were predominantly based on rural classes, especially the struggle of (mainly Muslim) 'Occupancy Tenants' (*de facto* landowners), for abolition of Zamindari overlordship, a cause upheld by the non-communal Krishak Proja Party led by A. K. Fazlul Haq.

Islam that came by the sea, with Arab control of overseas trade, resulted in a rather different class configuration of Muslims. (Our concern in this paper is primarily with northern India and we will ignore for the moment the logic and patterns of Muslim conversions in southern India.) In Gujerat (including Cutch and Kathiawar) on the west coast of India, Muslim conversions were mainly from trading communities, Sunnis such as Memons and Shi'as such as Bohras and Khojas (both Ismailis) and Ithna Asharis. This seems to be closely related to the fact that the bulk of the export trade from northern India went abroad through ports in this region, which were all under Hindu rule. Arabs dominated the trade of the Arabian sea. Substantial trading communities which

were engaged in export trade in Gujerat, not surprisingly, converted to Islam. The myths of origin of these communities speak of
benign and tolerant Hindu rulers who did not discourage this. One
can see the functionality of such tolerance and goodwill when rival
ports were competing with each other to attract Arab trade.
Contrary to the northern Indian pattern, no Muslim landlords
were installed in these areas and there was no dependent peasantry
therefore to take to Islam, except to the extent that the pattern
was to be modified later when Muslim rule itself was extended
southwards and was established in parts of Gujerat. During the
second half of the nineteenth century there was a diffusion of the
Muslim trading communities of Gujerat over various parts of India
when they began to move to the new expanding centres of colonial
trade, such as Bombay, Karachi, Calcutta, and elsewhere.
There was a push effect as well as a pull effect, for the development of the railway links between Bombay and Karachi with
northern India short-circuited the traditional trade routes from
northern India to Gujerat ports and the trading communities there
had to look for fresh pastures.

These Muslim trading communities of Gujerat were isolated,
with respect to language and culture, from the northern Indian,
Urdu-speaking, Muslim salariat. These trading communities set a
low value on higher education, which was functional for those
aspiring for salariat positions. In terms of their own values these
communities despised salaried employment, however eminent.
Their children were expected to join the family business after
secondary schooling. They missed therefore even the politicising
effects of university life. Nor were they impelled as a class into the
Muslim movement which at that time had little to offer them. In
the late 1940s Jinnah persuaded a few of them based in Bombay to
form a separate 'Muslim Chamber of Commerce'. But even that
remained a paper organisation. Their role in Muslim movements
was negligible, except for one or two individuals, notably, of
course, Mr Jinnah himself who, however, had cut himself off very
early from the modest background of his family and community in
Karachi and had assimilated himself, as an extremely successful
and very rich lawyer, into cosmopolitan upper-class Bombay society.

Much is made by some historians of another exceptional case of
a Gujerati businessmen, namely that of Sir Adamjee Pirbhai, a

Dawoodi Bohra industrialist who owned textile mills and the Matheran railway, amongst his varied interests. As a friend of the Agha Khan, he was made to preside over the conference of the Muslim League at Karachi in 1907, that is when the Muslim League had just been launched by the Muslim 'notables' and was about to be seized by the Muslim salariat who soon pushed the notables aside. They got little joy out of Sir Adamjee, whose Presidential Address had nothing to say about the aims and objectives and the anxieties of the Muslim salariat who had brought him there. Instead he spoke of the importance of 'industrialism' and declared with some pride how Muslim businessmen were participating fully in that enterprise, shoulder to shoulder with their Hindu brothers, adding a word of gratitude to the Viceroy and the (colonial) Government of India. As an enlightened liberal he advocated friendship between Hindus and Muslims. Sir Adamjee Pirbhai himself was soon to get embroiled in an anti-clerical movement within his own community for which he was to sacrifice his time and his fortune. He had little interest in or time for the Muslim League. It would be a mistake therefore to read in his momentary participation at the Muslim League conference (where he was out of tune with all that the League was trying to achieve) or similar participation of a very few such individuals in the Muslim movement, to imply the class involvement of the Gujerat-based Muslim bourgeoisie, much less its leadership of Muslim nationalism in India.

Islamic and secular ideologies of Muslims in India

There is a widespread tendency, in the language of scholars as well as in the rhetoric of politicians, to attribute political and ideological positions to Indian 'Muslims', in an over-generalised way, as if Muslims of different social strata and classes in different regions were equally involved. That is manifestly untrue. There were sharp differences in these respects not only between different classes and strata but also between Muslim majority provinces and Muslim minority provinces. It was in the Muslim *minority* provinces, especially in the UP, rather than those in which Muslims were in a majority, that specifically Muslim political and ideological movements were generated. Until the late 1940s, when Jinnah and the Muslim League managed to form an uneasy alliance with

TABLE 4.2

I. 'Muslim' positions in India

   i. *Islamic Traditionalism* The Ulama I: 'Deobandis'
  ii. *Islamic Traditionalism* The Ulama II: 'Barelvis', and Pirs
 iii. *Islamic Fundamentalism* Maududi and the Jamaat-e-Islami
 iv. *Islamic Modernism* Sir Syed Ahmad Khan, and Mohammad Iqbal
  v. *Secular Muslim Nationalism* exemplified by Jinnah

II Non-communal positions of Muslims in Muslim majority provinces

 vi. *Secular provincial non-communal transactional politics*
    Landlord-dominated right-wing Punjab Unionist Party and various political groups in Sind, being the ruling groups and parties
 vii. *Secular provincial non-communal radical politics*
    The Krishak Proja Party of Bengal, led by A. K. Fazlul Haq, the ruling party in Bengal
viii. *Secular non-communal 'Nationalist Muslims'*
    The ruling (Congress) party in the Sarhad

dominant groups in the Muslim majority provinces, their politics were not even Muslim nationalist, let alone 'Islamic'. They were, rather non-communal politics of landlord-dominated groups and political parties.

Broadly we can therefore identify eight ideological-political positions amongst Indian Muslims, before Independence, as shown in Table 4.2.

In addition to the groups mentioned in Table 4.2, there are also Shi'as, who are estimated to number about 15 per cent of the population of Pakistan; some estimates are considerably greater. No reliable data are available. Shi'as organised the All-India Shi'a Conference in 1907 to rival Sunni organisations. But leading Shi'as of the UP were active instead in the Muslim League and the Shi'a Conference did not make any headway. Lately some (minority) Shi'a organisations have surfaced in Pakistan, against the background of the Government's campaign for Islamisation, as well as the influence of the Iranian revolution, and they are demanding imposition in the country of *Fiqh Ja'faria*, the Shi'a code, rather than a Sunni code; a quite extraordinary and unrealistic demand which essentially expresses Shi'a fears of being forced to accept Sunni legislation. This is a minority militant movement which

illustrates where the logic of 'Islamisation' can lead. The main
current of Shi'a opinion in the country, however, seems to favour
the notion of a secular state. Contrariwise there have been equally
strident demands that Pakistan be declared a Sunni Hanafi republic and the Hanafi *fiqh*, or legal code, be made the law of the
land, that all other sects be declared minorities and be given
second-class citizenship. This has led to a great deal of sectarian
violence. But these developments are the logical extension of the
claim made by the Zia regime to impose Islamic Law in Pakistan:
the question is 'Which Islamic Law?'.

There were numerous other Muslim political movements (such
as Khaksars and Ahrars, especially, who were extremely hostile to
the Pakistan movement) and many sectarian divisions among
Sunni Hanafis. I have listed only three main sectarian categories,
namely the Traditionalist Deobandi and Barelvi Ulama and the
Islamic Fundamentalist Jamaat-e-Islami, whose beliefs and creeds
are quite incompatible with each other. We may also mention two
others, namely the Ahl-i-Hadith who deny the validity of the four
medieval schools of Islam and insist on a literal application of the
Qur'an and Hadith and the Ahl-i-Qur'an who go even further in
demanding absolute reliance only on the Qur'an, considering
reliability of Hadith, transmitted through fallible human channels,
also to be precarious. Each declares the others to be *kafirs* or
infidels. Summing up evidence taken from all major religious
groups, a high level judicial *Committee of Inquiry* (into sectarian
riots in 1953) headed by the country's two most eminent judges
concluded as follows: 'The net result of all this is that neither
Shi'as nor Sunnis, nor Deobandis nor Ahl-i-Hadith nor Barelvis
are Muslims and any change from one view to the other must be
accompanied in an Islamic State with the penalty of death, if the
State is in the hands of the party which considers the others to be
kafirs.'[12]

Traditionalist Islam: the ulama – 'Deobandi' and Barelvi

The 'ulama' (plural of *alim*, a man of – religious – learning) is a
grandiose term, which is often used quite loosely, as for example
in the results of a survey recently published by the Government of
Pakistan which finds the vast majority of them to be barely

literate. The 'ulama', properly so designated, however, are those who have been educated at a religious seminary and have gone through the *Dars-e-Nizami*, a syllabus that was laid down in medieval India and has hardly changed. Generally, they have little knowledge of the world that they live in, nor even perhaps of the world of Islam except for myths and legends. They inhabit little temples of their own uncomprehending and enclosed minds in which they intone slogans, petrified words and dogmas. Affairs of state and society are, generally, beyond their narrowed vision. There are only a few amongst them who have had the benefit of some tolerable education and who, in their own ways, try to follow current affairs.

The ulama of the Sunni Hanafi *Mazhab*, as mentioned above, are themselves divided into warring groups of whom the two main are popularly known as the 'Deobandis', after the great seminary at Deoband, and 'Barelvis', after the town of Bareilly in the UP, which was the seat of their mentor, Maulana Ahmad Raza Khan Barelvi. Deobandis and Barelvis differ in every respect, by virtue of their different doctrinal positions, the different classes (and regions) amongst whom they have influence and their different political stances. The hallmark of Deobandi ulama in the late nineteenth and early twentieth centuries was their unremitting anti-colonialism. Barelvi ulama and pirs, unlike the Deobandis, were not involved in anti-colonial ideology and struggle. On the contrary, most of them, with few exceptions, supported the colonial regime and, were in turn, favoured by it.

The 'Deobandi' ulama

It took the Deobandi ulama many decades of British rule before they began to show their eventual deep resentment against it. One should add, parenthetically, that the label 'Deobandi' is not wholly appropriate here, except for brevity, for the eponymous Dar-ul-Uloom at Deoband was not founded until 1867. Very few of these worthies played a part in the Wahabi movement of the early nineteenth century against colonial rule, with which they are often associated, which was led by men of the sword, the last defenders of Indian feudalism, rather than dispensers of law. Be that as it may, the belated hostility of these ulama to British rule was derived from changes that were being brought about during the middle decades of the nineteenth century by the colonial state, that directly impinged upon their lives and livelihood. There were three contexts in which the changes affected them. Firstly, in pre-colonial India Muslim ulama and Hindu pandits played a central role in the judicial system and held lucrative and influential positions. That continued in the early years of colonial rule. But soon a new legal system was being established to meet the new needs of the expanding colonial capitalist economy. The old feudal dispensations were no longer appropriate. Along with the new laws and new types of courts to adjudicate them, a new class of English-educated lawyers and judges took over from the ulama who were pushed out of their high status and lucrative jobs. Secondly, the ulama were also being pushed out of the educational system. That process was a little slower, though that was not because the colonial regime spared any efforts to speed it up. Indian clerks were needed who would be educated along lines that would prepare them for service in the apparatus of colonial government. The traditional schools run by ulamas (and Hindu pandits), with their emphasis on classical learning, Arabic, Persian and Sanskrit, were no longer suited to that purpose. They were replaced by new anglo-vernacular schools, with the active sponsorship and support from the colonial state. The hostility of the ulama to the colonial regime no doubt owed much to these bread-and-butter questions, although it was expressed and legitimised in terms of moral outrage. A third factor underlying the anti-colonialism of the ulama was the plight of Indian weavers, the *julahas*, who were their most fervent followers. Indian weavers, once the most prosperous of the Indian artisan classes, were devasted by the colonial impact and consequent destruction of Indian textile manufacturing. *Julahas* were therefore amongst the most embittered opponents of colonialism. They became extremely bigoted and developed an uncompromising attitude towards the West. The ulama's outlook reflected that also.

All these factors bound the ulama to the Indian nationalist cause. They never argued for the setting up of an 'Islamic' state nor a Muslim state. Quite the contrary: they called upon Muslims to join hands with their Hindu brothers in the patriotic cause against foreign rule. To rationalise that position they put forward a theory that constituted an essentially secular public philosophy. They separated the domain of faith, as a private domain, from the public domain of politics and government. This was formulated quite explicitly by Maulana Hasan Ahmad Madani of Deoband who argued that

(i) faith was universal and could not be contained within national boundaries, but
(ii) nationality was a matter of geography and Muslims were bound to the nation of their birth by obligations of loyalty along with their non-Muslim fellow citizens.

They would live together in harmony in independent India which, although not *dar-ul-Islam*, under Muslim rule, would be *dar-ul-amn*, the land of peace, where Muslims would be guaranteed freedom to practice their faith, where it would be the duty of Muslims to live as loyal and law abiding citizens. It was the duty of the Muslim in India to fight with a sense of dedication for the freedom and independence of his country quite as much as he was obliged to fight for the liberty of his conscience and the sanctity of his faith. The political philosophy of the ulama was a peculiar amalgam of pan-Islamic ideas and Indian nationalist ideas which were fused in their anti-imperialism.[13]

   This contradictory amalgam of ideas came together in the Khilafat Movement (1919–23) in the aftermath of the First World War, which was the climactic moment in the political struggles of the Deobandi ulama. The aim of the movement was to resist the liquidation of the Ottoman Empire and the office of the Ottoman Caliph. It was a bizarre movement of religious obscurantism that unleashed rabid and atavistic passions among Indian Muslims. It was strongly disapproved of by Jinnah. But, ironically, it was powerfully backed by Gandhi, the wordly-wise leader of secular Indian Nationalism, notwithstanding the fact that it ran counter to the aspirations of Turkish and Arab nationalism! It was Gandhi's intervention and organisational genius, and the resources of the Congress Party, that transformed a relatively minor movement into a mass phenomenon. It was a cynical tactical political move that promised to isolate the Muslim salariat leadership from Muslim masses by arousing their fanatical passions behind a hopeless and anachronistic cause. The Muslim League was eclipsed; it was virtually suspended and did not meet as a body between 1919 and 1924. Gandhi had achieved his purpose. In 1919, under the leadership of Deoband and in the wake of the Khilafat movement, the

Jamiat-ul-Ulama-e-Hind was formed as the political organisation of the ulama. It was during that movement, that they made their biggest, though somewhat brief, impact on the Indian political scene. But they left behind a bitter legacy of narrow communalism especially amongst some sections of the Muslim urban, subordinate classes. In the late 1940s the Muslim League made great efforts to win over the ulama to the Pakistan cause. They eventually succeeded in November 1945, when Pakistan was already in prospect, in winning over a breakaway group from the *Jamiat-ul-Ulama-e-Hind* to form the *Jamiat-ul-Ulama-e-Islam* which has established itself as a political party in Pakistan.

Barelvi ulama and pirs

In contrast to the Deobandi ulama, Barelvis profess a populist Islam, more infused with superstition, and also syncretism, that make up the religious beliefs of the peasantry. The Barelvi version of Islam emphasises belief in miracles and and powers of saints and pirs (*mashaikh*), worship at shrines and the dispensing of amulets and charms, which are all condemned by Deobandis as un-Islamic, Deobandis and Barelvis detest each other and much sectarian conflict consists of fights between the two.

Pirs or sufi shaikhs, play an important part in the religious life of the peasantry. Barelvi Islam is closely tied to devotion to pirs and belief in their powers of intercession (*wasilah*), whereas Deobandis emphasise personal redemption by rigorous performance of religious ritual and avoidance of sin. However, in the course of extended research in Punjab villages I found that the peasant makes a clear distinction between the powers of the spirit of dead pirs and those of living pirs. He goes to shrines of dead pirs and prays for his intercession for a variety of purposes. He believes that the spirit of the dead pir can hear him so that he communicates with him directly and has no need for intermediaries. He may show some deferrence but not too much reverence for the *Sajjada Nashins*, the guardians of the shrines, who are usually descendants of the dead saint. The *Sajjada Nashins* are credited by scholars with having spiritual powers. But the peasant himself does not seem to recognise that. Propositions in the literature about the powers of the *Sajjada Nashins* over the peasant,[14] not least in the political arena, are a myth which cannot survive close scrutiny in the light of actual observation of what goes on. Where *Sajjada Nashins* do play a role in local level politics, as they often do, they do so by virtue of their rather more material powers as landowners rather than some spiritual hold that they are presumed to have over the peasants.

Living pirs fall into two categories. Firstly there are pirs as petty practitioners, dealers in miracles and magic, at a price. They provide amulets or anointed oil to protect the peasant from evil, or specific remedies which he buys from them. Such pirs can make barren wombs fertile, or ease the pain of incurable disease, and so on. They take their lucrative business seriously and avoid getting involved in politics for, given the factional division of local level politics, they would run the risk of losing half their clientele if they were to get politically involved. During my period of fieldwork in Punjab villages I came across only one solitary case where such a pir did intervene in politics, due to some exceptional circumstances. He declared that as a man of God politics was not a matter that he would care to get involved in. But he was also able to invoke some high moral principles to explain why on that particular occasion he was compelled to do so. In the event his intervention was totally unsuccessful. Everyone (including the pir himself) could see who, in the event, were those that disobeyed him. The dissident group, in explaining their behaviour to me, made a distinction between the spiritual domain in which the pir had powers and the wordly domain in which he did not, so that they were not obliged to follow the pir's call in a matter which should not concern him.

Secondly there are pirs of an altogether different kind who operate on a much higher level. Their relationship with peasants is not a direct one based on 'spiritual powers' but is rather a mediated one, through landlords and local faction leaders who control the peasantry politically. Such pirs have *mureeds* or disciples, who take an oath of allegiance (*bai'a*, or, in Punjabi, *bait*) to the pir. At the core of such pir's coterie of *mureeds* are powerful landlords, village-level faction leaders, and not least government officials, who together constitute a freemasonry exchanging patronage and favours, which is tightly organised and controlled by the pir. They operate with great effect in the political arena, as well as in the dispensing of government patronage and favours.

Their mutual bonds are expressed in the language of kinship and the *mureeds* consider each other *pirbhais*, or pir-brothers. The pir himself, being at the centre of such a structure of 'generalised reciprocity' wields considerable power. But that is not direct power over the peasantry and it has little to do with religious beliefs of the peasantry. It is a myth to suppose that such pirs, by virtue of charismatic power, have political authority over the peasants in general, although where their landlords are *mureeds* pirs may indirectly control peasant followers in the political arena. In most cases such pirs are big and powerful landowners in their own right and control their own peasants. Political recruitment of peasants by such pirs therefore takes place on the basis of distinctly non-spiritual powers.[15]

Deobandi and Barelvi ulama in Pakistan

Historically, Deobandis have tended to be mainly urban and from the middle and upper strata of society, whereas Barelvi influence has been mainly in rural areas, with a populist appeal. This has changed somewhat in recent decades, for Barelvi influence has extended to towns and cities, amongst the lumpenproletariat (peasants in cities) and an insecure urban petty bourgeoisie. Traditionally Barelvi influence has been weaker in the UP (with the exception perhaps of the peasantry of South-Western UP) than in the Punjab and to some degree in Sind. On the other hand the main base of Deobandis was in the UP especially among urban Muslims, who are the *muhajirs* (refugees from India), in Pakistan. As an unmerited legacy of the Wahabi movement they are also well entrenched amongst Pathans of the Sarhad (the NWFP) and northern (Pushtun) districts of Baluchistan. That influence now extends to Pathan workers and lumpenproletariat in Pakistan's cities, especially in Karachi. These groups are their storm-troopers in sectarian riots against Shi'as and Barelvis.

In Pakistan both Deobandis and Barelvis have organised themselves as political parties, the former as the Jamiat-ul-Ulama-e-Islam (JUI) founded in November 1945 and the latter as the Jamiat-ul-Ulama-e-Pakistan (JUP) which was founded in 1948. The political influence of each is much more limited than their sectarian following. In Pakistan's first General Election in 1970 the

JUI won only seven seats (out of a total of 138 for West Pakistan). Not surprisingly six of these were from Sarhad and one from a Pushtun constituency of Baluchistan. The JUP too won seven seats, all from West Pakistan, of which four were from Punjab and three from Sind, one of which was from the city of Karachi.[16] In both cases the rural seats were won not so much on the strength of religious commitment to the Party concerned but rather because the JUI candidates were allied to influential tribal leaders, whereas in the case of the JUP they relied on powerful landlords and pirs.

Before we leave the ulama, we must take note of their position (both Deobandi and Barelvi) on a doctrinal point which is pivotal in the political debate between them and the Islamic fundamentalists on the one hand and Islamic modernists on the other hand. That is the concept of *ijtihad* or interpretative development of doctrine in keeping with the spirit of Islam, on issues that cannot be decided by direct applicability of injunctions of the Qur'an or Hadith, or a solution offered by other prescribed rules. *Ijtihad* is the final remedy and there are recognised methods by which it may be accomplished. The traditionalist ulama will not accept *ijtihad*. For them the doctrine, formulated by the ninth century AD, consisting of the teachings of the four orthodox Sunni schools, their received tradition, is fixed for eternity. Islamic modernists and Islamic fundamentalists each reject this traditionalist view of the immutability and rigidity of the doctrine of the faith, the principle of *taqlid*, or doctrinal conformity that the ulama consider to be fundamental. They each insist on both the possibility and the necessity of *ijtihad*, to revivify Islam in keeping with new questions and issues that arise with new conditions. Their different political positions turn on their different solutions to the question of *ijtihad*.

Religious reform movements in India: background to Islamic modernism

The colonial restructuration of India's political system shifted the centre of gravity of status and influence in Indian society from the landed gentry to the emerging salariat, members of the colonial bureaucratised state. This newly emerging class had different needs and outlook from those of pre-colonial upper classes. They began to develop a new life style and new ways and these found expression in new ideas. There was a 'Hindu Renaissance' which was followed, after an interval of a few decades by a 'Muslim Renaissance'. This time-lag is usually explained by an assumption of Muslim 'backwardness', attributed to a variety of factors. A more plausible explanation may lie in the fact that in places where the colonial transformation first got under way, namely the initial nodal points of colonial rule in Bengal, Bombay and Madras, the Muslim component of the new salariat was negligible in size and it was much later that these changes reached the UP, the heartland of the Muslim salariat. There Muslims were far from backward; while their proportion in the population was quite small, they held a preponderant position in the salariat. Not surprisingly it was in the UP where 'Muslim Renaissance' soon got under way.

The Hindu Renaissance in India began with the Brahmo Samaj movement in the 1830s in Bengal, under the intellectual leadership of Raja Ram Mohan Roy. There were parallel movements in the other two major centres of colonialism in India, namely the Vedic Samaj in Madras and the Prarthna Samaj in Bombay. Some social anthropologists have misconceived the nature and purport of this movement and speak of it as 'an intellectual nativistic revival' and saying, as Maloney does, that 'Ram Mohan Roy tried to recover and rationalise the spiritual essence of Hinduism'.[17] Such a view, one would suggest, fails to appreciate the rather more positive and forward-looking rather than nostalgic concerns of these movements. They attempted to articulate quite new ideas though in the idiom of the established religion.

An opposite kind of misconception about these movements, far more common, is that they simply packaged ideas imported from Europe in locally made boxes; that these are examples of mere reflection of Western ideas, a borrowing and mechanical transmission from one culture to another. Such a view seems plausible, for liberal ideas were in the ascendancy in the colonial metropolis, though it would be difficult to accuse British colonial officials of being the bearers of liberal ideas which they did not consider suited to India. The diffusionist theory of transmission of Western ideas to the colonised society fails to account for the fact that the ideas that were locally produced by intellectuals of the 'Hindu Renaissance' and the 'Muslim Renaissance' in India bore clearly the stamp of India's colonial situation and the peculiar character of its social structure. Their 'liberalism' was not that (at least formally) of free and equal individuals nor of *laissez faire*, the slogans of triumphant capitalism in England. It would be more accurate to describe these ideas as rationalism. David Kopf, a perceptive scholar, referring to these movements, writes: 'Such radical notions as secularism, humanism and rationalism had to be reinterpreted to fit the Indian situation'. He points out that the new Indian classes produced a new ideology to suit their own circumstances and needs. These movements repudiated tyrannies of religious orthodoxy from sources within their own tradition.[18]

Islamic modernism: Sir Syed Ahmad Khan and Mohammad Iqbal

The 'Hindu Renaissance' was followed by 'Muslim Renaissance' which was pre-figured by writers and poets such as Mirza Ghalib and, later, articulated most clearly and forcefully by Sir Syed Ahmad Khan, the most outstanding figure of the 'Muslim Renaissance'. Sir Syed Ahmad was a very effective practical organiser as well as a theoretician and major intellectual figure. His role and mission in life was to facilitate the transition of upper-class UP Muslims into the colonial salariat and to encourage them therefore to move out of the traditional system of education, which was controlled by the backward-looking ulama, and instead take to English and Western education. His own personal life reflects such a transition, of a member of the old UP aristocracy to the new salariat. He was from a noble family with long connections with Moghul Imperial rule, now less prosperous. He joined the service of the East India Company, against the wishes of his family, and rose to be a *munsif*, or sub-judge, which was as high a position in the colonial state apparatus as an Indian could aspire to at the time. He soon became the leading pioneer of a new rationalist public philosophy that was expressed in the idiom of Islam. He was much attacked and reviled by the ulama. Embroidered tales of his persecution by bigots have become a part of the mythology of the Muslim salariat.

It is not too surprising that Sir Syed Ahmad, the father of Islamic modernism was directly influenced by Raja Ram Mohan Roy, the father of the Hindu Renaissance. As an impressionable young man Sir Syed Ahmad met Roy, who was on a visit to the

Moghul court in 1831. He gave much prominence to an account of Roy's visit in his book *Sirat-e-Faridiyah*. A leading scholar on the life and work of Sir Syed Ahmad is of the opinion that 'The personality and work of Ram Mohan Roy were a formative influence in Sayyid Ahmad Khan's life'.[19] It is no accident that parallel religious reform movements arose in different parts of India both amongst Hindus and Muslims during the mid-nineteenth century (as well as a Buddhist religious reform movement in Sri Lanka), for they all reflected similar social developments, the emergence of different sections of the same class, the new salariat. It might be more illuminating to think of them therefore as different ethnic components of a single class and the Hindu and Muslim reform movements as different strands of a single intellectual movement, expressing rationalist ideologies and a commitment to a scientific outlook of the newly emerging Hindu and Muslim salariats, in their respective religious idioms.

Sir Syed Ahmad's political philosophy, as appropriate to the concerns of the emerging Muslim salariat in the UP, was cast in ethnic terms (rather than 'communal', which is a pejorative term) striving for numerical equality of Muslim representation in the services with Hindus, although in the UP Muslims were only about 13 per cent of the population. He argued that Muslims, as a community, were entitled to an equal share because they made up for their lack of overall numbers by their preponderence amongst the upper classes. That view did not entail hostility towards Hindus as such, nor was it a question of religion. The issue was that of equating the two communities, irrespective of their relative size and demanding an equal share for each. This was nicely expressed in his much quoted statement that India was a bride adorned by Hindus and Muslims who were her two beautiful eyes. The bride would be disfigured if the two eyes were not equal.

Sir Syed Ahmad did not argue for a restoration of Muslim power, much less an Islamic state. Nor did he want independence or democracy. His hopes were pinned, rather, on an indefinite continuation of British rule for that, in his eyes, was the only impartial guarantee of protection of Muslim interests which lay in their securing equality with Hindus within the Indian salariat. He was very suspicious of the Indian National Congress, and feared that independence and democracy would mean that Hindus would overwhelm the small numbers of *ashraf* Muslims, Muslims of the upper classes, who would then have no one to protect them. It is clear from this that Sir Syed Ahmad's political horizons were defined by the boundaries of the UP and he did not extend the logic of his argument to Muslim majority provinces where it could be inverted.

Education was the sovereign remedy for reversing the decline of (the UP upper-class) Muslim society. The main thrust of Sir Syed Ahmad's writing and indefatigable organisational activity therefore lay in the pursuit of modern education for Muslims. He founded the Muhammadan Anglo-Oriental College at Aligarh in 1877 which later became the famous Aligarh Muslim University, the heart of Muslim Nationalism in India. In other parts of India too, Muslim nationalists were preoccupied with the task of promotion of the new education, setting up educational movements and educational institutions for Muslims.

Sir Syed Ahmad had to fight the bigoted ulama at all levels, not least on their own ground of theology. His writings on religion were prolific and reflected a high level of scholarship. Without going into details of particular controversies one particular issue can be singled out. This was the burden of the received and congealed orthodoxy, the immutable Traditions of the Four Sunni schools, in the name of which the ulama fought him. His counter-attack was simplicity itself, the wielding of 'Occam's Razor'. He wiped the slate clean of the hidebound traditions of the four schools as handed down by the ulama over ten centuries, by declaring that they had become cluttered with accretions of *bid'at* ('innovations'), in other words, misconceptions and misinterpretations.[20] The only alternative was to go back to the source, the Qur'an and the Hadith of the Prophet. By that bold stroke he swept orthodoxy out of the way and gave himself freedom to write on the cleaned slate a message of a rationalist social philosophy, invoking the fundamental sources of Islam.

Sir Syed Ahmad's work opened the way for a liberal reinterpretation of Islamic political philosophy by Mohammad Iqbal. Iqbal attacked the dogma of the traditionalist ulama that the received doctrine was immutable. He passionately attacked the ulama's commitment to the principle of *taqlid*, or doctrinal conformity, which he argued had ossified Islam and made it remote from realities of the contemporary world. That was the root cause of the present decline of Muslims. To revitalise Muslim society, *ijtihad* had to be reinstated.[21] That could be done through *ijma*, or consensus of the community, which he considered to be 'The third source of Mohammedan Law [after the Qur'an and Hadith of the Prophet] . . . which is in my opinion perhaps the most important legal notion in Islam'.[22] He argued further that 'The transfer of *ijtihad* from individual representatives of schools to a legislative assembly . . . is the only possible form *ijma* can take in modern times.'[23] Iqbal was quite as hostile to the decadent and obscurantist views of the ulama as they were to his. Referring to provisions of the Persian Constitution of 1906 he repudiated as 'dangerous' the idea of giving powers to the ulama to supervise legislative activity. 'The only effective remedy for the possibilities of erroneous interpretations is to reform the present system of legal education,' he added.[24] By that formula, of securing *ijma* through a legislative body, he legitimised the liberal principle of representative self-government, the system that the political leadership of the professionals and the salariat (though not necessarily its bureaucratic and military components) best understood and wanted.

Islamic fundamentalism

The Islamic traditionalism of the ulama and Islamic modernism of Sir Syed and Mohammad Iqbal as I have suggested, were each identified with certain social classes whose concerns and aspirations they expressed. The social roots of the Islamic fundamentalism of the Jamaat-e-Islami cannot be so clearly identified. It originated entirely as an ideological movement and its appeal was initially limited to a small number of dedicated followers whom it offered a dream of a utopian future. It drew to itself a small band of idealists in search of a better society. Many of them were quickly disenchanted and left the Party, often joining left-wing groups and organisations. Their numbers and weight in that party have dwindled steadily. The Jamaat was soon to get generous support from powerful vested interests for whom it began to serve a political purpose. That changed its character radically.

The Jamaat-e-Islami was founded in 1941 by Maulana Maududi, a scholar-journalist with a classical education. Maududi was an opponent of Muslim nationalism and the Pakistan movement. But when Pakistan was created he found it prudent to migrate to Pakistan. With that his political philosophy went through a radical transformation. Maududi's opposition to the Pakistan movement was on the ground that the true vocation of an Islamic militant was a proselytising one, that Islam was a universal religion that knew of no national boundaries. After the creation of Pakistan, Maududi revised the conception of his mission and that of the rationale of the Pakistan movement. He now argued that the sole object of the creation of Pakistan was to establish an Islamic state and that it was his Party alone which possessed a true understanding of Islam and commitment to bring that about.

To build an Islamic state the existing state must first be captured and brought under the control of those who, by Maududi's definition, were the only true bearers of militant and authentic Islam, namely himself and his Party. Unlike the ulama, control of the state apparatus was therefore his first priority. His conception of the Islamic state was a strongly centralised one, run on authoritarian lines, with the help of a strong, effective and dedicated army, under the authority of the Commander of the Faithful. Democracy was despised, for it gave power to the ignorant and those whose commitment, and understanding, of the faith could be doubtful. The onus lay therefore on his Party and on himself as its Guide and Leader, to take Muslim society forward to its true destiny. His Party's constitution illustrates this authoritarian philosophy, for it demands unquestioning and total obedience from members of the Party to its *Amir*, its Supreme Head, namely himself. His ideas, justifying dictatorship in the name of Islam have, not surprisingly, found much favour with Pakistan's authoritarian military rulers.

The Jamaat is not a mass party but one with selected cadre members. Because of its shallow roots in society, the Jamaat has been quite ineffective as a political party. The full extent of its isolation from popular support was brought home recently to the Jamaat as well as its surprised opponents, by its débâcle in the controlled elections staged by the Zia regime in January 1985, for conditions for its electoral success could not have been made more favourable. All opposition parties were under a ban and their leaders and local activists were in prison or in exile. The field was therefore clear for the Jamaat to make a clean sweep of it. But it was routed completely.

The Jamaat's electoral bankruptcy ought not to lead anyone into underestimating its power and influence in today's Pakistan, which are derived primarily from its symbiotic relationship with the ruling regime. It tends to function as a pressure group rather than a political party and uses its influence with government agencies and power to blackmail and terrorise individuals to achieve its objectives. The Jamaat has acquired a firm grip over the universities and the entire educational system, its prime objective. It has also acquired a powerful influence on the government-owned and controlled broadcasting media. Its tentacles are believed to extend everywhere so that its opponents live in fear. The party, in turn, enjoys enormous capacity of patronage and thereby attracts support from all kinds of opportunists and careerists, which further reinforces its influence within the apparatus of the government and the army quite apart from its influence directly at the top.

After the Partition the Jamaat attracted a new following among Urdu-speaking refugees from India, the *muhajirs*, who felt insecure and bitter about India, because of their suffering in the course of their enforced migration. They responded readily to the chauvinistic rhetoric of the Jamaat. But, over the years, this support has been withering away. In part this is because muhajirs who have settled in the interior of Sind have developed linkages with the Sindhi community, being traders and professionals who serve Sindhi peasants and landlords. They have become the 'New Sindhis', and sympathise with the Sindhi movement which has got under way quite powerfully in recent years. They dislike the anti-democratic support by the Jamaat of the repression let loose by the military regime against Sindhi nationalism. Even in big cities, like Karachi, where *muhajir* support for Sindhis is much less, there are elements within the Jamaat, like Professor Ghafoor Ahmad of Karachi and Jan Mohammad Abbasi, who are critical of their party's support of the martial law regime because that has been losing the Jamaat popular support.

The leadership of the Jamaat has passed into non-ideologist hands, although exploitation of their ideology remains their principal political weapon. Its bosses seem to feel that its diminishing support from its meagre popular base, mostly amongst the *muha-*

jirs is of less consequence than the support that it is deriving from powerful classes in Pakistan for whom its value lies in its ability to bludgeon radical and left-wing groups, very often literally so. The Jamaat receives generous donations from big businessmen and landlords and is believed to be a recipient of generous donations from the Americans and from potentates in the Middle East. But an excess of money and, for that matter, influence, has also brought problems. New vested interests have grown up in the Party bureaucracy and its old ideological wing, in decline, resents this. There is a considerable tension (to say the least) between the ideologists in the Party, mainly Karachi based, and those whose political ambitions lie in what they can get from the military regime. This latter consists mainly of the Punjab-based, so-called 'pragmatic' wing of the Jamaat, led by Mian Tufail Mohammed, the Amir of the Jamaat and successor of Maududi. However, to retrieve its standing amongst the people the Party has begun to voice carefully measured criticism of the military regime, to distance itself from it. There is also a third element in the Party, namely armed thugs, an element that was reinforced by the repatriation from East Pakistan of members of Al-Badar and As-Shams, its fascist paramilitary organisations, after the liberation of Bangladesh. They go about beating up opponents and breaking-up meetings. These elements are especially associated with the *Islami-Jamiyat-e-Tulaba*, the student organisation of the Jamaat, which maintains an armed presence on university campuses.

To end our account of the Jamaat-e-Islami, we return to the central doctrinal issue of *ijtihad*, or interpretative development of doctrine, around which the political debate about the Islamic state has turned. The Jamaat stands for *ijtihad*, contrary to the traditionalist ulama position, but at the same time derides the method proposed by the modernist Iqbal for achieving it under contemporary conditions, by legitimating representative democracy in the name of *ijma*. Maududi contends against this that this could not lead to a reliable interpretation of Islam, for the voters may not be Muslim and even if they are, they may not have a 'true understanding' of Islam, such as only Maududi and his followers have. Iqbal's exhortation to educate the people was no solution either. Scholarship was no guarantee, for even the ulama were misled and ignorant.

The logic of that argument, leads Maududi to an authoritarian solution, for by his lights there is only one true and reliable interpretation of Islam and Maududi and his Jamaat are the custodians of that true knowledge. They are a gifted and select elite, and amongst them only its great leader knows what Islam is. 'According to Maududi', says K. K. Aziz,

> there is always a person (*Mizaj Shanas-i Rasool*) who alone is competent to decide what the Holy Prophet would have done in a given situation if he were alive. . . . He left no doubt in the minds of his followers that he was the only candidate for this supreme pontifical office. And his chief lieutenant, Maulana Islahi declared before the Punjab Disturbances Inquiry Committee that he wholeheartedly and unreservedly accepted Maududi as the *Mizaj Shanas-i Rasool*.[25]

As far as the Jamaat claims and ideology are concerned, there can be no objective or logical criteria by which their validity can be settled. They can be accepted only as an act of faith, by a religious conversion in effect, to the Maududi sect, which may therefore be properly regarded to be yet another sect of Islam which, like every sect, claims to be the only true one.

Paradoxically Maududi's elitism itself militates against a principle which would be regarded as a central tenet of Islam, namely that *ijtihad* by *ijma*, the consensus of the community, has precedence over *ijtihad* by the *alim*, the man of religious learning, because an individual, however learned he may be, is fallible, but Allah in his mercy would not allow his community collectively to go in error. This has always been recognised as the principle of democracy in Islam. Maududi's argument contradicts that. The Jamaat-e-Islami ideology while insisting on *ijtihad* in effect rejects *ijma*.

It must be said that by virtue of reinterpretation of Islam to suit the needs of the feudal Abbasid empire in the eighth century AD, the concept of *ijma* was narrowed down to that of a consensus between 'qualified' scholars, which took away the power from the community and abolished its power of representation in the state. But even this narrowed conception contradicts Maududi's claim, quite apart from the impossibility of such a 'consensus' of scholars in a world in which those of different sectarian persuasions call each other *kafirs*. So on doctrinal grounds we can see that there are contradictions underlying every position. There is no way of resolving it except by either imposing one sectarian position over all the others or by accepting a secular conception of the political process and the state so that every individual, whatever his or her religious persuasion may be, would be free to participate in the democratic process, following his or her own private faith and conscience, to shape policies of the state. We will refrain from pursuing this arcane and insoluble debate any further, for it cannot be resolved by logic.

Secular Muslim nationalism – Jinnah

Most of the salariat in fact, implicitly or explicitly, espoused a secular conception of being part of a Muslim nation. Jinnah, their spokesman, was always quite explicit about it and on this issue he put his position quite unambiguously. In recent years there has been a systematic attempt by Pakistan's captive media to misrepresent Jinnah on this point and they are trying hard to build up an image of the Father of the Nation as a religious bigot. The reality was very different. Jinnah was a member of cosmopolitan Bombay society, a close colleague and friend of Sir Pherozeshah Mehta, a Parsi Indian nationalist and, along with M. K. Gandhi, a protégé and close friend of G. K. Gokhale, the great Indian liberal leader. Jinnah began as an active member of the Congress Party. He was not among the founders of the Muslim League in 1907. He joined it much later, in 1913, at the invitation of Muslim League leaders, by which time the Congress and the Muslim League were already drawing steadily closer together, holding their annual conferences at the same time and in the same place. The high point of that *rapprochement* was the Lucknow Pact of 1916 between the Congress and the League. Ironically, the basis of this growing unity was destroyed by a decision to pander to Muslim bigotry not by the League but by the Congress, much to the disgust and resentment of the league leadership. This was by virtue of Gandhi's decision to back fanatical Muslim ulama in launching the Khilafat movement (1919–23). If there had been any intention to drive a wedge between the secular-minded Muslim salariat and the Muslim masses and to shift leadership in the direction of the obscurantist ulama, the Congress could not have taken up a more potent issue.

It is true that it was Muslim notables, so-called 'feudals', who presided over the birth of the Muslim League in December 1906 at Dacca. This has misled too many historians about the class character of the Muslim League. The fact of the matter is that the Muslim League, soon after its initiation by Muslim notables, was taken over by the Muslim salariat. At the initial meeting at Dacca two leading lights of Aligarh, Mohsin-ul Mulk and Viqar-ul Mulk, were appointed as joint secretaries and two-fifths of the Provisional Committee were from the UP. These were as yet 'men of property and influence' although quite committed to the salariat cause. Later, by 1910, the leadership and control of the Muslim League passed into the hands of men from a relatively more modest background who have been described as 'men of progressive tendencies', under the leadership of Wazir Hassan and others like him, who were based at Lucknow. They pushed the Muslim League in a new direction and sought co-operation with the larger Indian nationalist movement and the Congress, provided Muslim salariat rights were protected.

Jinnah himself was to be brought into the Muslim League by these elements three years later. It would be a mistake to think that the Muslim League was dominated and controlled by the so-called 'feudals' during the four decades after its inception. That is the nub of a complicated story, of which a most perceptive account will be found in Robinson's excellent study of the early Muslim Movement in the UP.[26] Naturally, like all great political and social movements, there are many different strands that are interwoven in the tapestry of Muslim history in India during the nineteenth and twentieth centuries. But its essential features were engraved on the map of Indian politics by the aspirations and anxieties of the Muslim salariat, the force behind Muslim nationalism.

A number of factors contributed to a new turn in the development of Muslim politics in India by the first decade of this century. The Muslim salariat was by now detached from its total reliance on the goodwill and patronage of the colonial regime. It turned towards its own self-reliant political organisation for which it looked to Muslim professionals to provide political leadership. That was prompted above all by the prospective constitutional

changes that offered an opportunity and need for representation in
the state apparatus. It is not an accident that the Muslim salariat's
political organisation took shape in that decade. Nawab Salimullah
Khan's initiative and invitation to Dacca had merely provided an
opportunity and an occasion for that.

The Muslim salariat had begun to crystallise its political identity.
Its key objectives were, again, defined by the narrow perspectives
of the privileged UP Muslim salariat in the light of its sharply
deteriorating position relative to Hindus, whilst still remaining a
privileged minority. Its demands corresponded to the problems of
a group that felt itself to be beleaguered in a Muslim minority
province. They do not make too much sense in the context of
Muslim majority provinces. Their central demand was for a separate electorate for Muslims so that they may not be outvoted by the
overwhelming Hindu majority in the UP. Robinson sums up
developments in the first decade of the century as follows: 'By 1909
a Muslim identity was firmly established in Indian politics . . . [by
virtue of] the creation of a Muslim political organisation . . . [and]
the winning of separate Muslim electorate. . . . The creation of a
protected share of power for Muslims . . . stimulated the further
development of Muslim politics.'[27] Jinnah, who was brought into
the Muslim League in 1913, reassessed the situation and recognised the value of an organised Muslim constituency and a role for
himself as a spokesman for Muslims but as yet within the Indian
nationalist movement. Robinson comments 'He brought to the
League leadership important connections with all India Congress
circles and the distinction of having been a close friend of Gokhale.'[28]

Jinnah eventually began to get disillusioned with the Congress
Party, from the 1920s, not because he was a Muslim communalist
but quite the reverse. It was the Congress, under Gandhi's leadership, which had embarked upon a course that encouraged Muslim
fanaticism under the leadership of the ulama, by taking up the
cause of the Khilafat movement and giving it a thrust that it could
not have achieved without that support. Jinnah was quite outraged
by this cynical move. No greater disservice could have been done
to the cause of inter-communal harmony in India. Nothing that the
Muslim League ever did or wanted to do could have done more to
excite Muslim communalist passions and to evoke corresponding
responses from Hindus.

The failure to reach an accommodation with the Congress after the 1937 elections finally forced Jinnah to reconsider his strategy. So far the Muslim League's influence was limited to the salariat; hence its relative ineffectiveness in elections in a society in which landlords controlled the mainly rural vote. Jinnah decided now to secure Muslim landlord support at any price and he soon set about making deals with those of them who were in power in Muslim majority provinces, persuading them to accept the Muslim League label, even if it was to be only nominally. In return he gave them *carte blanche*, and in effect surrendered the local Muslim League organisations to them. Jinnah's objective in this was to secure at least the formal position of the Muslim League as the nominally 'ruling Party' in Muslim majority provinces. This would legitimise his claim that the Muslim League was the sole and legitimate spokesman for the Muslims of India.

The alliance with the landed magnates did not deliver the landowners into the hands of the Muslim League – quite the reverse. It delivered the League into their hands. In the Punjab there was a wide gulf between the urban Punjabi salariat and the powerful landowners. In Sindh there was no ethnic Sindhi Muslim salariat to speak of. In the alliance between the landed magnates of the Punjab and Sindh and the Muslim salariat, it was the former who were the senior partners, the holders of power. The alliance was effected between the national leadership of the salariat, Jinnah and the All India Muslim League and the landed magnates. The local leadership of the salariat counted for little. The national leadership of the Muslim League had something to offer to the regional power-holders by way of ensuring that the post-Independence government would not be in the hands of the Congress Party (which was committed to land reform) but rather a party that was dependent on them and under their control and which would ensure their own survival as a class.

In contrast to the character of the alliance between the rural magnates of Punjab and Sind and the All India Muslim League during the Pakistan movement, the relationship between the movements of the salariats of Bengal and Sindh in regional ethnic movements that arose after Independence, was quite different in character. That is because in both those cases there was an *organic alliance* or bond between the respective salariats and the dominant rural classes of these provinces, for the ethnic Bengali and Sindhi salariats, respectively, were the sons of well-to-do peasants and landlords big and small of those provinces. Their interests were linked through ties of kinship. Such organic ties are often over-looked when questions of class formation and class alignment are considered entirely in the abstract, and analytic divisions in society are thought to imply the existence of the respective groups in separate compartments. That is not always the case. Landlords and well-off peasants who could give their sons a decent education were concerned about their prospects for employment and ad-vancement in government service. The motivations for the deci-sion of landlords of Muslim majority provinces to back the Muslim League in the late 1940s were quite different from those that elicited powerful support from rural power-holders for the Bengali and Sindhi movements later.

Jinnah looked upon the landed magnates, the political bosses of the Muslim majority provinces, with contempt and dislike quite as much as they in turn showed little inclination to allow him and the central Muslim League leadership to encroach on their domains of power. In Punjab the Jinnah–Sikander Pact of 1936 was the first of these one-sided arrangements between the Unionist Party and the Muslim League. The Unionist Party was an alliance of Muslim, Hindu and Sikh landowners. In return for the Muslim Unionists' nominal allegiance to the League it delivered the Punjab League into the hands of the Unionists' leader, Sir Sikandar Hayat Khan. The political cleavage in the Punjab was urban–rural and the rural magnates had always shown contempt for the urban salariat, which was the Muslim League's mainstay. The Unionist Party, especially earlier under Sir Fazl-i-Husain, was determined to keep Punjab politics 'non-communal'. Fazl-i-Husain's closest and most trusted associate was Sir Chhotu Ram, a Hindu, another close associate being Sir Sunder Singh Majithia, a Sikh landowner. Although he was prepared to patronise members of the Muslim salariat, Sir Fazl-i-Husain and his associates had no intention of letting the urbanites, on whom they looked down with some disdain, en-croach on their power. Iqbal complained of Sir Fazl-i-Husain's anti-urban bias in a speech in 1935 and his associate Malik Barkat Ali did so too; both were urban stalwarts of the Muslim League.[29] Later Iqbal was to protest repeatedly to Jinnah about his pact with Sir Sikandar Hayat, Sir Fazl-i-Husain's successor. In a series of letters in October and November 1937, Iqbal complained to Jinnah that 'Sir Sikandar wants nothing less than complete control of the League and the Provincial Parliamentary Board.'[30] Jinnah maintained a prudent silence over the matter and did not reply to Iqbal's repeated letters. Having handed over the League to Sir Sikandar Hayat Khan and the Unionists, there was little that he could have said.

In Sindh the story was no different, for there the local base of the Muslim salariat was narrower than that in the Punjab; it was minute. The urban leadership of the Muslim League, mainly in Karachi, was mainly ethnic non-Sindhi. The rural-based ethnic Sindhi leadership was divided into warring factions led by Sir Ghulam Hussain Hidayatullah and G. M. Syed. In terms of its social composition Hidayatullah's faction was a replica of the Punjab Unionist Party. Jinnah decided to put his bets on the Hidayatullah faction, which was the more powerful; but it was evidently an unpalatable decision. Jinnah confided his views about his Party colleagues to Sir Hugh Dow, Governor of Sind (which itself is an extraordinary reflection on Jinnah's relationship with the servitors of Empire). Dow, in a secret letter to Wavell, the Viceroy, reporting on political developments, wrote:

> Jinnah made a prolonged stay in Karachi . . . and held pro-
> longed conferences with the 'leaders'. . . . Jinnah dislikes them
> all (he once told me that he could buy the lot of them for 5 lakhs
> of rupees to which I replied that I could do it much cheaper) and
> has been mainly concerned that the League ticket should go to
> the man who was most likely to be returned, his previous and
> subsequent loyalty to the League being a minor consideration.[31]

All that Jinnah was looking for was pinning the Muslim League label on the Provincial governments and little more.

It is not difficult to see the short-term advantages of this strategy for Jinnah, for it legitimised his All-India position and strengthened his bargaining position. The reason for the decision of the Provincial magnates to accept the Muslim League label is less obvious. It was not the vote-pulling power of the League, for it was the landed magnates themselves who controlled the mainly rural vote. What the League offered to the landed magnates of Punjab and Sindh is best understood only if we consider the fundamental shift in the long-term political prospects that began to be visible to the landed magnates whose eyes were so far focused too narrowly on the provincial scene. With Independence in sight, they had to look beyond their provincial horizons and some of them could see the writing on the wall earlier than others. It was clear that it was only a matter of time before colonial rule would end. With the departure of their colonial patrons they were faced with the prospects of the rule of the Congress Party, with its commitment to land reform. If they were to preserve their class position, the only viable option for them was a government, at the centre, of the Muslim League rather than the Congress. If that was to mean Pakistan, so be it. Whatever form it took it would guarantee their own survival, for the Muslim League was wholly dependent on them. It was they who would wield power in any autonomous regional grouping of Muslim majority provinces that would ensue. It was not a question of ideology but clearly understood class interest that lined them up behind the Muslim League. They were unimpressed by Muslim League politics until the imminence of Independence. Only at that juncture did they decide to jump on to the Muslim League bandwagon and, in fact, took it over.

When the Pakistan slogan was raised Jinnah's opponents continually complained that he was refusing to specify precisely what Pakistan was actually to be. As a seasoned negotiator evidently Jinnah did not lay all his cards prematurely on the table. But it was not difficult to see that what he was aiming for was a grouping of Muslim majority provinces enjoying a degree of regional autonomy, possibly within an overall Indian Federal Union rather than the Partition of India, especially if that was to entail carving up Punjab and Bengal. That he was quite happy to accept Pakistan as a regional grouping within an Indian federal union is testified by his ready acceptance of the three-tier Cabinet Mission Plan which offered just that in April 1946. It was the Congress who rejected it. Such a solution, resulting in a weak centre, would have undermined a major objective of the Congress and the Indian bourgeoisie, namely to embark on planned development of free India; one may well conclude that India's progress in planned industrial development has justified that strategic decision. For the Muslim League, the federal union solution was particularly important for the sake of the Muslims of the UP and the Muslim minority provinces, for that would have established a link between them and those in power in the Muslim majority regions within the federal union. This 'reciprocal hostages' theory was based on the idea that the fate of non-Muslims in the Muslim majority zone would be a guarantee for their own protection in the other zone in which they were in a minority. The issue revolved around the fate of minority communities on either side. Furthermore, if only to guarantee the safety and interests of the Muslims of the UP and Bihar, who were the backbone of the Pakistan movement, Pakistan, in whatever form, was not to be a theocracy.

Jinnah had consistently opposed theocratic ideas and influences and never minced his words about his commitment to a secular state. Speaking to students in Aligarh Muslim University, the heart of the Muslim salariat, in February 1938, he declared: 'What the League has done is to set you free from the reactionary elements of Muslims and to create the opinion that those who play their selfish game are traitors. It has certainly freed you from that undesirable element of Maulvis and Maulanas [a derogatory reference to the ulama]'.[32] He reiterated, time and again, that Pakistan would be 'without any distinction of caste, creed or sect.' Ayesha Jalal, in her excellent study of Jinnah's political role, records at least two occasions on which Jinnah successfully resisted attempts to commit the Muslim League to an 'Islamic Ideology'.[33] His inaugural address to the Pakistan Constituent Assembly on 11 August 1947 was a clarion call for the establishment of Pakistan as a secular state. From the principal forum of the new state he declared:

> You may belong to any religion or caste or creed – that has nothing to do with the business of the state . . . We are starting with this fundamental principle, that *we are all citizens of one state*. . . . I think we should keep that in front of us as our idea and you will find that *in the course of time Hindus will cease to be Hindus and Muslims will cease to be Muslims, not in the religious sense because that is the personal faith of each individual but in the political sense, as citizens of the state*.[34]

There could be no clearer statement of the secular principle as the basis of Pakistan.

The true heirs in today's Pakistan of what the Pakistan ideology really was, are the secularists, many of them practising Muslims, who reject and repudiate the idea of exploitation of Islamic ideology in pursuit of political ends. If Islamic modernism was the initial ideology of the emerging Muslim salariat, it has long ceased to be a live intellectual movement and has been marginalised. It exists in small and peripheral groupings such as the Tulu-e Islam group led by Ghulam Ahmad Parvaiz. Many of the basic ideas of Islamic modernism, have passed into conventional wisdom. In so far as they still have currency, they are accommodated within secular political attitudes. It may help to put things into perspective if we quote from an account by Rosenthal, a renowned Islamic scholar, of his investigations in Pakistan, even though his report is over twenty-two years old. He summed up his impressions of attitudes in Pakistan with the words

> On balance, I should say that among the academic youth there is a minority in favour of an Islamic state in substance, not just in name. The majority are divided in their allegiance to Islam from personal faith to indifference and outright rejection as being out of date and dividing men instead of unifying and leading them to a world state.[35]

More recently this issue has been dealt with sensitively and perceptively by Sibte Hassan in his influential book *Naveed-e-Fikr*,[36] where he arrives at similar conclusions.

Islam in Pakistan

Muslim ethnicity had outlived its original purpose when Pakistan was created, for the 'Muslim' salariat, no longer stood in opposition to Hindus. Instead a new dominant ethnic group identified itself, the ruling Punjabis. In turn, other sections of the once-Muslim salariat now redefined their respective ethnic identities, as Bengalis, Sindhis, Pathans and Baluch, who were underprivileged in the new state. They demanded fairer shares for themselves. They had left Muslim ethnicity behind in the pre-Partition world. Now the regional question was to be at the centre of politics in Pakistan, ill-concealed by the rhetoric of Islamic ideology that was deployed against them to deny the legitimacy of their newly affirmed separate regional and cultural identities.

There was a fresh process of accounting of regional privilege and deprivation. Although there were 41.9 million East Pakistanis, as

against only 33.7 million West Pakistanis (1951 census), shares in
public appointments bore no comparison to that, not even re-
motely. In 1948 East Pakistanis numbered only 11 per cent of the
members of the CSP, the Civil Service of Pakistan, the elite cadre
that controlled the bureaucracy and thereby the state in Pakistan.
East Pakistani share in the army was even worse, for only 1.5 per
cent of army officers were East Pakistani. Bengali Muslims owned
no more than 3.5 per cent of the assets of all private Muslim
firms.[37] A wave of political militancy swept through the whole of
East Pakistan. The Bengali language movement erupted with
dramatic force in February 1952 when, for a few days, the writ of
the government ceased to run in that province. Every Bengali
government employee went on strike. That movement, significantly, started on the Dacca University Campus. The Bengali
language movement repudiated the ruling Muslim League's claim
to represent the people of East Pakistan. In the 1954 provincial
elections the ruling Muslim League Party won no more than 10
seats out of a total of 309, notwithstanding repression of opposition parties and the fact that many of the elected candidates were
in prison at the time. The opposition United Front, which articulated Bengali nationalism, swept the elections. Sindhis, Pathans
and Baluch movements were soon to develop likewise.

At first in Pakistan the secular tradition of Jinnah was maintained. In March 1949, moving the 'Objectives Resolution' in the
Constituent Assembly, Prime Minister Liaquat Ali Khan declared:
'The people are the real recipients of power. This naturally elimin-
ates any danger of the establishment of a theocracy.'[38] Choudhury,
editor of *Documents and Speeches on the Constitution of Pakistan*,
a champion of Islamic ideology, complained that 'The Ulama were
also not happy with the first draft constitution [that is, the Interim
Report of the Basic Principles Committee, 1950] as it contained
very little, if at all any, provisions as to the Islamic character of the
proposed constitution'.[39]

As soon as the regional protest against Punjabi rule began to get
under way, the ideological tune changed. Suddenly Islam and the
notion of Islamic brotherhood became the order of the day. It was
unpatriotic on the part of Bengalis, Sindhis, Pathans and Baluch to
make demands in terms of their regional ethnic identities because
all Pakistanis were brothers in Islam. The constitutional proposals
were quickly redrafted. Choudhury happily reported that 'The

Second Draft Constitution [the Report of the Basic Principles Committee, 1952] was noted for elaborate provisions relating to the Islamic character of the proposed Constitution. The most noble feature of the Islamic provision was a board of ulama which would examine if any law was repugnant to Qur'an and Sunnah'.[40]

All that this 'noble feature' added up to was a smokescreen, for it went little beyond setting up a 'Board of *Talimat-i-Islamia*' (Board of Islamic Learning) which had some advisory functions, and existed only on paper, for the ruling bureaucratic-military oligarchy (with the Punjabi salariat in the saddle) had no intention of giving the mullahs a share in power. The only concrete result of all this, after years of rhetorical Islamisation, was a decision to change the name of the Republic to 'The Islamic Republic of Pakistan' and, further, a provision was inserted in the Constitution that the President shall be a Muslim. The ruling oligarchy would not make any concessions of substance to the Islamic ideologists. But all this was quite enough to serve its purpose, namely to generate rhetorical steam on behalf of the dominant Punjabis who made it plain that 'Islamic' Pakistan would not tolerate any regional movements.

The secular mood of the country was dramatically demonstrated by the rout of 'Islam Loving' Parties in the first national election of Pakistan in 1970. The secular Awami League, predominantly Bengali with no influence in West Pakistan, swept the board in East Pakistan, winning every seat but one, that one seat for the Chittagong Hill Tracts being uncontested to allow its tribal leader to be elected there. In West Pakistan the Pakistan People's Party, with its secular slogan of '*Roti, Kapra aur Makan*' ('Bread, Cloth and Shelter') got a landslide victory in Sind and Punjab and the left-wing National Awami Party made a very good showing in Sarhad and Baluchistan. The Islamic parties got nowhere.

The Bengali movement was eventually to lead to the liberation of Bangladesh. It was the Bengali salariat which spearheaded that movement, although it had deep roots in the countryside. In a predominantly rural country (the urban population in 1960 being only about 5 per cent) most members of the Bengali salariat were sons of well-to-do peasants or the landed gentry and had solid support from the rural power base. The same is happening today with the powerful Sindhi movement that has erupted with force in the last few years. Its ideology too is explicitly secular.

The Sindhi salariat is backed by the entire rural population, as happened in Bengal. Their grievances are compounded by those of all other ethnic-Sindhi classes. Sindhi landlords and peasants are concerned about the question of equitable sharing of the waters of the Indus river system between Sindh and Punjab, of which the Sindhis feel they get less than their due share. Dispossessed Sindhi sharecroppers thrown out of their traditional source of livelihood by farm mechanisation and driven to the cities to look for work, find that the Sindhi urban society, of Karachi, Hyderabad and Sukkur, the major industrial cities of Sindh, has become non-Sindhi. They are therefore strangers in their own cities and are denied working-class jobs which are monopolised by immigrants from Sarhad and the Punjab. There is therefore an accumulation of grievances of all classes of the Sindhi people. The Sindhi movement therefore erupted with great force in 1983, drawing together all sections of the ethnic Sindhi people. It is not confined to the Sindhi salariat. But the Sindhi movement failed to build a united front with the predominantly non-Sindhi working class in Sindh, which isolated it in urban areas and made it ineffective. Currently leaders of the Sindhi movement, aware of this problem, have redefined and expanded the concept of Sindhi ethnicity so as to include also the Urdu-speaking *muhajirs* from India who pre-dominate in Sindhi cities. They declare that ethnicity is not a matter of language or culture or of origin but, rather, it is a question of roots. *Muhajirs*, victims of the history of the Partition, have nowhere else to go and have put down their roots in Sindh. They are Sindhis. But that is not so in the case of Punjabis, mainly bureaucrats and army personnel or their relatives, who have been granted lands in Sindh and have brought with them their own Punjabi workers. They have come as invaders and conquerors, they say, and must be made to return to Punjab and return the lands to Sindhi hands.

With the assumption of power by the Zia regime another factor has come into play, namely the exploitation of Islamic ideology to legitimate state power in the hands of the military. Afraid to face a free electorate and having no mandate to govern, the General turned to Allah. But he was forced to go much beyond the worn-out old rhetoric and had to show to a cynical public, who had heard it all before, that he actually meant business. But there was not much that he could do in practice, at least with regard to the economy. He is charged with the business of running a peripheral capitalist economy which has its own rules and logic and its own imperatives that he cannot afford to disregard. So he drew the lines clearly. He would make symbolic changes but he could not afford to interfere with the economy. In the Act setting up *Sharia* Courts, under the Constitution (Amendment) Order 1980, issued by Presidential decree, to Islamise Pakistan's laws, everything connected with the working of the economy is explicitly excluded from the jurisdiction of these Courts, under subsection (c) of section 203 A.

All that was left to the regime to do, in the name of Islamisation, was to undertake cosmetic measures, although the word 'cosmetic' is an outrageous word to describe the barbaric punishments that were prescribed under *Hudud* ordinances. The regime also launched a systematic attack, both symbolically and practically, on the status and privileges of women in Pakistan society. That in turn sparked off a women's movement which has generated a force that is unknown in Pakistan's history. The only measure that can properly be called cosmetic is 'interest free banking', the regime's pride and joy in its record of 'Islamisation'. Banks, instead of charging interest, are required, technically, to 'buy' their customers' goods which otherwise would have been hypothecated to the bank against the loan. Simultaneously the bank has to 'resell' the same goods to the customers, at a higher price. The difference between the nominal 'purchase' and 'sale' prices is thereby 'profit' and not un-Islamic interest, though in practice it makes no difference. This is just petty deception leaving the essentials unchanged.

The Zia regime seemed to have reached a dead-end in its Islamisation strategy by 1984. Its strident rhetoric about the Islamic basis of the Pakistan ideology failed to give it the basis of legitimacy that it sought. On the contrary, it only compounded its problems by raising the hopes of some naïve ideologists and Islamic fundamentalists that it was in no position to fulfil. Its bigoted supporters were already getting disillusioned and especially in the light of their electoral débâcle, they began to voice criticism of the regime that had so far patronised and protected them. There were soon signs that the regime had begun to soft-pedal the slogan of Islamic ideology. It turned instead to figure out alternative ways to build legitimacy, and has experimented with an Assembly elected under controlled conditions with all the opposition Parties under ban and their political activists under arrest. But even this does not seem to be working very well for the purposes of the regime and its problem remains unresolved.

Notes and references

1. See Ram Gopal, *Indian Muslims* (London, 1959), ch. 11 for an Indian nationalist view, and R. Palme Dutt, *India Today* (Bombay, 1970), pp. 456–9 and D. N. Pritt 'India', in *Labour Monthly*, XXIV (April 1942), for the Communist view. This view was reiterated by R. Palme Dutt, 'India and Pakistan', in *Labour Monthly*, XXVIII (March 1946).
2. G. Adhikari, *Pakistan and Indian National Unity* (Bombay, 1943) and also R. Palme Dutt, 'Notes of the Month', *Labour Monthly*, XXIV (September 1942).
3. Y. Gankovsky and L. Gordon-Polanskaya, *A History of Pakistan* (Lahore, n.d.).
4. Edward Mortimer, *Faith and Power: The Politics of Islam* (London, 1982).
5. H. A. Alavi, 'The State in Post-Colonial Societies', *New Left Review* 74 July–August 1972, reprinted in Kathleen Gough and H. Sharma (eds), *Imperialism and Revolution in South Asia* (1973), and in H. Goulbourne, *Politics and the State in the Third World* (London, 1979).
6. B. T. McCully, *English Education and the Origins of Indian Nationalism* (Williamsburg, 1940), and Aparna Basu, *The Growth of Education and Political Development in India 1897–1920* (Delhi, 1974).
7. Francis Robinson, *Separatism Among Indian Muslims: The Politics of the UP Muslims 1860–1923* (Cambridge, 1974), p. 46.
8. For an analysis of the role of the bureaucratic-military oligarchy in Pakistan see Hamza Alavi, 'Class and State in Pakistan', in H. N. Gardezi and J. Rashid (eds), *Pakistan: The Roots of Dictatorship: The Political Economy of a Praetorian State* (London, 1983). Within the bureaucratic-military oligarchy, the military emerged as the senior partner by the 1970s and the coherence of the once tightly-knit bureaucracy, controlled by the CSP cadres, has been largely undermined. Punjabis dominate both the military as well as the civil bureaucracy.
9. Abdul Hamid, *Muslim Separatism in India* (Lahore, 1967).
10. McKim Marriott, *Caste Ranking and Community Structure in Five Regions of India and Pakistan* (Poona, 1960).
11. Aparna Basu, *The Growth of Education*, p. 151.
12. *Report of the Court of Inquiry . . . into the Punjab Disturbances, 1953* (Munir Report) (Lahore: Government of West Pakistan Press, 1954), p. 219.
13. Zia-ul-Hassan Faruqi, *The Deoband School and the Demand for*

Pakistan (London, 1963); Barbara Metcalf, *Islamic Revival in British India: Deoband 1860–1900* (Princeton, 1982), passim.

14. David Gilmartin, 'Religious Leadership and the Pakistan Movement in the Punjab', in *Modern Asian Studies*, vol. XIII, No. 3 (1979); Barbara Metcalf (ed.), *Moral Conduct and Authority* (London, 1984) – articles by David Gilmartin and Richard Eaton.

15. For an account of political factions dominated by landlords and pirs, see Hamza Alavi, 'Politics of Dependence: A Village in West Punjab', *South Asian Review*, vol. IV, no. 4 (January 1971).

16. Iftikhar Ahmad, *Pakistan General Elections 1970* (Lahore, 1976).

17. Clarence Maloney, *Peoples of South Asia* (New York, 1974), p. 506.

18. David Kopf, *The Brahmo Samaj and the Shaping of the Modern Indian Mind* (Princeton, 1979).

19. Christian W. Troll, *Sayyid Ahmad Khan: A Reinterpretation of Muslim Theology* (Karachi, 1979), p. 18 and n. 75.

20. Sir Syed Ahmad Khan, *Rah-e-Sunnat dar Radd-e-Bid'at*, *Tasanif-e-Ahmadiya* vol. I (Aligarh, 1883).

21. Mohammad Iqbal, *The Reconstruction of Religious Thought in Islam* (Lahore, 1958 reprint).

22. Ibid., p. 173.

23. Ibid., p. 174.

24. Ibid., pp. 175–6.

25. K. K. Aziz, *Party Politics in Pakistan 1947–58* (Islamabad, 1976), pp. 143–4.

26. Francis Robinson, *Separatism*, passim.

27. Ibid., pp. 173–5.

28. Ibid., p. 252.

29. Azim Husain, *Fazl-i-Husain: A Political Biography* (Bombay, 1946), pp. 315–16.

30. Mohammad Iqbal, *Letters of Iqbal to Jinnah* (Lahore, 1963), pp. 28–32.

31. Dow to Wavell, 20 September 1945, *Fortnightly Reports – Sind, L / P & J / 5–261*, Jan.–Dec. 1945, India Office Records.

32. Jamil-ud-Din Ahmad (ed.), *Speeches and Writings of Mr. Jinnah*, vol. I (6th edition, Lahore, 1960), p. 43.

33. Ayesha Jalal, *The Sole Spokesman: Jinnah, Muslim League and the Demand for Pakistan* (Cambridge, 1985), pp. 95–6.

34. G. W. Choudhury (ed.), *Documents and Speeches on the Constitution of Pakistan* (Dacca, 1967), pp. 21–2.

35. E. I. J. Rosenthal, *Islam and the Modern National State* (Cambridge, 1965), p. 245.

36. S. Sibte Hassan, *Naveed-e-Fikr*, (Urdu) (Karachi, 1983).

37. Rounaq Jehan, *Pakistan: A Failure in National Integration* (London, 1972), pp. 25–7.

38. G. W. Choudhury, *Documents and Speeches*, p. 25.

39. Ibid., p. 30.

40. Ibid., p. 31.

5 Syria's Muslim Brethren

HANNA BATATU

Who are the Muslim Brethren in Syria? What is their significance socially? How are they related to Syria's social structure? What is the social meaning of their ideas and values? Are these ideas and values responses to distinguishable conditions and interests of one or more identifiable social groups? Are the Muslim Brethren, in other words, an incidental phenomenon or the organisational expression of a basic structural force? For the most part, this chapter deals with these and related questions. It provides a tentative, exploratory interpretation, with some vivid and sharp images, rather than a thorough and refined picture of the movement.[1]

Programme and ideas

The Muslim Brethren of Syria can initially be identified by the ideas which they have espoused. At first, they had no clear thoughts on social or economic issues or the problems of government. In the late 1940s and the 1950s they flirted with an undefined 'Islamic socialism',[2] but by 1961 they had excised the term altogether from their political vocabulary. Their earliest programme – that of 1954 – offered only generalities. It committed them to such objectives as 'the combating of ignorance, disease, want, fear, and indignity' and 'the establishment of a virtuous polity which would carry out the rules and teachings of Islam.'[3] Their central slogans were no more definite: 'God is our End; His Messenger our Example; the Qur'an our Constitution: the Jihad our Path; and Death for God's Cause our Highest Desire.'[4] These formulas had an immense weight of popular sentiment behind

112

them, but their practical implications were vague and difficult to ascertain. The Qur'an and the Muslim heritage, like the Bible and the Christian traditions, contain rich and varied elements which can be and were in the past interpreted in different directions by different Muslims according to their circumstances.

In 1980, in the light of the accumulating experience of the intervening decades and under the red-hot pressure of the bloody events in Aleppo, Hamah, and Palmyra, the Muslim Brethren published a new programme. Here they spelled out their position on several issues in somewhat clearer and more concrete terms. A number of points stand out.

First, there is a forthright appeal to the 'wise men' of the 'Alawi community. '9 or 10 per cent of the population,' the appeal reads, 'cannot [indefinitely] dominate the majority in Syria.' This would be against 'the logic of things.' 'The ['Alawi] minority has forgotten itself and is ignoring the facts of history.' This state of affairs and 'the provocative and aggressive practices' of the regime with which it has linked its fate 'could ignite a murderous civil war.' The appeal ends with the hope that the 'Alawi community would shake off the 'guardianship' of Hafiz al-Asad and his brother Rif'at and thus 'prevent the tragedy from reaching its sad end.'[5]

In this appeal, the Muslim Brethren clearly put themselves forward as the natural spokesmen of the Sunni community, and define their conflict with Syria's rulers as a conflict between Sunnis and 'Alawis. To no little extent, the conflict has indeed taken on this aspect in the past few years. At the same time, it is quite plain that the conflict is not about religion. It is not the beliefs of the Sunnis that have been in danger or under attack since the Ba'thist take-over in 1963, but the social interests of the upper and middle elements of their landed, mercantile, and manufacturing classes.

It should be noted parenthetically that the 1980 programme is remarkable for the absence of any mention of Iran's Islamic Revolution. This is easily explained. The Muslim Brethren had appealed to Ruhullah al-Khomeini in 1979 for moral support against Syria's regime but received no response whatever. It did not escape their leaders that an informal coalition embracing Syria's rulers, the Shi'i *Amal* movement in Lebanon, and Iran's theocracy had taken shape. Moreover, they could not afford to displease the Iraq government which had been helping them with money and military supplies[6] and continues to be their principal

source of support. Over and above this, Sa'id Hawwa, the chief
ideologist of Syria's Muslim Brethren, had made clear in no
uncertain terms that the authentic community of Muslims is 'the
community in which has appeared the only form of truth conven-
tionally recognised through history and which finds its embodiment in the People of the Sunnah.'[7] This appears to exclude, at
least tacitly, an ideological accommodation with a regime so
uncompromisingly Shi'i as that of present-day Iran.

More to the point is the great emphasis which the Muslim
Brethren place in their 1980 programme on the political emancipa-
tion of the common citizens: 'the need of the nation to regain its
freedom is as vital as its need for air, water, and food.' They
strongly condemn martial law, arbitrary decrees, and inhuman
police practices and proclaim their attachment to the freedom of
the citizenry to think, publish, assemble, protest, oppose, and
form political parties and trade unions. They also declare themselves firmly for the principles of the separation of powers and the
independence of the judiciary, and for a government subordinate
to the rule of law and resting on *shura* (mutual consultation).[8]

Except for the last point, there is nothing characteristically
Islamic about these values. They are obviously drawn from the
moral armouries of classical liberalism. There may be a temptation
to dismiss them as empty formulas in an uncongenial context, but
the temptation ought to be resisted. The recurring rise to power in
the past three decades or so in Syria and other parts of the Arab
world of unrepresentative and narrowly-based groups, their discharge of public affairs in manners prejudicial to the general
interest, their violent and often bloody suppression of dissenters,
their bringing of writers, journalists, and teachers to low esteem,
and the sad deterioration of Arab thought have pushed the question of basic freedoms to the political forefront. Through bitter
experiences, increasing numbers of politically conscious Syrians
have realised that these freedoms are very important human
values and have incalculable practical significance. What may have
been in the 1940s mere catchwords have become now a living faith.
By hoisting high the standard of political and civil liberties, the
Muslim Brethren hope to press this faith into the service of their
cause.

No less interesting are the economic demands of the Muslim
Brethren. They insist on the need for vesting 'full ownership of the
land' in the farmers and for their liberation from middlemen,

guardians, and officials who 'suck [their] blood in the name of the state, party, and socialism'. They call for the transfer of the ownership of public industrial establishments unrelated to national security from the state to the workers. They favour adequate rewards and better conditions for the labourers in factories owned by private individuals, but in the same breath castigate workers who 'think they are entitled to everything and others possess no right to demand anything from them' and who 'convert factories into *takaya* [hospices] for the lazy and the indolent'. They also call for the encouragement of artisans, and the freedom of private capital to export, import and manufacture within the limits of a 'studied plan approved by the *shura* [consultative council]'. While conceding that 'some merchants may be excessively greedy' and 'inclined towards monopolism', they express their conviction that 'the state is bound to fail . . . when it turns into a merchant.'[9]

In brief, the economic programme of the Muslim Brethren is consonant with the outlook and interests of the urban Sunni trading and manufacturing middle and lower middle classes. Can it be inferred from this that the Muslim Brethren are the organised expression and forward arm of these classes? To answer this question, it is necessary to cast a glance at the origins and evolution of this movement.

Roots of the movement

The Syrian branch of the Society of the Muslim Brethren struck roots first among young men who were for the most part students of the *sharia* (Islamic law). Some of them had attended courses at Cairo's al-Azhar University; there they had come under the influence of the ideas of Hasan al-Banna, the society's founder. Others had apparently been won over by Egyptian Muslim Brethren who toured Syria in the mid-1930s.

With few exceptions, the earliest of the society's Syrian devotees stemmed from families of 'men of religion'.[10] Thus Mohammad al-Mubarak and Salah ash-Shash, who founded its Damascus branch in 1937, belonged to families of '*ulama*' of middling income and status. Mustafa as-Siba'i, the first superintendent general[11] of the society in Syria and its foremost leader from 1945 to 1961, came from a family which had for long provided the *khatibs* (preachers) of the Grand Mosque of Homs. His successor, 'Isam al-'Attar, who guided the entire organisation from 1961 until the rift in its ranks in 1972 and continued up to 1980 to inspire only its Homs, Dayr az-Zur, and Damascus branches, also sprang from *ulama* of intermediate social standing and was himself the *imam* (prayer leader) at the mosque of Damascus University. 'Abd-ul Fattah Abu Ghuddah, who led the seceding elements in 1972 and had set up the Aleppo branch in 1935, descended from a family of artisans and began life as a weaver but subsequently became a *mudarris* (teacher) of the *sharia*.[12]

The religious class with which the Muslim Brethren were and still are closely connected is not, relatively speaking, very large in Syria. It is not, in a numerical sense, anything like its Iranian counterpart. According to an informed Shi'i source, the *mullahs* in Iran counted no fewer than 120 000 in 1979;[13] if correct, this would translate roughly into one *mullah* for every 308 Iranians. By contrast there were in Syria among all denominations in 1960 only 1761 and in 1970 only 2843 'men of religion and persons connected with them',[14] including *muwaqqits* (timekeepers), mosque servants, and reciters of Qur'anic verses. In other words, there was one man from this broadly defined religious class for every 2592 Syrians in 1960[15] and for every 2217 Syrians in 1970.[16] The ratio was higher in urban than in rural areas: one for every 1638 city-dwellers as against one for every 3042 rural inhabitants in 1970. In clearer terms, there were in 1970 only 1173 urban men of religion and related functionaries and servants for no fewer than 5000 villages.[17] Due allowance must be made for statistical imperfections, but the figures confirm the discernible absence of men of religion from many of Syria's villages.

The bulk of the 'men of religion' were and are very poorly remunerated, as is evident from Table 5.1. The meagreness of the *imam* compensation can be gathered from whispers among merchants relating to the income of senior army officers: they are said, not perhaps without exaggeration, to average no less than 8000 Syrians pounds (about $1840) monthly. In addition, they can purchase subsidised goods from army co-operatives, build apartments or villas with state loans obtained on very easy terms, and – as the merchants wistfully point out – have the use of the cars not subject to customs' inspection at official borders. By contrast, the minimum pay of the *khatib* and the *mudarris* is lower than that of the mosque servant; their maximum pay is higher only by 9 and 18 per cent respectively. Even the *imam*'s maximum salary exceeds that of the servant by only 58 per cent.

TABLE 5.1 Monthly pay scales, in Syrian pounds,* of 'men of religion' and of 'persons connected to them' as of 6 March 1980

imam (prayer leader)	385–610
mudarris (teacher)	285–455
khatib (preacher)	250–420
mu'azzin (announcer of the hour of prayer)	285–320
qari' (reciter of Qur'anic verses)	190–270
muwaqqit (timekeeper)	180–250
khadim (servant)	305–385

* The Syrian pound exchanged for roughly 23 US cents in 1980.
† Excluding *muftis* (consultative jurists) and *qadis* (judges in *sharian* cases).

Source: Prime Minister's Decision No. 61 of March 6, 1980, Syrian Arab Republic, Al-Jaridah ar-Rasmiyyah . . . [Official Gazette], Part I, No. 11 of 1980, pp. 466–467.

Of course, the servant puts in long hours at the mosque, whereas the *imam* merely leads the assembly of the faithful in reciting the five daily prayers, and the *khatib* preaches to them only on Fridays. Moreover, a 'man of religion' may discharge two or more religious functions. He may also receive fees on the occasion of ceremonies attendant upon circumcision, marriage, and death. Even so, except for the *muftis* and *qadis*, who draw much higher salaries – and there are no *muftis* and few *qadis* among the Muslim Brethren – the 'men of religion' cannot, as a rule, live on the income they derive from religious service. They must frequently engage in petty trade or handicraft. Many of them are drapers or stationers or booksellers or perfume vendors.

In fact, there is a substantial degree of coincidence between the class of tradesmen and the religious shaikhly class. The shops of the tradesmen-shaikhs are usually located in the neighbourhood of mosques. In Damascus, for example, they are established in the *suqs* (markets) of al-'Asruniyyah and al-Madinah close to the Umayyad Mosque. Some of the founders and earliest devotees of the Society of Muslim Brethren descended from this class of people, as is apparent from their family names: 'Attar is the Arabic for perfumist, Tunji[18] for goldsmith, ash-Shash for muslin or white cloth. Incidentally, the father of Hasan al-Banna belonged also to this class: he was both a religious *mudarris* and a watch-repairer, and thus known as as-Sa'ati.

The economic self-support of the bulk of the Muslim 'men of religion' has had important consequences. In as much as they have not depended for their livelihood on the government, they have not on the whole truckled to it or cringed at its feet. On the other hand, by dint of their trading interests and the government's ability to damage or impair these interests, and in view of the appropriation by the government in 1965 of the right to appoint and dismiss the *khatibs* in the mosques, the 'men of religion' have on the whole been careful – unless ideologically provoked or economically injured, as at some points in the Ba'thist period – not to take sharp political positions.

This is true not only of the tradesmen-shaikhs but of the whole small-scale trading and artisan class among whom, as could be expected, the Muslim Brethren penetrated deeply and with ease. But in this regard two distinctions must be made. According to the society's deputy superintendent general, 'Adnan Sa'd-ud-Din, craftsmen and petty traders indeed form a major component of its membership, but its most militant activists are drawn from their offspring or their educated elements – students and members of the intelligentsia by and large[19] – who are in their teens, twenties and thirties and, being youthful, are more daring and reckless than their elders and more prone to take uncomplicated and brisk attitudes. To the generational difference must be added regional dissimilarities. The Damascene Muslim Brethren, like other Damascenes, are in general milder, more flexible, more subtle, more cautious, and less inclined to violence than, say, the Aleppans, possibly by reason of climatic and environmental differences. There is nothing similar to Damascus' fertile oasis of Ghutah on any side of Aleppo. Its landscape is more barren, its climate drier and more severe. Damascus, being the principal seat of government, has also been more favoured economically in recent decades.

There has been another consequence of the economic self-reliance of the Muslim 'men of religion'. Since most of them have lived by their own effort rather than on exactions from the people and since their class has not, on the whole, enjoyed privileges or special rights, they have not been viewed by the mass of Syrians as a parasitic body or an economic burden upon society. Moreover, they have never been a highly organised or closely integrated group, and, at least in recent times, have not presented a united ideological front or constituted a powerful or insurmountable impediment to the advance of secular ideas. This explains the absence in Syria (and in other Arab countries) of strong anti-shaikh or anti-religious trends. There were, in the past, protests or demonstrations against individual arbitrary or unpopular *muftis* or *qadis*, but not against the shaikhs as such. Irreligion or indifference to ancestral beliefs or doubt concerning basic *sharia* principles have progressed among leftist intellectuals but have not resulted in intense anti-religious feeling. In the 1920s, the Communists frontally attacked the men of religion. Making no headway among the populace, they quickly desisted from this course.

Significance of the small traders

The small-scale trading class has a number of features which throw some light on the ideas, policies, and history of the Muslim Brethren. First, the urban small tradesmen and artisans were and still are the most religiously orientated class in Syria. They by and large observe faithfully and regularly the precepts of Islam. Their idiom is that of the religious shaikhs, and they are akin to the religious shaikhs in values and way of life.

Second, they are strongly attached to 'free enterprise'. They favour competition among the big merchants and simultaneously fear it in their own sphere. The terms of trade between them and the big merchants are often not to their advantage. In this sense the interests of the two classes are opposed. In another sense, however, they are complementary. Under certain conditions, when the big merchants suffer they are also affected. After the rise of the Ba'thists to power in 1963, some of the functions of the big merchants, like the wholesale import and export of goods, were assimilated by new public organisations. Small-scale traders had to deal with government employees who were often of rural origin and, if not hostile to the urban trading community, had little understanding of the intricacies of trade and thus wittingly or unwittingly raised all sorts of impediments in its path. The small-scale traders had clearly been more comfortable with the traditional big merchants who, in addition, were Muslim Sunni like themselves.

Interestingly enough, some of the important merchants of the *suq* of Hamidiyyah somehow continued all along to exercise influence over the small tradesmen of Damascus. The adoption by Hafiz al-Asad in 1970 of the policy of 'economic liberalisation' greatly enhanced their position. Subsequently, they appeared not only to control the small traders but also to maintain relations with influential army officers and with the Ba'th party apparatus. In fact, there is reason to believe that the merchants of *suq al-Hamidiyyah* were playing a double game. At least some of them were thought to be liberally subsidising the Muslim Brethren. Others, by gestures of support to the government through the Chamber of Commerce which they controlled were obtaining concessions for the class as a whole. In 1980, for instance, when the activities of the Muslim Brethren were at one of their peaks, the import quotas of the merchants for consumer goods were sharply increased.

The trading class as a whole has been adversely affected by the rise of agricultural co-operatives in rural districts and consumers' co-operatives in urban areas. Sellers who travel from village to village and constitute a large group at Hamah, where they are known as *al-muta'iyyishin*, have apparently been similarly hurt. Co-operative stores were the first establishments to be destroyed in a rising organised by the Muslim Brethren in 1980 in Aleppo.

One other point needs to be underlined: the small-scale artisan and trading class is very significant not only in terms of skills and economic *savoir-faire* but also numerically. The traditional big landowners and their mercantile allies consisted of a few hundred families and were hit or overthrown with relative ease. By contrast the small-scale traders and artisans counted in 1970 nearly a quarter of a million.[20] With their dependents, they easily accounted for one-sixth of the entire population. They are not a force that can be discounted or effortlessly suppressed.

The movement in Syria

At this point it is appropriate to highlight and explain the major events in the history of the Muslim Brethren.

One thing that at once attracts our attention is that the movement first took shape in Aleppo. It appeared there in 1935 under the name of 'The House of al-Arqam' and was so-called after al-Arqam b. 'Abd Manaf b. Asad who was one of the earliest converts to Islam and in AD 614 offered his house at Mecca as a meeting-place for the Prophet Muhammad and his followers.[21] The 'House of al-Arqam' at Aleppo remained for several years the most active centre of the Brotherhood and served as its head-quarters until 1944. How can one account for this fact?

Of course, the Aleppan Muslims were deeply disturbed by the passage of Syria after the First World War from Turkish Muslim into 'infidel' French hands. But this feeling was shared by the believers in the rest of the country. More to the point is that Aleppo was at that time the largest and most important city in Syria. Moreover, the Aleppan Muslims had special reasons to be aggrieved. Between 1919 and 1925 no fewer than 89 000 Arme-nians moved from Turkey to Syria, most of whom settled in Aleppo[22] and, by virtue of their industrial skills and aptitude for making money, not only disturbed the denominational balance of the population in the city but also the position of its trading class. Much more seriously, the artificial detachment from Syria – to the benefit of Turkey and in defiance of the factors of trade, history, and ethnic origin – of the port and district of Alexandretta in the late 1930s and of the Cilician wheatlands, the cities of 'Aintab and Urfah, and the Baghdad railway territory across northern Syria in the wake of the First World War, cut off Aleppo from its natural outlet to the sea and from its natural markets and hinterland and limited its commerce to the district lying within a radius of some twenty miles from the city.[23] The Muslim trading community in all its components suffered more profoundly than the Christian mer-chants, who were connected with the European rather than with inter-Ottoman trade. By the mid-1930s, the Muslim men of com-merce had not yet adapted to their shrunken markets.[24] All these factors resulted in the revival of Muslim sentiments and in move-ments against European and for native products[25] and no doubt assisted the advance of the ideas of the Muslim Brethren.

In 1944, sensing, in the light of an open and sharp clash between French and British interests, the approach of political independ-ence, the society shifted its main center to Damascus. In the following year it adopted the appellation of 'Muslim Brethren'[26] and elected Mustafa as-Siba'i[27] as its first superintendent-general.

The short supply of consumer goods during the Second World War, which was then nearing its end, and the accompanying inflated prices, heightened by speculation and profiteering, en-riched the local merchants and improved the conditions of the small traders. This decreased their susceptibility to the views of the Muslim Brethren who, however, gained some support among lower middle-class state employees, and especially schoolteachers, with fixed incomes.[28]

It was the defeat of the Arab armies and the creation of the state of Israel in 1948 which gave a considerable impetus to the movement. The disruption of a large part of the Palestinian community and of its economic structures inflicted special harm on the Damascene merchants and traders for whom Palestine had, for generations, served as an important market. Indeed, the interests of the mercantile classes of Damascus were far more closely interwoven with the interests of the Palestinian trading families than with the interests of the commercial communities of Aleppo and northern Syria.[29]

The rise of the Nasserist pan-Arab trend in the second half of the 1950s tangibly reduced the appeal of the movement. The Egyptian leader drew part of his strength in Syria from the very same urban Sunni petty trading elements which nourished the Brotherhood. In 1958, upon the creation of the United Arab Republic, Mustafa as-Siba'i yielded unconditionally to Nasser and officially dissolved the society.

The attitude of the Muslim Brethren towards the break-up of the UAR in 1961 was ambiguous. 'Isam al-'Attar,[30] who had just succeeded Siba'i as superintendent-general, refused to sign the historic manifesto issued by eighteen of Syria's foremost politicians in support of secession. At the same time, Lieutenant-Colonel 'Abd-ul-Karim an-Nahlawi, the principal author of the separatist *coup*, who descended from a family of traders and artisans and shaikhs of the defunct Ahmadi mystic order,[31] moved in an ideological environment pretty much dominated by the Muslim Brethren. After the *coup* he relied on them and gave them a free hand.[32] This led to a noticeable expansion of their ranks.

The comparative strength of the Muslim Brethren in the fourteen years or so prior to the conquest of state power by the Ba'thists in 1963 may be gathered from the figures in Tables 5.2 and 5.3. For the proper interpretation of these figures, it is necessary to keep in mind that every district and the chief centre of every province and the villages attached to it constituted single electoral districts. Thus, in 1961, the city of Damascus and six of its surrounding villages formed only one constituency. Moreover, every

TABLE 5.2 Distribution of Parliament seats in the pre-Ba'thi period

Year	Total seats	Parties of big land-owners and merchants		Akram Hurani's Socialists	Ba'th Party and allies	Muslim Brethren and allies	Independent deputies	Other elements
		People's Party	National Party					
1949	114	43	14	1	4	3 (2.6%)	45[a]	4[b]
1954	141	27	14	5	13	5 (3.5%)	64[c]	13[d]
1961	173	25	13	7	8	10 (5.8%)	96[e]	14[f]

[a] Includes 9 tribal representatives
[b] Includes 1 seat for Parti Populaire Syrien (PPS)
[c] Includes 18 tribal representatives
[d] Includes 2 seats for PPS and 1 seat for Communists
[e] Includes 13 tribal representatives
[f] Includes 5 Nasserists and 1 Arab Nationalist

Sources: Great Britain, F.O. 371/75541/XL/A/11644 E 14487E. Letter of 28 November 1949 from British Legation. Damascus to Foreign Office, London: Khalid Al'Azm. *Mudhakkirat* [Memoirs], vol. II (Beirut, 1973), pp. 300–7; Amin Isbir, *Tatawwur-un-Nuzum as-Siyasiyyah wa-d-Dusturiyyah fi Suriyyah* (Development of Political and Constitutional Systems in Syria) (Beirut, 1979), p. 89, and 'Adnan Sa'd-un-Din, deputy superintendent-general of the Muslim Brethren, conversation, January 1982.

TABLE 5.3 Distribution of Parliament seats in the pre-Ba'thi period

Year	Total seats in Damascus	Parties of big land owners and merchants		Ba'th Party	Muslim brethren	Independent deputies	Other elements
		People's Party	National Party				
1949	13	2	—	—	3 (23.0%)	6	2[a]
1954	16	2	2	1	3 (18.7%)	5	3[b]
1961	17	1	4	—	3 (17.6%)	8	1

[a] Includes 1 seat for Parti Populaire Syrien (PPS)
[b] Includes 1 seat for PPS and 1 for Communist Party

Sources: Great Britain, Foreign Office, FO 371 75541 XL A 11644 E 13908. Telegram no. 618 of 17 November 1949, from British Legation. Damascus to Foreign Office London: Khahd al-'Azm, *Mudhakkirat*, vol. III (Beirut, 1973), pp. 220–1, and Amin Isbir. *Tatawwur-un-Nuzum as-Siyasiyyah wa-d-Dusturiyyah fi Suriyyah*, p. 93.

eligible voter could cast as many votes as there were candidates in his district and could thus endorse more than one list. The big merchants and landowners of Damascus, for example, threw their principal weight behind the People's Party and the National Party, but they and their supporters also voted for the Muslim Brethren, not out of sympathy for them but out of their fear of the Communists and Ba'thists. At the same time, in the hope of enhancing their electoral chances, the Muslim Brethren pursued, at least in 1961, the tactic of voting exclusively for their own candidates. For these reasons, the figures may not provide an accurate index of the actual distribution of the influence of the Muslim Brethren or of their rivals. The favour they enjoyed with Lieutenant-Colonel 'Abd-ul-Karim an-Nahlawi in 1961 may also have had a distorting effect.

Even though at that time they were making headway, they did not enjoy wide support in the country as a whole. In the parliamentary elections they won only 2.6 per cent of the seats in 1949, 3.5 per cent in 1954, and 5.8 per cent in 1961. In Damascus, though, in striking contrast to the marked frailness of the Ba'th Party, they occupied a relatively strong position: they captured 23 per cent of the seats in 1949, but 18.7 per cent in 1954 and 17.6 per cent in 1961.

While showing vitality in Damascus and other Syrian cities, the Muslim Brethren had scarcely any foothold in the countryside. Indeed, until 1975 there was, according to their deputy superintendent-general,[33] a discernible resistance within the society to any orientation towards the peasants: influential leaders in the organisation apparently did not think it desirable to politicise country people. On the eve of the Ba'th's seizure of power, therefore, the movement of the Muslim Brethren was and has, to a lesser extent, remained to this very day essentially a movement of the cities, in sharp contradistinction to the rurally orientated and rurally supported Ba'th party. Of this point we should not lose sight, if only to understand the conflicts to which Syria fell prey in the last two decades.

Stages under the Ba'th

For the same purpose, and in order to grasp the meaning of the policies and tactics of the Muslim Brethren in the Ba'thi period, it will help to emphasise the three main stages that the Ba'th regime has gone through.

Its first stage began in 1963 and ended in 1968. The regime was then more broadly based than it is at the present time. At bottom, it rested on an authentic if uneasy alliance within the army between varying groups which shared similar rural roots and similar rural orientations and included 'Alawis from the Latakia province. Druzes from the Jabal al-'Arab, and Sunnis from the region of Hawran and the district of Dayr az-Zur, and from different small country towns. The inadequately studied and rather carelessly applied socialist policies with which these groups became identified, and the rapid penetration of the bureaucratic apparatus by rural elements allied to them, severely damaged the interests not only of the big men of commerce, industry, and finance but also of the broad class of urban artisans, petty traders, middling state employees, and members of the professions. Indeed, on the whole, the intermediate urban classes viewed the 'socialism' of the day as a weapon by which the more conscious segments of the long neglected and long suppressed rural people sought revenge against the main cities and the decisive impoverishment of their inhabitants. Consequently, in this period the political conflict took on much the aspect of an urban–rural conflict, and the Sunni element of the population itself split clearly along urban–rural lines.

To understand better the dynamics of the conflict, it would help to focus briefly on the relationships between the Sunni Hawran and Sunni Damascus. For a very long time, the Hawran was the granary of Damascus. Its people, who were for the most part small farmers, sold their produce in markets controlled by the merchants of the capital. Even in the towns of Hawran, the shopkeepers were more often than not Damascenes. Their relationships became in essence relationships of debtors and creditors. This is in part explicable by the improvidence of the Hawranis: *'isrif ma fi-j-jayb, ya'tika ma fi-l-ghayb'* ('spend what is in the pocket and you will share in that which is in invisible') runs one of their favourite sayings. The Damascenes, on the other hand, prefer the adage *'khabbi irshak-il-abyad liyomak-il-aswad'* ('save your white piaster for your black day'). But the merchants of the capital were also more artful than the Hawranis in money matters, and markedly more calculating. Moreover, in the past the state machine was pliable to their wishes. They were, therefore, able to set the conditions of trade in manners consistent with their interests.

As the merchants of Damascus dominated the Hawran, so did the entrepreneurs of Aleppo dominate Dayr az-Zur and the Jazirah. But here there was also a tribal division at work. For example, at Dayr az-Zur the affluent traditional leaders stemmed from the Albu Saraya, a section of the Baggarah tribe, whereas many of the Ba'thists descended from such inferior clans as the Khorshan and Shuyukh.

In this many-sided situation, the Muslim Brethren emerged in the mid-1960s as the most implacable opponents of the Ba'this and the forward arm of the endangered urban traders. They promoted a campaign of civil disobedience, using the mosques as their centres and mobilising or encouraging for this purpose *ulama* hostile to the secular orientation of the Ba'thists, including Shaikh Hasan Habannakah, a popular figure in the Damascus district of al-Maydan.

Their agitation attained such a force that it succeeded in bringing about in 1965 a *partial* polarisation within the officer corps along sectarian lines, with many of the rural Sunni officers gravitating towards the compromise-minded Sunni General Amin al-Hafiz and the 'Alawi Druze, and part of the Sunni Hawrani officers towards an inflexible bloc led by the 'Alawi Salah Jadid and the Druze Hamad 'Ubayd.

From the ensuing tug-of-war, Jadid emerged supreme. He pulled down Amin al-Hafiz in 1966 and, not long afterward, got rid of his erstwhile Druze and Hawrani allies. By 1968, the 'Alawi dominance of the armed forces was well-nigh complete.

But at this point as the regime entered its second stage, which was to last until 1970, the military 'Alawis split. One section, buttressed by the bulk of the civilian component of the Ba'th Party, gave its loyalty to Salah Jadid, the other to Hafiz al-Asad. The division arose partly out of a conflict of personalities. It may also have had a tribal aspect: Salah Jadid belonged to the 'Alawi tribe of al-Haddadin, Hafiz al-Asad to the 'Alawi tribe of al-Matawirah. Publicly, the division assumed the form of a clash of policies, with the more pragmatic Asad insisting on the need for moderating the urban–rural conflict and Jadid bent on a radical 'socialist' line.

Dissensions also set in within the Society of the Muslim Brethren in this period. The younger members of the Aleppo and

Hamah branches, shaken by the Arab military defeat of 1967, agitated for the continuance of the policy of confrontation with the regime. The Society's superintendent-general, 'Isam al-'Attar, backed by the bulk of the membership in Damascus and Homs, determinedly and successfully opposed this tendency.[34] Strengthening the hand of Asad in his contest with Jadid served better the interests of the natural supporters of the Muslim Brethren, the urban artisans and petty traders.

In 1968 irreconcilable young militants led by Marwan Hadid, a 34-year-old agronomist and the son of a small agricultural entrepreneur from Hamah, left Syria for Jordan. There they joined Fatah, the principal arm of the Palestinian resistance movement, and received commando training in one of its camps. This marks the beginning of the militarisation of the policy of the Muslim Brethren.

The third phase in the development of the Ba'th regime opened in 1970, with the triumph of Asad over Jadid and his seizure of the reins of government. Throughout the first half of the 1970s, he steered Syria in a manner congenial to the urban traders and the Damascus leadership of the Muslim Brethren. He drew close to Egypt, waged with Sadat the October War of 1973, and mended Syria's relations with the Saudis and the Jordanians. He simultaneously liberalised the country's economic policies, attracting wide-scale aid and some investment capital from the Arab Gulf states. A sort of *de facto* axis developed between military 'Alawis and the commercially-minded Damascenes. The traders of *suq al-Hamidiyyah* never had it so good as in these years.

The Brethren against the Ba'th

After 1975, however, things began to change. The flow of Arab oil money, which had been copious, diminished sharply. The heightened scale of peasant migration and a mounting rate of inflation deepened the injury to the social fabric of the principal cities.[35] Rents became inaccessible for the middle and humbler classes, with modest apartments in the better parts of the capital going for 60 000 or even 80 000 Syrian pounds a year. An honest man could no longer live on his salary. Labourers and petty state employees had to take two jobs just to survive. The growth of a parasitic class of state contractors, the rampant corruption in the upper layers of the bureaucracy, and the fat commissions made on government contracts by men close to the pinnacle of power added to the popular discontent. Even more aggravating was the intervention of the Syrian regime against the Palestinians in the Lebanese conflict: at one point, in 1976, the Syrian units pinned down the main Palestinian forces in the mountains, allowing the Maronite Phalange to destroy completely the camp of Tal az-Za'tar with considerable loss of life. Since 1917, no regime in Syria, whatever its colouring, had taken an anti-Palestinian stand. It was a policy without precedent, and shocked and alienated wide segments of Syrian opinion.

But what above all incurred the hostility of the Muslim Brethren was the sharpened 'Alawi bias of the regime and the deepening erosion of the status and power of the Sunni community. Two political orders, both headed by President Asad, had by now crystallised in the country and still function at the present time. In the first, which consists of a Council of Ministers, a People's Assembly, the Ba'th Party Command, and their subordinate organs, the Sunnis play conspicuous roles. But all these bodies have merely an apparent or derivative authority. Real power lies on another, more fundamental level. It is held by Asad and the 'Alawi leaders of the intelligence apparatuses and the crucial armoured divisions and air and missile units which underpin the whole structure.

The Muslim Brethren began their offensive against this order of things in 1976, not long after the intervention of Syria's armed forces in Lebanon. At first they confined themselves to persistent minor blows in the hope of provoking Syria's rulers, involving them in repressive policies, and estranging them further from the people. They concentrated on hit-and-run killings of 'Alawi functionaries, security agents, and professional men, focusing attention on their origins and the origins of Hafiz al-Asad outside the Sunni Muslim main current of Syria's life.

In a second stage, they escalated their acts and widened their scope: they carried out attacks on government buildings, police stations, Ba'th party institutions, and army units. They provoked demonstrations and large-scale shutdowns of shops and schools as at Hamah and Aleppo on 8–10 March 1980, and at Hamah in February 1982. They also struck spectacular blows at the ruling power: in June 1979, with the help of a Ba'thi Sunni officer who had been won over to their cause, they assailed with grenades and machine-gun fire 200 or so 'Alawi cadets of the Artillery Academy at Aleppo, killing 83 of them and wounding many others.[36]

The violence produced an atmosphere of crisis and great danger. The Muslim Brethren's defiance of the authorities also emboldened other opposition forces to follow along.

The militants who carried out these acts were men in their 20s or early 30s, ardently attached to their beliefs, daring to the point of recklessness. In large part, they were university students, schoolteachers, engineers, physicians, and the like. This is evident from the occupational distribution of the activists – mostly Muslim Brethren – who fell into the hands of the government between 1976 and May 1981. Out of a total of 1384 no fewer than 27.7 per cent were students 7.9 per cent schoolteachers, and 13.3 per cent members of the professions, including 79 engineers, 57 physicians, 25 lawyers, and 10 pharmacists.[37] The profiles of the leaders of the Military Sections of the Muslim Brethren point to the same conclusion. 'Adnan 'Uqlah, who led the latest rising at Hamah, is a civil engineer and the son of a baker. His predecessor, 'Abd-us-Sattar az-Za'im, was a dentist and the son of a tradesman. Husni Abbu, who was the chief of the Military Branch of the Aleppo region in 1979, was a teacher of French, the son of a well-to-do merchant, and the son-in-law of Shaikh Zayn-ud-Din Khayr-ul-Lah, the *Imam* of the Grand Mosque of Aleppo.[38]

What have the Muslim Brethren achieved? They have succeeded in widening the distance between the government and the majority of the people, but not in destabilising the regime. Instead of splitting the 'Alawis and thus weakening their foothold in the army, they have, by their anti-'Alawi practical line, frightened the 'Alawi community into rallying behind Asad. They have also provoked a ferocious response on the part of the government. In June 1980, in putting down an attempted breakout by political prisoners at Palmyra, the security forces killed no fewer than 100 men.[39] In February 1982, in order to suppress a rising by the Muslim Brethren at Hamah, the government went to the length of leveling whole sections of the northern and eastern parts of the city. In the process, they killed at least 5000 people, according to Western diplomats,[40] but eye witnesses from Hamah insist that no fewer than 25 000 perished. About 1000 government troops are also said to have died in the fighting.

What is the outlook for the Muslim Brethren? In the past decade, the movement underwent acute shifts in its strength. For example, on the reckoning of its own leaders, its membership in the city of Aleppo did not exceed 800 in 1975, but had by 1978 swollen to an estimated maximum of 5000 to 7000.[41] There is reason to believe that its numerical weight – but not moral sympathy for its cause – shrank noticeably after the passage of Law no. 49 of 8 July 1980, which regarded adherence to the Muslim Brethren as 'a crime' punishable by death.[42] Its total strength at the beginning of 1982 probably did not surpass 5000. At Hamah it suffered a deep wound from which it will not recover easily. Many of its natural supporters in Syria's other cities may have come to entertain second thoughts about its tactics, which have no doubt been too costly in human lives and material possessions. However, so long as the present regime remains narrowly based and unrepresentative of the country's majority, there is bound to be a revival of the spirit of revolt which no repression, however brutal, can extinguish.

Notes and references

1. I am grateful for comments on this paper by Hafiz ash-Shaikh, a knowledgeable journalist from Bahrain.
2. See, for example, Mustafa as-Siba'i (the then superintendent-general of the Society), 'Al-Ikhwan al-Muslimun' [the Muslim Brethren], House of ar-Ruwwad, *al-Ahzab as-Siyasiyyah fi Suriyyah* [*The Political Parties in Syria*] (Damascus, 1954), pp. 30–1.
3. Article 6 of the Society's Basic Rules of 1954, The Muslim Brethren, Syria, *an-Nizam al-Asasi* (Aleppo, 1954), pp. 8–9.
4. Quoted by Sa'id Hawwa (the Syrian Muslim Brethren's principal ideologist) in his *Fi Afaq-it-ta'alim* [*In the Horizons of the (Society's) Instructions*] Cairo, 1980), p. 162.
5. The Command of the Islamic Revolution in Syria, *Bayan-uth-Thawrat-il-Islamiyyah fi Suriyyah wa Minhajuha* [*The Declaration and Program of the Islamic Revolution in Syria*] (Damascus, November 9, 1980), pp. 10–12. The Declaration was signed by Sa'id Hawwa. 'Ali al-Bayanuni. and 'Adnan Sa'd-ud-din, members of the Executive Bureau of the Society of Muslim Brethren.
6. Letters dated July 26 and August 8, 1980 from Iraq's First Deputy Premier Taha Yasin aj-Jazrawi to 'Adnan 'Uqlah, Chief of the Military Section of the Muslim Brethren, attest to this fact. For photocopies of these letters, whose authenticity has not been called into question, see *Tishrin* (Damascus), 26 October, 1980.

7. Sa'id Hawwa, *al-Madkhal ila Da'wat-il-Ikhwan-il-Muslimin* [*Intro-duction to the Mission of the Muslim Brethren*] second edition. ('Amman, 1979), p. 22.
8. The Command of the Islamic Revolution in Syria, *Bayan-uth-Thawrah.* . . , pp. 14–20.
9. Ibid., pp. 20–32.
10. The Muslim Brethren insist that strictly speaking, there are no 'men of religion' in Islam but only 'men of the *sharia*' or 'men of 'ilm (Islamic knowledge).' However, they are clearly distinguishable from others by their religious functions and titles, even though they may revert to purely civilian occupation and thus do not necessarily form a fixed or stable group. The term 'men of religion' will be used in this paper with these qualifications in mind.
11. The Arabic terms is *'al-Muraqib al-' Am'*.
12. The foregoing observations are essentially based on a conversation with 'Adnan Sa'd-ud-Din, deputy superintendent-general of Syria's Muslim Brethren, January 1982.
13. Conversation with this writer, November 1980. Paul Balta and Claudine Rulleau, in *L'Iran insurge* (Paris, 1979), p. 152, gave the higher figure of 180 000.
14. The Syrian Republic, Ministry of Planning, *At-Ti'dad-Am li-s-Sukkan li'Am 1960.* . . [*The Population Census of 1960 in the Syrian Republic*] (Damascus, n.d.), pp. 224–225 and 230–231; and Central Statistical Office, *Nata'ij at-Ti dad al-Am li-s-Sukkan* . . . , 1970 [*The Results of the Population Census for 1970 in the Syrian Arab Republic*], p. 225.
15. The total population of Syria in 1960 was 44 565 121.
16. The total population of Syria in 1970 was 6 304 685.
17. There were 5,476 towns and villages in 1952, Syrian Republic, *At-taqsimat al-Idariyyah fi-j-Jumhuriyyah as-Suriyyah* [*Administrative Divisions in the Syrian Republic*] (Damascus, 1952), pp. 295–301.
18. Abd-ul-Wahhab at-Tunji was one of the founders of the society's Aleppo branch.
19. Conversation with this writer, January 1982.
20. Consult the Syrian Arab Republic, *Nata'ij at-Ti'dad al-'Am li-s-Sukkan* . . . *1970*, Part I, pp. 247–250
21. Conversation with 'Adnan Sa'd-ud-Din, January 1982.
22. In 1928, out of an estimated population of 300 000, not less than 50 000 were Armenians: see Great Britain, Foreign Office, F.O. 406/62/4694 E5338/141/89 Letter of October 30, 1928 from Consul Monck-Mason, Aleppo, to Lord Cushendun.
23. Consult Great Britain, Foreign Office, F.O. 406/46/4694 E5774/117/89 Letter of April 23, 1921 and F.O. 406/51/4694 E2345/2204/89 Letter of February 12, 1923, both from Consul Smart, Aleppo to Earl Curzon, London: and F.O. 406/75/4694 E196/3/89 Memorandum of January 11, 1937 by J.G. Ward of the Eastern Department.
24. Great Britain, F.O. 406/74/4694 E961/195/89 Letter of February 15, 1936 from Consul Parr, Aleppo to Mr. Eden, London.
25. Movements of this kind first appeared in the 1920s. See Great Britain,

F.O. 406/51/4694 E6332/867/89 Letter of May 31, 1921, from Consul Smart, Aleppo, to the Marquess Curzon of Kedleston.

26. Mustafa as-Siba'i, 'al-Ikhwan al-Muslimun', House of ar-Ruwwad, al-Ahzab. . . , op. cit., p. 11.
27. For Siba'i, see ibid., p. 6.
28. According to the Society's deputy superintendent-general, inferior state officials and schoolteachers still constitute a substantial portion of the Society's membership: conversation with this writer, January 1982.
29. In the 1930s, Palestine was the most important customer of Syria: consult the figures for Syria's exports provided in Great Britain, F.O. 406/74 E4121/1403/89 Letters of April 13 and June 24, 1936 from Consul-General Havard, Beirut, to Mr Eden and F.O. 406/74 E6898/1403/89 Letter of 22 October 1936 from Acting Consul General Furlonge, Beirut, to Mr Eden.
30. For al-'Attar, see p. 6.
31. Muhammad Adib Al-Taqi-ud Din al-Husni, *Kitab Muntakhabat at-Tawarikh li-Dimashq* [*Selections from the Histories of Damascus*], Beirut, 1979, p. 885.
32. Sami aj-Jundi, *al-Ba'th*, Beirut, 1969, p. 101.
33. Adnan Sa'd-ud-Din, conversation, January 1982.
34. The particulars relating to the dissension in the ranks of the Muslim Brethren provided in this and the succeeding passages are based on 'Adnan Sa'd-ud-Din's account.
35. The official wholesale price index rose from 100 in the base year 1962 to 226 in 1973 and 350 in 1979 for cereals and flour and, in the same years, to 294 and 509 for vegetables and to 328 and 483 for meat. (Central Bureau of Statistics, *Statistical Abstract, 1980* [Damascus, 1980]).
36. *An-Nadhir* (underground organ of the Muslim Brethren) No. 16 of April 29, 1980, pp. 7–10 and No. 17 of May 25, 1980, pp. 26–7: *Le Monde Diplomatique* (Paris), April 1980, pp. 4–5 and October 1979, p. 7; and *The New York Times*, June 23, 26, 29 and September 4, 1979.
37. Based on figures provided by the Committee for the Defence of Freedom and Political Prisoners in Syria, in its organ *al-Minbar* (Geneva), No. 3 of January 1981, pp. i–xl, and No. 4 of May 1981, annex after p. 95.
38. The particulars concerning these leaders were obtained from 'Adnan Sa'd-ud-Din, conversation, January 1982.
39. The leaders of the Syrian opposition estimated the number of killed at Palmyra prison at between 550 and 700 in their letter of May 18, 1981 addressed to the secretary-general of the United Nations and published in *an-Nadhir* No. 35 of 17 June 1981, pp. 40–3.
40. *The New York Times*, 29 May 1982.
41. 'Adnan Sa'd-ud-Din, conversation, January 1982.
42. Article of the Law, Syrian Arab Republic, *al-Jaridah ar-Rasmiyyah* . . . , Part I, No. 29 of 1980, pp. 1450–1.

6 State and Ideology in Republican Egypt: 1952–82

MARIE-CHRISTINE AULAS

On 23 July 1982 the Egyptian republic was thirty-years old – the age when a generation reaches maturity. Although it was a public holiday and the Ramadan fast had recently ended, the Nile Valley did not take the opportunity for one of its characteristic displays of exuberance. The authorities celebrated in a mood of respect for tradition: a speech here, a bunch of flowers there, amid the nervous ritual of starchy official ceremonies. The popular symbols of the event, however, were almost entirely absent, as if republican Egypt feared to look at itself in the mirror of recollection.

At the time Israeli and American bombs were raining down on Beirut. But even without them, it would have been rather improper to commemorate the tremendous wave of hopes which, thirty years earlier, had spread over Egypt and so many other countries in the region. It would not have been wise to evoke the earlier dreams of independence and development, at a time when Egypt, though once again territorially intact,[1] was unable to recognise itself and was searching more than ever to understand where its future lay. In more senses than one, its situation might be compared to the background of the 1950s revolt – a situation in which social inequalities and external dependence impregnate and mould the panorama of everyday life.

Egypt does present a continuity in that its regime is the legal inheritor of the July Revolution. The men have changed over

133

time, but the state apparatus still functions within republican structures which, despite the harsh trial of military defeat in 1967 and the assassination of the head of state by members of his own army in 1981, have remained essentially the same since 1952. It is somewhat as if the body, deprived of its soul, were clinging to life through an eternity reflex of this old nation-state.

How has Egypt come to this pass within a mere generation? How could the republic have spawned opposite principles to those it initially bore?

The construction of Republican Egypt

New foundations for an old project

The whole story began on 23 July 1952, when a group of twelve officers managed to seize power in one of those *coups d'état* that involve a discontinuity of the political order. The Republic took the place of the monarchy. But there was also a profound upheaval in the social order. Before the various changes had taken shape, the new regime announced its twin goals: to secure independence from any foreign tutelage, and to develop the country's economy. It was certainly a vote-winning platform, corresponding to the ideological spectrum of the Free Officers themselves, some of whom were close to Islamic currents such as the Muslim Brotherhood, and others to secular currents such as the Communist parties.[2] There was even a possibility that the programme would win over some of the old rulers – above all, the 'national bourgeoisie' in the Wafd Party, one of whose leaders, Mustafa El Nahas Pasha, had been prime minister until the great Cairo fire of January 1952.[3] After all, independence had been the main goal of the Wafd Party since its creation in 1918. And even in its decline, as late as October 1951, it had yet again denounced the treaty of 26 August 1936[4] and refused to join the proto-Baghdad Pact, the 'Middle East Supreme Command'. As to economic development, this was already the great aspiration of the national bourgeoisie, which had set up the Bank Misr and fostered other such projects as long ago as the 1920s. To be sure, development still required not only industrialisation but also agrarian reform. But that was not a particularly revolutionary demand: the UN had itself embraced it in 1950 on the proposal of the United States; and it had been widely sounded by the big bourgeois Miritt Butros Ghali,[5] and even debated in Parliament. In short, the objectives of the new regime corresponded to evident needs that were the subject of deep and widely held aspirations.

The group of officers, who had barely turned thirty and were united by an ardent nationalism, were taking charge of the country in the name of the most traditional ideals. But these did not add up to a project that would immediately go beyond a merely political break with the previous order. Like so many other Third World leaders on the morrow of independence (including the Algerian FLN), the Free Officers sorely lacked a programme of action. Yet the challenge that lay ahead would concern the fundamental issues of the battle for development and national security, and even such unprecedented problems as the nationalisation of the Suez Canal Company.[6] The years brought no correction of this gap – at most there were short-term measures of one kind or another. New institutions, and the Action Charter of 1962, then tried to give a form and a content to those measures, infusing an *ad hoc* mobilising ideology.

With the benefit of hindsight, it is easy to see that the often bold initiatives of the new regime were more a reaction to events than the implementation of a coherent programme.[7] Still, the pragmatic approach did have its hours of glory for a decade or more. From 1954 to 1967 Egypt lived at a furious pace, as the British withdrawal was followed by Cairo's rejection of the Baghdad Pact, the Bandung Conference, the Suez nationalisation, the blocked invasion of 1956, the creation of the Non-Aligned Movement, the union with Syria, and so on. At a less spectacular level, closer to everyday reality, there were also major internal achievements: agrarian reform, the development of an industrial infrastructure and of numerous public services (health, education, housing, and so on), and the construction of the High Dam, the country's main energy resource. It was an impressive list, which could hardly have failed to convince its originators that they were on the right track.

As it shook the old social equilibrium and the tacit rules of the international game, Nasser's Egypt had the illusion of controlling the new course of post-war history. In reality, however, it was merely riding the crest of a wave, and its successes could not last forever. After careful and prolonged study, the host of Western research centres would come up with ways of countering the new pattern. And by then Egypt's internal social dialectic would have run out of steam, never having really been allowed to develop freely by those who had control of it.

For reality was deeply ingrained in those who held power on the banks of the Nile. In socio-economic terms, those impertinent young officers could not be described as bourgeois, since they did not own any property. Nor were they proletarian, since they had not been directly linked to the production process. As army men, they belonged to that layer of state functionaries whose weight, in the land of the 'crouching scribe', can be truly enormous. Their perception of world realities, like their underlying aspirations, were those of the middle-class milieu from which they had issued. It is true that this class has still to be satisfactorily defined. But above all in the Third World, it is a fractured class and hence a nest of contradictions. It is mainly given over to tertiary activities, which most often developed under the impetus of economic necessities in the colonial period. The middle class is torn between its essentially traditionalist cultural attachments, and its thirst to climb the social ladder through education that is usually modernist and Western in its left–right, capitalist–socialist dichotomies of political and ideological discourse. In short, as the Free Officers group itself testifies, we are dealing with a class in which the most diverse and contradictory ideologies, whether Islamic or Marxist in origin, are caught up and jumbled together. A nationalist orientation will clearly have a large following among this class, because its affective virtues attract opposites and dispense with the need for analysis. In Egypt, where history has a quite special weight, nationalism appears as more coherent perhaps than elsewhere. But beyond the short-term mobilising effect of nationalist discourse, the eternal dilemma of 'tradition' and 'modernity' continues to traverse particularly the middle class, and inevitably resurfaces in the end.

Nasser's Egypt would obscure the cultural and ideological dimensions of the dilemma by perceiving it only in political and economic terms. In fact, although the accents were different, it took over the basic problematic of the Nahda movement of a century before. The Arab 'renaissance' had then sought to breathe new life into Arab-Islamic civilisation by drawing inspiration from the European advances in science and technology. However, the intellectual upsurge had been unable to stem the process of colonisation, which began in 1882, after Mohammed Ali's first steps in industrialisation, after the creation of a publishing industry, the completion of the Suez Canal, and the opening of an Egyptian Parliament in 1876. Just like its unacknowledged forerunners, the Nasser regime was unconsciously mined by the dilemma and condemned to eventual failure. For even if it is not explicitly formulated, the choice between 'tradition' (an ideological and cultural identity, of which the economy is but one dimension) and 'modernity' (a goal imposed by the West in its 'capitalist' or 'social-Marxist' variant[8]) cannot fail to make itself felt – whether in the way of directing development or in the model fostered by the class in power.

Only today are we in a position to ask how Egypt could claim to be freeing itself, while it strove to imitate the very forces against which it was locked in political and economic struggle. At the time, Egypt was not the only country to live such an illusion.

The building of state capitalism

Once in power, the stratum that had emerged from the middle class imposed a new *de facto* social order by supplanting the old ruling class that had taken shape a century before around the Mohammed Ali dynasty. By its very nature, this stratum identified with the state as the bulwark of national independence, and as the key instrument of political and economic action. In the stage of construction, the state would forge the structures that assured the legitimacy of its controllers: the armed forces, and then the single party. In a parallel process, it became the country's principal entrepreneur, if not its only employer: as one nationalisation measure followed another[9] and development assumed an industrialist inflection, the state acquired supreme control over the bulk of industrial production and a sizeable portion of agriculture. Outside the state, no salvation for the Egyptian people! There can be no doubt that this statist, authoritarian dynamic did raise many structural blocks and resistances in a number of areas. Yet the transformation of economic structures proceeded on the basis of a state capitalism which in no way altered the capitalist relations of production. On the contrary, these now spread to sectors of the economy and society which had formerly lived on their margin.

Once the initial stage was over, the concentration of responsibilities in the expanding bureaucratic order gave birth to a form of economic statism and internal political rivalries. These rigid tensions had all the more paralysing an effect in that the nationalist momentum never structured a broad social base or a will to sweep away the old social order. However great the aspirations and initial steps towards equality, any further progress was rendered highly problematic by the essential incapacity of this social class to formulate a coherent project. Its very nationalism, which had been intended as a revolutionary force, later served to mystify the crucial socio-economic differentiation of the traditional classes and of the privileged layer emerging from the new state-capitalist class.

Ideological elaboration

As the Egyptian leaders empirically developed new state structures and a new political orientation, they gradually became aware of the ideological holes in their project. They never tired of inventing new forms to motivate and regiment the population, but they did so less from ideological conviction than out of a pragmatic need to acquire a broad popular following. This explains their fascination with the experience of the Communist countries, whose ideology explains and justifies an apparatus of popular mobilisation. Indeed, during the ascendancy of its nationalist discourse, Nasserism sought to rally the masses by borrowing a number of ideological elements that it felt to be either imposed or justified by the circumstances. This approach underlay the role given to intellectuals, and it allows us to understand the mistrustful and ambivalent way in which the regime always related to them. Conflictual for the first ten years, this relationship improved after the intervention of Mohammed Heikal, the enterprising editor of *Al-Ahram* and the regime's chief ideologue – if ever there was one.

Explicit ideologies

Arab nationalist ideology was advanced at the time when Cairo's triumphant acts of defiance (rejection of the Baghdad Pact, the 1956 nationalisation, and so on) galvanised the Arab masses from Baghdad to Rabat. To be sure, Nasser had strongly evoked Egypt's

Arab identity in the theory of 'the three circles' in his one and only work, *The Philosophy of the Revolution*. But that would seem to be an obvious fact of culture and geography, of politics and history. Many others in Egypt had already said as much, and various pacts signed with Arab countries since 1952 provided the proof, if any were necessary. One would have expected from Cairo a more sustained analysis of its Arab nationalist ideology – for the heart of the Arab world beats in the Egyptian capital, even if it is not there that the greatest Arab thinkers have been produced. Most often they went there – from Syria, Lebanon, Palestine – to achieve recognition and freedom of expression. The Nasser period did little to reverse this trend: none of its intellectual output, painted on to reality in order to justify or flatter, has proved able to withstand the test of time. Not by chance did Doctor Hussein Fawzi's *Sinbad al-masri* ('*An Egyptian Sinbad*') enjoy such success during those years.[10] Nor was it the only systematic study of the Egyptian personality: Gamal Hamdan's *Shakhsiyat Masr* ('*Egypt's Personality*'), for example, was a geo-strategic variation on the same theme. But where were the basic works on Arab national-ism? It is true, however, that the official encouragement of pan-Arabism drew attention to several great works of classical Arabic literature, as well as to contemporary non-Egyptian Arab writers. When the schools and universities were opened to all, this opening to Arab culture would form a whole generation.

In the cultural domain proper, Arab nationalism and the Palesti-nian question bore little fruit. The cinema, for instance, then bursting with creativity, could only produce a clumsy epic, *Salah-el-Din*,[11] in which the features of Nasser, the Ra'is, were barely disguised. The lack of anything solid on the Palestinian drama or the Algerian war of liberation also marked the literature of the period. Only after the defeat of 1967 did Egypt face the Arab world with a few films and literary works of interest concerning Palestine and the conflict with Israel. Sinai had just been occupied.

Given the image in the West of Nasser's Egypt,[12] it is strange to note the marginal place of the Palestinian problem in the cultural life of the time. Even when the problem was addressed, it was analysed in such a feeble way that it appeared as a question of duty or solidarity *vis-à-vis* despoiled Arab brothers, never as an in-trinsic part of the Egyptian national cause. Similarly, Egypt's total ignorance of Zionist ideology, though explicable in terms of the denial of the Jewish state, hindered a concrete knowledge of Israel. Later, all these things would smooth the way for Sadat's trip to Jerusalem, the signing of the Camp David accords, and so on.

As for *socialist ideology*, Nasser's Egypt took even longer to develop its distinctive themes. Political discourse turned to them only after a transitional stage of 'positive neutralism' and at the same time as the Non-Aligned Movement was coming to the fore. These semantic precautions tell us a great deal about the constraints and reservations standing in the way of such an ideological orientation. Like many other Third World countries, Nasser's Egypt became socialist by economic determinism (choice of a development model) and strategic necessity (US–European collusion with Israel forcing an alliance with the USSR), rather than from a concern for equality, as is usually the case in the West.

During the same period, the positions of the USSR *vis-à-vis* decolonising Third World countries underwent a significant evolution. Khrushchev's advent to power was followed by de-Stalinisation and a thaw in the international situation, and the Twentieth Congress of the CPSU moved away from the old line, defined by Zhdanov in 1949, which denounced 'the putrid idea of the possibility of some third, middle road between communism and capitalism'.[13] The new approach, which was more adapted to the needs of the Third World leaders, stressed the concepts of 'national democracy' and 'a non-capitalist path of development'. Eschewing any class analysis of the anti-imperialist states, a stream of articles substituted definitions in terms of 'unity' or 'working together' in the general interest. Such theorisations, corresponding to the bloc interests of the Soviet Union, entailed that local Communist parties should dissolve themselves in the national effort, while the USSR sought an alliance with the new national bourgeoisies.

Both Cairo and Moscow had an interest in such a convergence. However, Egypt wanted to chart its own path of development and its own socialism. Already in the late 1950s a number of working groups and research institutes were set up to develop a 'scientific' approach that would result in a specifically 'Egyptian road to socialism'.[14] Yet despite the scientistic phrases, dear to every type of socialism, the research projects often merely compounded the ideological confusion. In 1962 – a full ten years after the seizure of power – a Charter of National Action finally set the guidelines for the regime's political activity, but without coming near to a resolution of the fundamental contradictions. For how could Egypt claim to embrace socialism if the regime blocked the class struggle and strove to absorb and freeze any rank-and-file pressure within an all-powerful single party? How could Egypt be socialist if it interned for several years those of its citizens who were most ready to defend and advance socialism?

Egypt was the first, but not the only, Third World country to live these 'socialist' contradictions with the obliging approval of Moscow. The Egyptian Communists would be sacrificed on the altar of bloc politics and forced to participate in 'national democracy'. Within this framework the progressive intellectuals began to be released from detention, although they were not invited to help in drafting the Charter that was then under preparation. While the Communist Party was dissolved, Heikal intervened to encourage intellectuals to join the regime in its efforts along 'the non-capitalist path of development' – a theoretical novelty which made them prepared to accept the offer. However, they were being asked only to supply intellectual substance for analyses which the regime itself was far from living up to.

Emanating from the summit, with no grassroots consultation or participation, this rather intangible Egyptian socialism did not enter the national consciousness. Only in education, health, housing and purchasing co-operatives did it leave some trace and a fairly widespread nostalgia for a time when the state concerned itself with citizen's welfare.

The implicit ideology of modernisation

Neither Arab nationalism nor 'particularist socialism' managed to awaken a process of reflection that went beyond the passing conjuncture. By wedding themselves to practical necessities – whether of a political, economic or strategic order – these orientations would eventually run up against the regime's implicit ideology.

After all, it is undeniable that there was a Nasserite project, unconsciously conveyed by the 'fractured' social class in power. This project never appeared in speeches but only in actual deeds – for the good reason that it conflicted with the publicly declared anti-imperialist political options. We might summarise the Nasserite project as one of Western-style modernisation that borrowed the non-capitalist (or state-capitalist) path of development. The Western – or, to be more precise, American – model had also been the goal of Moscow in its pursuit of scientific and technological progress; and at about that time Khrushchev was continually uttering the challenge: 'We shall catch up with the Americans!' In this regard, a semantic approach to the material achievements of the Nasser regime may prove quite instructive. We can see this in many areas.

(a) *The production choices of the industrialisation programme, then in full swing.* Import substitution favoured those aspirations which the middle class had never managed to achieve: refrigerator, hot-water system, air conditioning, a Fiat Nasr car, and all the varieties of comfort propagated by American TV series in the newly-born Egyptian television network. Possession of such consumer goods was not just a question of greater well-being, but was dialectically related to social status. The harder they were to acquire for anyone without the right connections to the state apparatus, the more their owner was held in esteem. The alternative was to go to Gaza, which had a privileged import regime.[15]

(b) *House-building programmes geared to the social class identified with the state apparatus.* The most striking feature here was 'neo-Californian' architecture, whether in the private villas of Dokki Mohandessin and the new destricts of Cairo, or in the recreational complexes of the resort towns of Maamura and Gamassa, designed to meet the leisure needs of this class.

(c) *Co-operation with other Arab countries, particularly Syria (the Union of 1958–61) and North Yemen (after the overthrow of the Imam in 1962).* In each case, the haughty and contemptuous attitude of Cairo's officers and functionaries was so intolerable to the local population that the Egyptian presence was phased out by those who had requested it.

(d) *The magnetic attraction of Beirut.* Like West Berlin in Eastern Europe, Beirut serves as a shop-window of the West in the Arab world. At the time when Cairo was capitalising on regional political aspirations, the Egyptian petty bourgeoisie had its eyes firmly fixed on Hamra . . . on the road to Moscow.[16]

This 'modernising' perspective was basically continuous with the 'Nahda' of a century before. Yet the fact that it was only implicit excluded any reflection on its inevitable cultural impact. Modernisation involved no more than an often clumsy application of a borrowed model, in which no attention was paid to the ideological dimensions conveyed by science and technology. As it intoned the hymn to progress and aseptic science, Egypt believed that it was genuinely creating something. But it was merely relaying the ideological conceptions of the Euro-American West, from which it claimed to be freeing itself politically and economically.

Once it had passed the colonial stage, Egypt fell into the evolutionist trap of the 'stages of economic growth' theory developed in Washington.[17] Whole chapters of Rostow's work were translated and serialised in *Al-Ahram*, with the headline taken from Rostow's sub-title 'a non-communist manifesto'. And that was when the regime was deciding to embark on the socialist path!

The extension of school education to all layers of society, as well as Cairo's influence in a number of Arab and 'non-aligned' countries, helped to spread the 'model' beyond the limits that the West could hope to achieve through its own dynamic. North Yemen, for instance, which had been virtually closed to the world for centuries, was introduced by Egyptians to reinforced concrete and the tie-and-suit before anyone arrived from UN development agencies. Egypt thereby revived the pioneering role it had played a century before, when the Austro-Hungarian strategist Friedrich List could write:

No traveller doubts that [Mohammed] Ali has the strength of will and sufficient means so to found a power that would introduce European civilisation to the most beautiful countries in the world and beam, by the shortest route, the European sense of initiative to southern Asia and eastern and southern Africa.[18]

Ardently encouraged by progressives, Communists and Marxist-Leninists,[19] the Nasserite ideology of modernism helped to ease the spread of the Western capitalist market and to topple the whole Arab world irresistibly into a new kind of ideological alienation (the Western model implicitly conveyed by modernisation). This was done in the name of socialism and Arab nationalism, in accents which celebrated the regaining of freedom and independence.

Furthermore, the regime's monopoly of expression (education, the printing and distribution of books and magazines, and so on, and its ideological monolithism froze any creative thought outside the institutional channels. Unable to free the social dialectic and the expressions of national culture, the institutions gradually became constricting forces whose wooden language, fed by taboos, silences, artifices and stereotypes, distorted information when it did not obscure it completely. In this sense it was the Soviet model that was at work in Egypt – although the regime's conception of its intellectuals was much more restrictive than in Moscow. The intellectual had to discard any critical spirit and become a mere scribe in the service of a regime whose cultural horizon, unlike that of the Nahda period, was extremely narrow and displayed all the ambiguity of the 'fractured' social class in power. The nationalist stage did produce some valuable achievements, but then the dynamic of the state came to petrify the intellectual capacities of a whole generation. Sooner or later, it seemed, there might be no one left but hacks ready to argue for any new course or decision of the regime.

The end of Nasserism

Wherever Egypt may have been heading, Washington could not wait for this internal revolution to run its course. This was because Egypt opened the way for the key international difference (one now conceived in the North–South vocabulary) to be converted into a tactical confrontation, one between East and West. The country's political weight and influence in the world was seen as intensifying the threat to the strategic balance; and as, after 1968, the British prepared to withdraw from East of Suez,[20] it became an urgent necessity to stem the Nasserite tide.

The tripartite attack on Egypt in 1956 had been a failure. So in June 1967, Israel was called upon to secure a clear-cut victory, by acting militarily on its own. As a result, after fifteen years of independence, Egypt found itself defeated militarily and with a partial occupation of its territory. The ideologies of Arab nationalism and a particularist socialism began to evaporate as Cairo strengthened its alliance with Moscow and disengaged from Yemen. The traumatic character of the defeat bred sceptical and self-critical attitudes, overturning certain shibboleths in favour of a few elementary truths. These could be seen emerging in the press, in various cultural, literary[21] and cinematic works,[22] and in the newly founded Palestinian Research Centre.[23] However, although the crisis did introduce a certain freedom of expression, it was not long before this was obstructed by the state apparatus, which had emerged unscathed, if emptied of all substance, from the war.

Despite the defeat, Nasser remained until his death in September 1970 the charismatic leader of both Egypt and the Arab world. He never ceased to be faithful to, or perhaps imprisoned by, his image: that of a man who would fight with the means available to assure his country's independence and security.

The end of state capitalism

The preconditions

Defeat in 1967 initiated the decomposition of state capitalism, even as Nasser still lived. Cracks appeared here and there in the hitherto monolithic structure of the state, leading not only to a relative cultural relaxation but also to a degree of economic liberalism *vis-à-vis* the national bourgeoisie. In 1968 student revolts broke out in Alexandria and Cairo, calling for the punishment of officers with operational responsibility in the June War, and for genuine popular participation.[24] In response, the National Charter of 1962 was amended in a few purely formal ways by the proclamation of 30 March 1968.

The country's dramatic situation made the choice of a policy all the more crucial. The regime could no longer get by on artificial ideological constructs, nor appeal to a nationalist mobilisation that abstracted from the social dynamic. The Israeli occupation of the Sinai imposed a new priority, one that would take precedence over the battle for development and constitute *the* national question in whose name the later compromises and political changes would be justified. In the meantime, Nasser devoted his final efforts to rebuilding the army and, in 1969, to a war of attrition that would only end with his acceptance of the Rogers Plan in July 1970. The mobilisation of military resources, culminating in the triumphant crossing of the Suez Canal, would dispense with the need for popular mobilisation.

Gathering momentum

Nasser's death removed the main obstacle to Egypt's integration into the capitalists sphere of influence. But his charisma was still so powerful that his successor had to await the momentous events of the October War before daring to proclaim the new orientation. In the half-light of the neither-war-nor peace period (1970–3), however, the new regime would introduce certain profound changes and various mechanisms that prepared the ground for the official re-integration.

Rivalries within Nasser's small group of legatees soon burst into the open. They took the form of an ideological conflict over whether Washington or Moscow could best allow the national question to be resolved. But this debate concealed what was no more than a struggle for power within the ruling class – a struggle in which the population remained completely marginal. Although, at this stage, each clan waged its struggle purely from its positions of power within the state apparatus, the rivalries heralded a gradual return to other forms of social differentiation.

Anwar al Sadat finally asserted himself as head of state on 14 May 1971. Under cover of eliminating rival 'centres of power', a huge process of reorganisation shifted the goals of the state apparatus while preserving its essential structures. In the trade unions, the single party, the national assembly and so forth, a series of elections brought forward new faces and new political currents. A new constitution[25] reaffirmed the commitment to socialism, 'which will prevent exploitation, and aim to dissolve class differences',[26] but it also strengthened the powers of the head of state and underlined the Islamic character of the regime. The press, brought into conformity with the other media, was purged. A few months later, in the wake of the student riots of January 1972, numerous intellectuals lost their job or were banned from publishing. The crisis also yielded a new government, most of whose main figures, though known from the previous regime, had the common feature of being Western-trained technocrats. In the 1960s many of them had helped to draft socialist measures, and now they were being called upon to assure the return to capitalism. Their actions spoke for themselves.

In 1971 the Aziz Sedki government decreed a reorganisation of the public sector, under which companies whose activity depended upon it would enjoy freedom of movement and initiative without being subject to government or other supervisory intervention. It was also decided to set up an international foreign-trade bank whose function would be to strengthen the ties with Arab countries, and to create free enterprise zones in which Arab and foreign capital would be encouraged to participate in industrial and commercial ventures. In summer 1973, a new government under the head of state himself (but with the economy and finance portfolio going to Abdel Aziz Hegazi) announced the broad lines of its economic policy, which included the creation of a parallel currency market free of import-export restrictions.

This series of measures naturally reassured those at whom they were aimed. They were certainly more than enough for the hitherto veiled class differences to express themselves with confidence: the wives of officials now dared to sport their jewellery at receptions, and 'top' weddings began to be celebrated at the only two big international hotels of the time (the Nile Hilton and the Sheraton). Nor was the ruling class of petty-bourgeois origin alone in displaying the economic resources it had acquired under state capitalism – it was soon joined by all those who had preserved the bulk of their fortune through the years of socialist austerity.

It was precisely to this kind of clientele that the new regime turned in order to build a social base. It produced one concession and one conciliatory advance after another: 800 landowners whose property had been sequestered ten years earlier were handed back their land; and 5000 more who had been affected by the 1967 land reform were given cash compensation.

Strict controls on trips abroad were lifted. Journalistic contacts with Western embassies were actively encouraged, after many years of strong official disapproval. Shawarbi Street, in the heart of Cairo and the centre of the black market, overflowed more than ever with anything from tights to washing-machines that had been smuggled in from Beirut. Both the government and the privileged classes had an interest in this nod-and-a-wink form of liberalisation. Yet it was still too early for it to be officially proclaimed.

Official discourse began to stammer as it tried to legitimate itself with references to Nasser while giving signs of a new departure. It was a difficult balancing act, not without danger in this period of uncertainty and looming war. Indeed, it was this weakness which lay at the root of the serious student disturbances in the winter of

1972. For President Sadat, having declared in June 1971 that this year would see the decisive conflict with Israel, had announced at the beginning of January 1972 that the 'fog' of the Indo-Pakistan war had ruled out a renewal of hostilities.

It was at this time that Sadat introduced two ideological surrogates that would serve him throughout his years in power. First, the espousal of Islam initially allowed him to broaden his social base by releasing the members of the Muslim Brotherhood who had been jailed in the repressive campaign of 1965. He then encouraged Islamic forces to enter the university in order to counter the influence of progressive-Nasserite groups. Characterising himself as '*Al-Raïs al-Mumen*' (the Believer President), he invited Egyptian television every Friday to film his participation in mosque services. The brown patch or *zebiba* that he marked on his brow offered tangible proof of his piety. Nor were these references to Islam entirely without an economic basis, since Egypt's relations with Libya (then in its anti-Soviet phase) and Saudi Arabia (previously disliked in Cairo) were continually undergoing expansion.

As a complement to religion, the head of state also invoked themes of traditional morality. In his first speech to the People's Assembly after the launching of the 'rectification movement', the President declared: 'I want us to return to the village source, to our origin . . . I want the constitution to take this into account, not only for the sake of the villages, but so that the whole of Egypt should take shape in this way and become a single village.' The wisdom of tradition and of the paterfamilias would become a recurrent theme of official discourse, constantly backed up by the President's trips to his home village, Mit Abul Kom, and illustrated by photos of him in the peasant *jallabieh*. The clear purpose was to substitute the wisdom of tradition for the perils of class struggle.

As for Egyptian nationalism, which lends itself so easily to popular mobilisation, the regime was content to strengthen its outward emblems. Having been known since 1958 as the United Arab Republic, the country was renamed Egypt. The falcon of the Qoraish appeared on the national flag, in place of the two stars that had symbolised the union with Syria.[27] But this nationalism no longer had the militant tone of defiance.

Throughout the period between 1970 and 1973, one marked by the political succession, clan rivalry and incipient economic liber-

alisation, the contradictions of Nasserite ideology were apparent
in Heikal's continuing role as chief ideologue of the regime.
Nasser's former confidant supplied Sadat with the arguments to
justify many of his new policy initiatives: the 'rectification movement'; Egyptian intervention against the pro-communist *coup
d'état* in Khartum, in July 1971; the *rapprochement* with Saudi
Arabia and the United States.[28] Heikal was truly the *eminence
grise* of the regime, writing most of the key speeches and using his
journalistic talent to launch a good number of media slogans, such
as that 'rectification movement' itself, which were later adopted by
others. Although Heikal was dismissed as *Al-Ahram* editor on 4
February 1974, many friends and disciples continued to occupy the
highest posts throughout the period of the Sadat regime.

Practical applications

Whatever the scope of the internal changes impelling Egypt towards the capitalist sphere of influence, they always came up against
the obstacle of the national question. Unless a solution could be
sketched out, it was difficult to see how diplomatic and economic
links could be restored with Washington[29] and a final shift made
towards the Western camp. All diplomatic endeavours – the
Rogers Plan, the Jarring mission, the initiative by African senior
statesmen – had so far failed to produce results. The only other
way of unblocking the situation was actually to initiate hostilities
with Israel – something never before attempted by Republican
Egypt. However, if the regime was to overcome the obstacles to
joining the camp of Israel's allies there would have to be an
appearance of victory.

In the name of 'Allah Akbar', the Egyptian army successfully
crossed the Suez Canal and the Bar Lev line. The general mood of
elation demonstrated that the 1973 October War was serving its
catalysing function: once again the conflict with Israel became a
crucial determinant of the evolution not only of Egypt but of the
whole Arab world. Anwar al-Sadat, the hero of the crossing of the
Canal, thereby managed to establish a new centre of his legitimacy. Having done what Nasser never achieved, he was able to
shake off the influence of his predecessor and uninhibitedly declare a new orientation of his own. The wave of national unity
swept aside the remaining detractors. Egypt had rediscovered
hope in victory.

Just as the war had not been confined to the sands of Sinai, so the euphoria did not stop at the Nile Valley. For the first time the 'moderate' Arab regimes took part in the battle by means of their oil weapon. Apart from the embargo, the price of the black gold was drastically increased – as James Akins, US ambassador to Saudi Arabia, had suggested a year earlier in the corridors of OPEC.[30]

Economic applications

Signs of a peaceful and prosperous era began to appear with Arab money and a *pax Americana* with Israel on the horizon. These seemed to offer a solution to all problems, particularly those which lay at the origins of Republican Egypt. But the original project – which, as we have seen, aimed at independence, national security and economic development – no longer revolved around dynamic internal initiatives but crucially required the assistance of external forces.

A single word sums up the whole new project: *infitah* or 'opening'. So rich are its semantic associations that it sounds like a magic password.[31] In its opposition to *inghilaq* ('closure'), *infitah* encompasses the ideological and political notions of socialism and capitalism, with all their components (bloc alignment, choice of another mode of development) and with all their consequences.

Officially announced on the morrow of the October War, the policy of economic opening followed the logic of the previous few years. There was no need for a change in the government, except for the appointment of Ismail Fahmi, one of Heikal's close collaborators, to head the ministry of foreign affairs. Abdel Aziz Hegazi combined his office as minister of economics and finance with that of prime minister. Together with Ismail Sabri Abdallah, the planning minister known for his Marxist leanings, Hegazi drew up the 'economic crossing plan' (a reference to the crossing of the Canal). If not exactly new, the goal of the Hegazi cabinet had the virtue of clarity: to stimulate national capitalism, both public and private, with the financial and technological assistance of Arab and Western capital. This showed conclusively that Egypt's state capitalists were unable to sustain their original project, and that new forms of social differentiation had emerged within the state-capitalist society. At the same time, however, there was a clear wish to keep the process of opening under control, and to give the economy a new impetus through the introduction of foreign capital and improved means of production. According to the logic of the time, Egypt was to contribute its manpower for a Brazilian or South Korean type of peripheral capitalist development that would be adapted to its own social formation.

The plan drawn up by the regime's technocrats only partially married with the thinking of the major international financial agencies, the IMF and the World Bank. Whereas the former set their sights on gradual development within a 'national' framework, the latter looked forward to radical change within a global perspective. The former considered that the traditional stage of state capitalism had been fully accomplished, but the latter saw *infitah* as itself the transition stage[32] that would adapt the structures of the Egyptian economy to the model of Milton Friedman and the Trilateral Commission. In practice, this meant that free competition was to become the sole regulator of economic activity, and that the public sector and the 'welfare state' were to be discarded. But in a Third World country more than elsewhere, the economic transition also requires a social 'transition': it is necessary to create capitalists who are capable of directing the take-off on the basis of a primitive accumulation of capital. Thus the Egyptian road to capitalism depended not on an internal evolution, one within the social formation, but on shock therapy designed to shake its very foundations. What already existed of the Egyptian economy was placed in a stranglehold – not only the public sector that had accounted for the bulk of production, but also the private sector that was assigned for development.

Political applications

Before the economy reached explosion point, the opening had to embrace the field of politics and to establish the system which capitalism claims as its prerogative: namely, democracy. The regime had already promised this as part of the 'rectification movement', in honour of Point 6 of the Revolution. But whereas it had hitherto remained a pious wish, pressure was now mounting on all sides: not only did the external allies want Egypt to abandon its socialist application, but the dynamic of *infitah* made this inevitable. How could new social classes be asked to make an active contribution if they were not allowed to express themselves or to participate in power? Besides, the evident incompetence of the single party, the Arab Socialist Union, was widely denounced even within the regime. Thus, in 1976, the date for renewal of the People's Assembly became associated with a democratisation process that had been the object of political debate since the October War.

In March 1976 the regime decided to create three 'platforms', with a view to their becoming parties. In this way it cut short the numerous grassroots initiatives and sought to define the rules of 'its' democracy: 'The experiment will begin with the constitution of three platforms representing the right, the centre (which is the key tendency in our country) and the left.'[33] This skilful manoeuvre illustrated the limits of the official conception of democracy. For it granted no place to the main currents of thought within society, those most likely to demand a say in the media and parliament. These were: the Nasserite current, which was not allowed a party of that name[34] since the regime claimed the heritage for itself alone; the Wafd current, whose nationalist discourse was dangerously attractive to citizens of every affiliation;[35] and the Islamic current around the old Muslim Brotherhood leaders, who were nevertheless granted permission by the head of state to publish a monthly magazine, *Al-Da'wa*. The elections of November 1976, like the new assembly that resulted from them, reproduced the mechanisms and defects of the old single party. A dozen deputies out of nearly 360 provided the democratic alibi.

Through the debate on democratisation, the broad ideological currents running across Egyptian society but on the margin of its institutions began to emerge into the light of day. The principal effect, however, was a 'de-Nasserisation' campaign. The new rulers very one-sidedly presented the previous regime as a state of the *mukhabarat* ('secret services'), one trapped in socialist austerity, and from which all the ills of contemporary Egypt derived. This way of defining themselves by negative opposition did not apply in one key area: the modernisation model. However, it was the Western–American model that was now so explicitly proclaimed and which formed the core of the dominant discourse. Modernisation was no longer presented as a goal of collective, auto-centred effort, but as an existing reality. Eventually peace and prosperity would bring the model to the whole population – and meanwhile the virtue, or even the miracle, of *infitah* was to make it accessible to some by introducing it ready-made into Egypt. Not only did imported consumer goods flood the market, but people were called on to 'modernise' their social practices and life-style. Official discourse was relayed by the numerous American and West European tourists and residents, while various experts arrived with a particular interest in Egypt's past difficulties and future options. Modernisation was at work in every practical and ideological area. Whether concrete or abstract, the model was asserted in an exclusivist manner. As a result, modernisation scorned any developmental imperative and produce nothing but mechanisms of alienation. The question became one of how to assuage consumer frustrations whose outward signs served more than ever as criteria of social belonging. How could one be modern and yet remain Egyptian?

If the economic dynamic of *infitah* profoundly unbalanced Egyptian society, the corresponding dynamic of 'modernism' had a very serious impact on the psycho-cultural foundations of society.

Egypt falls apart

The situation exploded in the early hours of 1977. From Aswam to Alexandria the people took to the streets as soon as the radio announced the ending of subsidies on basic goods. It was a long time since Egypt had witnessed demonstrations of such breadth and violence. The regime was caught unprepared. After hesitating for forty-eight hours,[36] it responded with a show of force and simultaneously went back on the measures imposed by the IMF. But it had been a full-scale alert. It was clear that the hopes raised three years earlier had still not been realised: neither those of economic prosperity nor the prospect of peace. A new policy had to be found that would solve these two crucial and inextricably linked problems.

Towards a rentier *economy*

Once it had been condemned by most of the population, the term *infitah* was banished from official discourse. But the regime remained faithful to the policy of an economic opening, while transforming its fundamental logic. Having failed to attract private investment into projects that would have boosted internal productivity and opened the road to a peripheral capitalist economy, the government tried to fend off the most pressing dangers by finding capital where it already existed. Prosperity could come later. This *rentier* quest[37] became the basic of the economy principle – if there was one at all – through a rare combination of factors:

(a) the urge to liquidate state capitalism;
(b) the possibility of supplying labour to Arab oil-producing countries with a low population; and
(c) Egypt's strategic weight, which the Arab-Israeli conflict turned into a source of income.

Such an an economic philosophy, in a Third World country with no major natural resources and a population of more than 40 million, distorted any perspective for the future by taking the present as its field of purposive action. This high-risk course launched Egypt on what was no longer anything but a headlong flight.

The state itself began to profit from 'rents' to a degree never seen before – whether it was the major oil strikes in the Red Sea, the reopening of the Suez Canal to international shipping, the SUMED oil pipeline,[38] or, less significantly, the growth of tourism. These sources of revenue – to which we should add the wages of expatriate workers – came to play a key role in the national budget. Yet they did not make Egypt a *rentier* state comparable to its neighbours in the Arabian Peninsula, and they were far from sufficient to meet the needs and commitments of the national economy. However much the regime may have wished to unburden itself of the socio-economic gains that the population inherited from state capitalism, the riots of January 1977 demonstrated just how great were the political risks of such an operation. After dismantling the public sector's production units, the authorities were not able to sell shares in these enterprises to Egyptian capitalists, nor to hand them over to foreign companies within the framework of joint venture agreements. Very often bureaucratic resistance from the layer of state employees prevented the process from going beyond very narrow limits. Thus, the state remained in charge of a public sector which, despite its falling productivity and exposure to repeated attacks, still occupied a dominant position within the production apparatus and still had no stimulus from local or foreign competition of the kind that the *infitah* policy had originally envisaged. Since the hoped-for rent cannot be derived from sales of public sector industry, it has been the latter's output which has allowed certain figures within, or close to, the regime to draw a rent.

In reality, however, it is on the external plane that state action has counted for most, both in balancing the country's finances and in securing food supplies (60 per cent of which now come from abroad). The sizeable financial contribution from Arab countries, although not originally intended for that purpose, has helped the state to carry out such activities. Egypt can also expect to receive aid from the West so long as it adopts its political goals. Foreign businessmen may have refused to invest in Egypt, but the West does not hesitate to provide government aid to an extent that many other Third World countries can only envy. In return, Cairo has only to make ever greater and ever less reversible political concessions. Egypt can command a price for its political and strategic weight.

All these sources of revenue have helped the Egyptian state to avert a new wave of popular disturbances. But this does not explain how the system has managed to survive the state's gradual unloading of its social obligations (health, education, employment, housing, transport, and so on), and the lack of any incentive to engage in productive activity. The fact is that the regime's slogans in favour of *al-Kasb* (profit) have invited citizens to adopt a *rentier* philosophy similar to its own. The dominant ideology frees the state of any responsibility for the problems of the hour. These are attributed not only to past socialism but also to the ungratefulness of the Arab countries and, more seriously, to personal incapacity on the part of those who cannot find a source of rent. Thus, several million dollars have gone into a birth control campaign whose purpose, apart from encouraging couples to have fewer children, is to demonstrate that population growth implies individual responsibility for the shortage of social, health and educational services, and for problems of work, transport and housing. Government is thereby absolved of blame: it has created the peacetime conditions for prosperity, and every citizen is (theoretically) free to make their fortune without constraints. The

156 *State and Ideology in Republican Egypt: 1952–82*

nsmyth of Osman Ahmed Osman,[39] overseer of the new economy and symbol of individual success, has played a role similar to that of Rockefeller in the collective imagination. Everyone who has the capacity can at least become a 'self-made man', if not exactly a millionaire. It is up to everyone to find the way.

The way is simple indeed to enter into the system introduced by the *infitah*, itself only a semi-legal one. This involves, on the one hand, activity in the commercial sector and foreign-linked services and, on the other, the receipt of state orders. These are the pillars on which the new Egyptian capitalism is developing, in complete divorce from the pre-revolutionary agrarian and then industrial bases of national capitalism. Indeed, the term 'capitalist' needs further specification before it can be applied to the new economic logic. Very few Egyptian capitalists can claim to be the head of a company, since it is hardly worth taking the risk when huge fortunes can be made through service activities requiring no more than an initial capital outlay. Even existing company bosses are being forced to halt operations in the face of foreign competition and labour emigration, and to take part in the *infitah* system in order to survive. Among the new capitalists are to be found old feudalists who have used their name, connections or knowledge of foreign languages to join the world of international business; many a chairman or member of a public sector board of directors who has used his influence to branch out into the private sector; and businessmen who have been spontaneously generated by the *infitah*. This third category is most clearly typified in the irresistible rise of Rashad Osman, an illiterate 40-year-old from the Alexandria dockland, a man of no fixed occupation who, after the October War, managed to smuggle in a large amount of hashish. With this illicit capital he launched into import-export activity and accumulated a fortune that has been estimated at several hundred million Egyptian pounds.[40] He was elected to parliament, where he enjoyed the support of certain high officials and won many a state contract.[41] His case is by no means exceptional, and there are a number of films which portray the theme of social success along similar lines.

The *infitah* does not, however, stop with these get-rich-quick millionaires. Its virtue is that it has been able to penetrate all layers of society, inducing the doctor to raise his fees, the teacher to make private lessons compulsory, the butcher to charge double the official price for meat, the grocer to sell deregulated foreign produce instead of controlled local foodstuffs, and the taxi-driver, plumber, garage-owner, hairdresser, and suchlike, to engage in a host of similar operations. In short, every social group without a fixed wage and without state or industrial employment is in on the act.

Another solution has been to run. The old barriers to emigration have been progressively removed, and the sharp rise in oil prices created a market for all kinds of labour in nearby Arab countries. Job difficulties and a rising cost of living forced many people into emigration, even though this is alien to the national tradition, unlike in Greece or Lebanon. By 1976 the authorities were citing a total of 1.4 million Egyptians living abroad – or 10 per cent of the economically active population. In subsequent years the official figure grew without interruption, and even that only recorded the 'stock' of stable *emigrés* and took no account of the large number of people working under contract in the Arab world. Whatever the precise figure, emigration remained a central feature of the *infitah* and of accompanying social and economic changes.

Emigration involved every layer of society – from lecturers to peasants, from bank clerks to skilled workers. Yet it was an option only for the chosen ones, who would later be able to use their accumulated income to return to the Nile Valley and significantly improve their material circumstances. In every social milieu, in country as well as town, there are now 'enclaves of modern life' which the regime and its devotees – Westerners for the most part – hold up as vindication of the dominant ideology and the policy of opening.

However, for the small peasant and artisan producers who have never left the country, for the growing numbers without any 'assets', the new dynamic has been a veritable catastrophe. Its economic thrust and the values it bears are driving them into poverty and marginalisation. The middle layer of state employees and civil servants, which provided the main social base for the Nasser regime, is also seriously affected as its fixed salaries have not kept pace with inflation. The state, to which it is tied both politically and economically, is disintegrating before its eyes. Many have been forced to assist the disintegration simply in order to survive – by absenting themselves from work to earn money elsewhere, and by cashing in on their status or influence and thereby joining the spiral of corruption.

The Egyptian social pyramid is being shaken to its foundations. The mechanisms of *infitah* and emigration affect all classes, disturbing their system of values and blurring their national, social and even family identity. In a situation devoid of economic cohesion, some are rich and others growing poor along the very faultline between 'tradition' and 'modernity' that defines the 'model'. Only those who are materially or intellectually closest to the Western model come through by one means or another. Those still attached to the national framework – to its culture, its values, its productive economy, its institutions – are thrown aside in the process. The faultline does not simply run through the field of the social; it is also tearing apart the identity of the individual. There is much here to challenge traditional analyses in terms of the nation-state or the class struggle. As state capitalism decomposes, Egypt is undergoing a mutation without precedent in its recent history, and without the emergence of another coherent system. Reduced to its coercive functions, which have become increasingly elaborate since January 1977, the state retains monopoly control of the ideological apparatus.

One solution: peace

Rentier logic is only one aspect of this headlong political flight. More important still – because it concerns the very stuff of the national question – has been the recovery of the occupied territories within the framework of a solution to the conflict with Israel. The October War had unblocked the situation by allowing the regime to find a new centre of legitimacy, to proclaim its new line of approach, and to enter diplomatic negotiations. Three years later, however, the process ran into an economic and diplomatic impasse, since the signing of the second Sinai accords in September 1975 was not followed up in practice. The task then was to take a sufficiently bold initiative to unblock the situation again, with the same policy aims in view. In other words, it had become a question of carrying the new political, economic and ideological course through to its logical conclusion.

On 9 November 1977 Sadat surprised his associates by announcing to the People's Assembly that he intended to go to

Israel. Ten days later he surprised the world by offering peace proposals in a speech to the Knesset. Even if his decision was a continuation of previous policy, the effect was still that of an electric shock. The prospect of peace caused hopes to rise anew.

For most Egyptians they were hopes of a solution to problems of a mainly economic order. Naturally this was the aspect underlined in the official speeches and newspaper articles of the time. Peace would be the road to prosperity. It would remove the need for spending on war;[42] it would attract foreign investors and lead the supposedly pro-Israeli banks and multinationals to take an interest in joint Egyptian–Israeli ventures. Some journalists, like Mustapha Amin in *Al-Akhbar*, went so far as to praise 'Egyptian genius and Israeli money'. Such talk did have some resonance: the head of Austria's Jewish community, the banker Kahan, visited Cairo in 1979 and helped in negotiations for a fabulous $1800 million contract to modernise Egypt's telecommunications system.[43] A delegation of 'thirty-six Swiss-Jewish millionaires' stated in Cairo that 'its visit could make a positive contribution to normalising relations between the Egyptian and Jewish peoples'.[44] Baron Edmond de Rothschild also paid a visit to Egypt and declared his readiness to finance construction projects.

The economic function of peace was not confined to such hopes. For the Egyptian state it was inserted within the logic of rent. In civil society, the appeal for peace was greatest for the *infitah* 'capitalists' who were expected to show the greatest dynamism. Any future co-operation with Israel would enable them to adopt more rational practices and to undertake more daring initiatives. Once more Osman Ahmed Osman came forward as a pioneer. He accompanied the head of state to Jerusalem and took to arguing that Egypt's future lay in high technology. (His state-funded Salheya agricultural project served this psychological role, even though it proved to be an economic disaster.)

When it was presented in this way to the Egyptian population, peace with Israel appeared not only as the solution to economic difficulties but also as the highest stage of modern life: civilisation. By choosing peace Egypt would become . . . civilised! Elizabeth Taylor made this clear on 18 September 1979, having been invited to Cairo by the head of state himself. But even official discourse and the dominant ideology said as much. Once again the regime was defining itself by opposition. Just as Egypt had become modern by setting itself against the austerity of socialism, so it would become civilised by counterposing itself to the Arabs and finally breaking down the two ideological bases of the Nasser regime (Arab nationalism and particularist socialism). As early as 5 December 1977, at a large popular demonstration before the presidential palace, President Sadat extolled the defiant breadth of vision that was supposedly lacking in Arabs of all political orientation, so numerous were their inborn defects. Sadat's very daring would spring from the age-old 'distinctiveness' of the Nile Valley. Before signing a separate peace treaty, Egypt was discovering its 'Egypticity' in a political form. This was, of course, the kind of formula used by European powers in order to detach Egypt from the regional whole. In the new context, it had the merit of accounting for Egypt's ties with the West, and indirectly of establishing a common heritage with the Jewish state.

The economic *infitah*, like political 'de-Nasserisation', had created the space in which to denounce a wide yet selective range of errors committed by the previous regime. This was done with the help of numerous Western experts and intellectuals, who came to lend a hand in the 'modernisation' of Egypt. But the new reading of history collided with the Egyptian view of Israel – a view shared by monarchical and republican governments and associated, in the Ministry of Foreign Affairs and other authorised milieux, with the fundamental problem of national security.[45] President Sadat's initiative offered a new line of approach: the conflict with Israel now involved nothing more than a clash of national psychologies; and peace, desired by one and all, was a question not of international law but of moral virtue. This argument, which the head of state expounded to the Knesset on 19 November 1977, carried all the more weight in that it belonged to the same register as the dominant Western conception of the psychological, or even religious, basis of the conflict. To preach peace, then, was to preach Reason itself. The last, ideological, barrier was removed to Egypt's full assimilation to the Western model. Egypt was at last embracing the full rationality of Civilisation.

There can be little doubt that most Egyptians approved of the head of state's initiative. Its surprise announcement and rapid execution did not leave any time for reflection. And the authorities took care to ensure that their arguments were the only ones heard.

No debate was allowed on the national question in the media or parliament. The non-Western foreign press was censored, and the regime set about staging media events and orchestrating a masterful publicity campaign. But how long could it last? The 'momentum' of peace – from the Camp David accords in September 1978 to the Washington treaty of March 1979 – allowed the flame of illusion to be rekindled. Yet it gradually lost strength as the results failed to materialise.

Having followed all the logical steps through to the end, the regime now faced growing unrest even among sections of the population who had initially been close to it. Sadat's discourse became more and more aggressive, especially since none of the few actively sympathetic journalists and intellectuals managed to utter a word against his incoherent decisions and frenzied attacks. By September 1981, when the head of state lashed out against all oppositional thinking, the repression was already taking a daily toll of individuals and grinding down one professional group after another: lawyers, journalists forbidden to publish, deputies expelled from parliament, well-known political figures driven into the cold, and so on. Now that Egypt had broken with its regional environment and its own history, intellectual activity centred more on the quest for a lost identity (the dominant theme of Yussef Shahin's films of this period, and of many poems and short stories), and on the exaltation of the most traditional symbols such as the Nile and the pyramids (used in many films and short stories to invoke hope and rooted identity), than on the celebration of a rediscovered self-assurance. There would be no celluloid depictions of peace; and no major voice would sing its praise after the death of Um Khalthum and Abdel Halim Hafez.

While the regime grew ever more isolated, the silenced parties of the legal opposition did not pick up any broad popular support. In fact neither the Socialist Labour Party,[46] with its bourgeois-nationalist discourse, nor the National Progressive Unionist Party,[47] with its blend of nostalgic and progressivist ideology, proved able to analyse the new realities of the country or to work out a coherent alternative.

An almost *fin-de-règne* atmosphere of despair settled over the Nile Valley, at the very time when the West was praising it to the skies. The Egyptian-Pharaonic style was high fashion in the shop windows of Fifth Avenue and the Avenue de l'Opéra, as it was on

Dizengoff Street in Tel Aviv. Literature, games, holidays – the big metropolitan newspapers were overflowing with articles about Egypt. President Sadat and his family were treated in exactly the way that had once been reserved for the Shah of Iran. Nor did the similarities end there: the Iranian scenario came to dominate the new 'scientific' analyses that the Egypt experts applied to the economic failure of the *infitah*. Ever careful to justify the basic model of modernisation, they explained all the difficulties by reference . . . to Islam. The rise of extremist groups was held up as proof of the positivist analysis that the Muslim religion is impermeable to modernisation.[48]

The assassination of the head of state by an Islamic fundamentalist soldier fitted in perfectly with this essentialist diagnosis. But as far as the mass of Egyptians were concerned, their apparent lack of emotion was not without significance. Very few official institutions or shops in the Cairo city centre followed the custom of displaying a black-rimmed portrait of the dead leader. Equally rare were the office-workers, teachers or civil servants who wore mourning. Silence filled the capital and other large towns; no sad song was heard to mark the occasion. And as soon as the funeral was over, those *naktas* (jokes) which tell so much about the popular view of politics began to compete in their irony, sarcasm and even contempt towards the tragic victim.

Mubarak's Egypt: the hour of realism

An epoch is coming to an end – not of Republican Egypt, but of the hopes that gave birth to it and the illusions that changed its shape. After thirty years of vain efforts the hour of realism can no longer be avoided.

In its structures, policy guidelines and personnel, the regime is still the same today. But its role is now just one of pragmatically managing the situation, however difficult that too may be. Its language has abandoned any talk of new orientations and instead enjoins acceptance of reality. Its tone, at once sober and frank, contrasts with the ideological flights of fancy of the high Nasser period, and with the psychological shocks of the Sadat years. Reassured by the lack of any political alternative, either internally or externally, the regime is able to use the trumps that the model itself has dropped into its hand. Social inequality is a fact that has to be accepted, just like external dependence. Any claim to find a remedy would be harking back to illusions. Thanks to a new generation of scribes trained on the other side of the Atlantic,[49] the West can transmit its message throughout the state-controlled ideological apparatus. A cover of tolerance is designed to gain acceptance for certain differences – particularly those of an economic nature – while masking others that might threaten the model's evolution towards global ideological uniformity. This is the goal that Mubarak's Egypt has set out to achieve, through the opening of non-institutionalised dialogue with the various currents in society, and through an attempt at economic rationality that will try to steer the *infitah* towards production.

What of the two national objectives – independence/security and economic development – which for the past two centuries have impelled history of this old nation-state? Political independence was achieved with the Republic, and territorial integrity with the return of Sinai. The economy has become a simple matter of managing reality, within the framework of an opening to the capitalist sphere of influence. Has Egypt, then, finally exhausted the sources of its own forward movement? Has it solved its own contradictions? Is Egypt's long history coming to a halt on the eve of the year 2000? Such a conclusion hardly seems credible: except to those, inside and outside the country, whose political, economic and ideological exertions have helped to anaesthetise it, for the time being.

Notes and references

1. Egypt regained its territorial integrity on 26 April 1982, except for the enclave of Taba which remained an object of litigation.
2. On the eve of the revolution there were several (clandestine) Communist parties in Egypt. The most important was the Hadeto, an acronym for the Arabic *al-haraka ad-demoqratiyya li-t-taharror al-watani* (the Democratic Movement for National Liberation).
3. This was the customary way of referring to the two wings of the Egyptian bourgeoisie – that is, the Wafd and the big bourgeoisie. See Anwar Abdel-Malek, *Egypt: Military Society* (New York, 1967).
4. Under the terms of this treaty, which was signed by the Wafd, British

military occupation was ended in law but retained in reality through a treaty of alliance.

5. In 1945, in the name of 'Gamaat al-nahda al-kawmiyya', Miritt Butros Ghali put forward a twenty-five year programme of agrarian reform. See Abdel-Malek, *Egypt*, p. 70.

6. The only previous nationalisation had been that of the Anglo-Iranian Oil Company in 1951. It is well known what became of Mosaddeq, who carried out this measure.

7. Mao Zedong's China did have one. . . .

8. Georges Corm, 'Saper l'idéologie du développement', *Le Monde Diplomatique*, April 1978; François Partant, *La fin du développement* (Paris: Maspero 1982) and 'The End of Development', *Democracy*, vol. III, no. 4 (1983).

9. The nationalisations were carried out in two stages: after the 1956 act of aggression in the cases of French and British property; after 1960 in the case of the large Egyptian enterprises.

10. Dean of the Alexandria Faculty of Sciences in 1948, under-secretary at Nasser's Ministry of Culture, Hussein Fawzi would be the first well-known Egyptian intellectual to go to Israel.

11. Directed by Yussef Shahin in 1962.

12. Paul Balta and Claudine Rulleau, *La vision nasserienne*, (Paris: Sindbad, 1982). These texts (speeches and articles) show the extent to which the main concern of the Nasser epoch was economic development.

13. E. Zhukov, 'Questions of the National and Colonial Struggle after the Second World War', in Hélène Carrère d'Encausse and Stuart Schram, *Marxism and Asia* (London: Allen Lane, 1969), p. 266.

14. Dar El-Maaref (ed.), *La voie egyptienne vers le socialisme* (Cairo, n.d. after 1964).

15. Only the Gaza Strip then enjoyed a special import regime, having been placed under a UN mandate in 1947.

16. The main commercial thoroughfare in Beirut.

17. E. Rostow, *The Stages of Economic Growth* (London, 1957).

18. J. Hajjar, *L'Europe et les destinées du Proche-Orient 1815–1848* (Belgium: Bloud & Gay, 1970), p. 172.

19. The Egyptian Marxist-Leninists were essentially intellectuals who stated their views in French or English from their place of exile in the West. Highly critical of the Nasser regime, their theoretical analyses referred only to problems of class struggle and ignored altogether the national dimension of the Egyptian 'case'. Still implicit in their positions, however, was a Western-style ideology of modernism.

20. Lotfallah Soliman, 'Aux origines de la guerre israélo-arabe de 1967', *Peuples Méditérranéens*, no. 1 (October–December 1977).

21. Among others Faruk Munib's short story *Pieces of Paper* (*Qusasat waraq*), published in *Al-Adab*, March 1969, and *Acre, My Homeland* (Watani Akka), a play in verse by Abdel Rahman al-Sharkawi (Cairo: Dar Al-Churur, 1970).

22. Aly Abdel Khalek's *Passage Song* (1971); Hussein Kamal's *Chats on the Nile* (1971); and Yussef Shahin's *The Sparrow*, which was only allowed to be shown in 1974, as part of the de-Nasserisation campaign.
23. Located at the Centre for Strategic Studies of the daily paper *Al-Ahram*.
24. Abdel-Hakim Amer, chief of staff and minister of defence at the time of the defeat, was found dead in his cell in 1968.
25. Until then Egypt had had only a provisional constitution. After the 1967 defeat, Nasser had promised that a parliamentary commission would be entrusted with drawing up a permanent constitution.
26. Article 4 of the chapter on the economy in the Constitution.
27. *al-Qoraish*, name of the Prophet Muhammed's tribe.
28. Mohammed Heikal, *The Road to Ramadan* (London: Collins, 1975).
29. Diplomatic links with Washington had been broken off in June 1967.
30. See his famous article in *Foreign Affairs*, April 1973.
31. Despite the connotations of *infitah* Egypt had not previously been closed. Foreign trade as a percentage of national income had risen from 36 per cent to 44 per cent during the first and only five-year plan.
32. See the World Bank report: Khalil Ikram, *Egypt: Economic Management in a Period of Transition* (Johns Hopkins University, 1980).
33. Speech of President Sadat, 14 March 1976.
34. While the 'left' Nasserites joined Marxists and other progressive elements in the 'left' platform, the 'right' Nasserites were not allowed to form a party.
35. The Wafd current only managed to create a party in January 1978. On 2 June 1978, however, it was scuttled as a result of a referendum which, among other things, forbade figures active before the 1952 Revolution to return to political life.
36. Sadat, who was on holiday at Aswan, thought it amounted to a *coup d'état*; while his government, led by Mamduh Salem, did not dare to take the initiative of calling in the army.
37. The term 'rent' is not used here in its Marxist sense, but refers to the wish to obtain money without work. See my article 'Anatomie d'une dépendance: Egypte', *Peuples Méditérranéens*, no. 19 (April–June 1982), part of which was translated in *MERIP Report*, no. 107 (July–August 1982).
38. The SUMED (Suez-Mediterranean) pipeline was opened in 1977 between Ain Sokhna on the Red Sea and Alexandria. It complements the Suez Canal, which is not accessible to large oil-tankers.
39. Originally a small public-works entrepreneur who made his fortune on the Aswan Dam. See Mohamed Sid Ahmed, 'Sadat's Alter Ego', *MERIP Report*, no. 107 (July–August 1982).
40. In November 1984 an Egyptian pound was on a par with sterling for commercial transactions, while the tourist rate of exchange was £1st.=£E1.4.
41. His case was the subject of a widely discussed trial in autumn 1981.

42. In fact Egypt's military spending would rise constantly in the following years. See 'Higher Spending Aims to Keep Armed Forces Happy', *Financial Times*, 4 October 1983.
43. Signed on 17 September 1979 by a European consortium headed by Siemens and its Austrian subsidiary.
44. *Le Progrès Egyptien*, 3 November 1979.
45. We should mention the resignations of Ismaïl Fahmi, minister of foreign affairs before Sadat's trip to Jerusalem; Ibrahim Kamel, minister of foreign affairs after the signing of the Camp David accords; and Murad Ghaleb, ambassador to Yugoslavia and former minister of foreign affairs under Sadat. See Mahmud Riad (one-time minister of foreign affairs under both Nasser and Sadat, and secretary-general of the Arab League), *The Struggle for Peace in the Middle East* (London: Quartet Books, 1981); Ismaïl Fahmi, *Negotiating Peace in the Middle East* (London: Croom Helm, 1983); and Ibrahim Kamel, *The Failed Peace* (in Arabic) (Cairo, 1983).
46. This party, led by Ibrahim Shukri, was created in 1978 on the initiative of President Sadat. Ibrahim Shukri was minister of agriculture at that time. In February 1981 this party denounced the Camp David accords, and in September of the same year several of its members were interned.
47. A party which grew out of the platform, led by the former Free Officer Khaled Mohieddin. It comprises 'left' Nasserites, former members of the Egyptian Communist Party that dissolved in 1965, some members of the Egyptian Communist Party that was formed in Beirut in 1 May 1975 (and worked underground in Egypt), and a variety of progressive forces. See Bertus Hendricks, 'The Legal Left in Egypt', *Arab Studies Quarterly*, vol. v no. 3 (Summer 1983).
48. It should be pointed out that 8 to 10 per cent of the Egyptian population are Coptic-Orthodox Christians, and that extremist groups are also to be found among them.
49. Marie-Christine Aulas, 'L'Egypte à la recherche d'une cohérence idéologique', *Le Monde Diplomatique* (December 1982).

This chapter was translated by Patrick Camiller.

7 Popular Islam and the State in Contemporary Egypt

MICHAEL GILSENAN

One of the most striking features of Egyptian society in the post-Nasser period has been the intensity and explicitness of attempts by different classes and strata to find modes of apprehension and expression through which the current Egyptian experience can be grasped and, in the same process, transformed and determined. There is a public emergence of various kinds of discourse for imaging and guiding the reconstruction, reform, or, more radically, reconstitution from the base up, of the structures and meaning of Egyptian society. Certain of these discourses are secular, non-religious, or anti-religious (as is the case with groups on the left, or with that heterogeneous set of forces clustered under the label of the Wafd, the old liberal bourgeois constitutional party dominated largely by landed interests with some fractions of the commercial and industrial bourgeoisie); others are religious (as, obviously, the Muslim Brothers and a range of groups who styled themselves as 'Islamic'); yet another is part of the ideological production of the Egyptian nation-state and those classes particularly associated with it. All are fragmentary, full of certain contradictions and incoherences and silences that their absolutist and totalist tendencies mask and try to eradicate to greater or lesser degrees. Their internal and external tensions with the social world resist such eradications at the level of language alone and recur again and again as problems not fully grasped, or even grasped at all.

167

At a deeper level that only partially finds its formulation, representation, systematisation in such social movements and their ideologies, are cultural and symbolic complexes whose relationship to the changes in Egyptian society are many-layered and difficult for a student to mould, even tentatively, into his own language.

All these various discourses and social patterns of association, however, have one element in common: a sense of replication and repetition, of a series of critical blockages that are both ideological and social in their nature. Languages evolved in the 1920s and 1930s and earlier reappear in the critically different circumstances of the 1970s, but without the transformation and development necessary to give an account for and of Egyptian society in its contemporary forms.

Sometimes it seems as though individuals and groups are aware of this and seek to break out to what they see as the true course and form that Egypt should take, through the power of pre-existing paradigms and symbols about what society is and should be. In other instances this sense of tension is subordinated to the formulaic, incantation of what is clearly regarded as a 'given' and 'known' set of propositions in some ultimately transcendental dimension. As social reality proves obstinately resistant to the power of verbal reiteration there is a spiralling into a mystifying, essentially magical rhetoric that is in turn ever more impermeable by the social experience to which it is none the less intimately linked. It becomes ever less capable of making real relations beyond the spell of the 'word' to that experience. A radical, indeed desperate, disjunction grows more acute. This growing acuteness of the separation between discourse and social reality accelerates the processes of magic and ritualised repetition still further.

The understanding of forms of popular religion can be approached in a general context which clarifies the relations between such forms and the state's and dominant classes' own conceptions of religion, and their attempted manipulations of religious forces. Such conceptions of religion (and what is considered to be appropriate religion for the masses) of the dominant strata also contain, of course, internal incoherences and tensions. Equally important are the contradictions and uncertainties that mark the relation of these religious conceptions to other interests, ideologies and structural relations within the state and ruling classes.

In local apprehensions of power in and over society the state itself, as dominating institution, and the symbolic-political role of the leader (the *za'im*), have a mixed and ambiguous ideological inheritance. Though there are very ancient traditional elements of rulership contained within it, there is a very specific and post-imperial component which has a limited historical depth and a very particular basis in social experience for Egyptians at all levels. It was formed predominantly by the highly concentrated and concrete but at the same time diffuse phenomenon of 'Nasser' (as symbolic construct, the *za'im*) and 'Nasserism'.

In the context of modern Egyptian history in its relationship to Europe the struggle for independence, realised by the Revolution of 1952, was 'appropriated' by the Free Officer group. The logic of the institution of rule by the military and those who were in whatever degrees its social and political allies and shared its conceptions of the nature of development and independence, demanded that other groups and tendencies who had in any sense helped to constitute for good or ill the period of imperial rule (and even the struggle against it) were to be excluded from, or discredited in, the new history of the Revolution. The struggle was generalised to that of 'the people' for independence from colonialism. But the concrete forms that struggle had in fact historically taken (in the liberal bourgeois Wafd party, the Communists, the Muslim Brothers, and so on) were ideologically eliminated without a developed, critical history being produced. Within initially very limited and conservative notions of property and strong etatist ideas of social development imposed from above, the new nation-state that came into being consigned the 'pre-Nasser' period largely to oblivion. History, liberation and dignity took their true course with the army and the Free Officers.

The latter were not a mass movement, though they represented an overwhelming concern of the masses already seen in years of protest, demonstration and opposition that the British, the Palace and the landed and commercial classes had never been able totally to channel or control. The Free Officers were never to form the basis for a mass movement either and, as new state forms appeared, they were to do everything possible to block any such movement emerging save as tame official organisations.

The new regime that was becoming the director of the nation-state was therefore seen 'from below', even while it could well claim to incarnate for the first time Egyptian rulership of Egypt, the voice of the people, its *only* voice. The great landowners of the agrarian bourgeoisie were to be politically neutralised and progressively economically displaced by land reform. Their class, and what was seen as the vehicle for that class's interests and the means for controlling the countryside, the Wafd Party, was to become a thing of the past. On the other hand, those movements sharing much of the class basis of the Free Officers in that vast and heterogeneous complex of social levels schematically included in the ranks of the petite bourgeoisie, were suppressed and forbidden political activity. This was to include the Society of the Muslim Brothers, who had enormous mass appeal in the cities in the immediate post-war period of the 1940s particularly, and were deeply opposed to the left. They also possessed ideological appeal in terms both of a commitment to fighting the British and the Zionists, and on the grounds of religion and the reforming of an idealised social totality of 'Egyptian society', a restoring to wholeness of what had been dislocated and fragmented by alien and unbelieving rule and the social inequity of capitalism. They were suppressed after two uneasy years of relations following the Revolution, not on the basis of an understanding of what had made them so significant a force, but on the basis of superceding them *by the mere fact of controlling*, of having the power, of incarnating power in Egyptian society and taking on the mantle of Egypt's triumph.

It was the Free Officers who were to be sole guardians of the new nation-state, new in that for the first time it was figured as the representative and expression of the Egyptian people and not as an entity imposed upon them. History, as it were, began again *de novo*. The regime created in the 1950s and the emergence of the enormously powerful person of Nasser and the cult that became associated with him, a combination of an age-old set of symbols of the dominant centre, the army, the ruler, with a new aspect of directing one's *own* society, of leading national forces through domestic transformation *outwards* against Egypt's enemies and to the victory of the regional (even global) currents of anti-imperialism. Society would determine itself, transform itself, *but through the unique agency of the state*. The nation-state, and the *za'im*, would bind together what imperialism and the old classes had torn apart. The disarticulations of society in the economic, political and ideological spheres would be resolved into a comprehensive wholeness at all three levels by the same means. If village communities had been ruptured by the fragmentation of the lower peasantry, the increasing numbers of landless, the dominance of capitalism through the dominance of cotton in the agrarian sector, and migration to the cities, 'Nasserism' and the transcendent personal symbol of the *za'im* himself would in some way restore coherence and a historical purpose, autonomy and meaning to the otherwise meaningless and externally determined processes imposed upon Egyptian society in the colonial period.

Victory over the imperialist forces in 1952, the clearing of the Canal Zone and the Gaza Strip of British troops, the Suez War, the apparently irresistible tide of the Third World and nationalism, Bandung and the flow of neutralist leaders to one of the new world centres that was Cairo, gave a dynamic to this new ideology. Yet the same period was marked by a growing and complementary division between the figure of the *za'im* incarnating in personal but abstract form a collective personality, and the apparatus of the state organs of control (not least the Army intelligence which became more and more vital, the *mukhabarat*). Identification with the people in a ritualised cult of symbolic relationships went hand in hand with the development of the control function of the nation-state, the formation of an elite of army officers, and the use of rubber stamp organisation and assemblies.

Imperialism and changes in class relations that were part of Egypt's incorporation in the world system of nineteenth and twentieth-century capitalism had politicised broad strata of society. Parties, movements, associations, clubs, disparate groupings and tendencies reflecting often contradictory interests, had all developed. Forms of nationalism, forms of reaction had emerged, sometimes in bitter opposition. A 'street politics' of demonstrations, slogans and riots had developed. Now, with the Revolution, nationalism was to attain its unique realisation and fulfilment in the nation-state and its discourse of liberation. What was inchoate and contradictory within the previous phase was to be unified and shaped, controlled and directed. This meant a powerful mobilisation and crystallising of unity around the Revolution. It also meant, as the nation-state became more reliant on the bureaucracy and intelligence services and its internal blockages emerged, that there was a kind of radical depoliticisation or ossifying of the political dimensions of society. A genuine liberation, in the context of immense external threat that seemed to require imperatively a vigilant and omnipresent state to ensure that no factions within Egyptian society could be used by outside powers to undermine Arab nationalism from within, had as its other face a repression and negation on the plane of ideology and association.

Alternative readings of economic and political development, of Egyptian history, were blocked. Groups and movements were suppressed. Members of the Communist Party at different times were in prison camps or exile and their social base severely damaged. Leftist critiques became largely impossible, outside the fluctuating forms of 'Nasserism'. Leaders and activists of the Muslim Brotherhood fled or were imprisoned while the membership and those diverse social elements who found expression in them were silenced. Groups and organisations, such as the Wafd, were dissolved *as groups*, but *not* in their social base of economic and political relations which remained intact to a degree far greater than was realised at the time.

In short, opposition seems frequently to have been defined in terms of formal institutions rather than as sets of economic and political relations. Ideological transformation appeared comprehensive and monolithic and the ideology of the *za'im* and the nation-state was comprehensively and monolithically imposed. Yet this naturally entailed a futher blockage, in this instance to the state's own conceptions of its relations to the society and the nature of the forces operating within society. It made it difficult to gauge the diversities and contradictions that might exist at the base (except where 'plots' or 'enemies' were specifically revealed). The increasing expansion of control meant also increasing ossification of state forms in their relation to society, as the growth of the bureaucracy brought chaos to the administration whose servant and instrument it was intended to be. Censure and imposed silence had their price.

Such blocking factors, insidious, gradual, multi-faceted, were of course not emerging or grasped as a totality or as a counter-logic developing within the heart of the nation-state system. The expansion of the state at different levels rather seemed the dynamic and over-riding social force, especially in the impact of Nasserism and the pan-Arab and Third World and neutralist front against colonialism (at the same time as neo-colonial types of dependency were in fact being established, a new form of relationship less immediate and 'transparent' than the political and military dimensions of imperialism). The struggle enhanced the identification of army, state and nation, and the army itself was presented as the agent, representative and symbol of the new Egypt.

The nation-state was not, therefore, based on an ideology of the reconstitution of society on the basis of a return to the past, to a golden age, to a remodelling on the inspiration of eternal and pre-existent paradigms. Rather it was founded on a conception of a constant forward motion and an active forming of history and national destiny in the only possible total framework that would and could make a new Egypt. There was no critical recuperation of the past, which was rather 'put in brackets' or 'frozen'. It was frozen, too, in the sense that there were actually relatively few radical changes in the overall structures and processes of the economy. Cotton remained dominant in agricultural production and agriculture as a whole remained in disequilibrium as a result. Co-operative policies largely benefited an expanding middle peasantry. The fragmentation of small plots continued and the numbers of landless and migrants to evermore infrastructurally inadequate cities grew.

Development meant state-created heavy industries that absorbed enormous amounts of capital and tended to increase the general imbalance of the economy. The industrial and state bourgeoisie took on a greater importance and the state's interests were identified at this level of management and control. Trade unions were therefore weak and subject to stringent regulation. Political and economic hegemony and the mystification of 'the people' and the *za'im* in the realm of the transcendent 'nation' proceeded, but the practices of the state and the experience of Egyptians made the structures more vulnerable than they seemed at the time.

Over and above the blockages to which I have referred, state ideologies obscured the degree to which the conditions for a re-emergence of the 'old' ideologies and discourses still existed. It disguised the intensification of those conditions, not least by the disjuncture between the language of the nation-state and the group and class interests and practices that it actually represented.

The key 'visible' moment of disjuncture came in the defeat of 1967. Here was a moment of political and ideological reversal of traumatic proportions. That defeat, which coincided with the growing power of finance capital in the conservative oil states (and especially with the movement of the arch-enemy of Nasserism,

Saudi Arabia, towards a leading position), left the army in total discredit and humiliation. The terms on which 'the nation' had been ideologically constituted were abruptly revealed as false, illusory, lacking precisely the powers and capacities they were supposed to enshrine and realise in practice. They produced, not the fulfilment of an ever-expanding role for Egypt, but disaster. Uncertainties born of the collapse of the union with Syria or of the war in the Yemen which had cost more than had ever been foreseen became, almost overnight, the conviction of betrayal. The whole logic and symbolism of the nation-state, which had been developed as *the* only authentic language, was undercut and revealed as without substance in exactly those dimensions where it had most claimed to be powerful.

What was, however, intact and was increasingly able to exert itself because of Egypt's *de facto* dependency on foreign powers, her large external debts, and the vacuum left by the desecration of and by the ideologically sacralised forces of the Army, were elements of the state bureaucratic, management and technocratic cadres. These were allied with those sections of the bourgeoisie who operated both in the state sector of the public corporations and in those many areas of the private sector that fed into it, depended on it and creamed off a lot of its profits. To this social level the discredit of Arab socialism and progressivism and the whole heterogeneous vision that Nasserism had carried as a new, the new, true language of Egypt, came as a release. These elements were, and have become ever more, able to follow out a narrower class ideology of Western-dominated 'modernisation' and 'non-ideological', business-orientated and technocratic conceptions of Egypt's future that under Sadat was growingly and profitably linked to the West and capitalist notions of what constitutes 'social change'.

The Revolution of 1952 had defeated the old feudal order of the Pashas (the agrarian bourgeoisie and rural notables led by the great landowners linked to the international market through foreign control of Egypt's exports). That order seemed irrevocably tainted. Now the Revolution itself was also tainted, defiled and dishonoured. Experience of capitalism and of Arab socialism, for the *petites gens* and the masses, had entailed both experience of domination and economic and political exclusion and contradiction.

For many occupying quite different class and status positions, only one total conception of social order, one language, retained its pristine and unqualified authenticity: Islam.

Islam was of course 'used' by the state as an ideological support. Reference can be made to the control of the mosque-university of Al Azhar and to the later emphasis on 'Islamic socialism' or 'Islam and socialism' and the way in which Islam would ensure justice in the form of Arab socialism in the years of the early 1960s. It is possible, however, to see the Islamic element as relatively limited – organisationally, politically and ideologically – for any fundamental purposes.

In the first phase of the Revolution much of what Nasserism opposed was framed in terms of 'Islam' and Western hopes of 'Islamic pacts' of conservative client regimes that would stand against revolutionary forces in the Middle East. The attempted appropriation of an Islamic discourse by governments dominated by the West reinforced deeper elements in the ideological bases of the strata supporting the Revolution of 1952. For though many, of course, were deeply religious, and were not far from movements such as the Muslim Brothers in their personal orientations, religion in the public sense was in multiple ways identified as obstructive to the full realisation of the nation-state, unless rigorously channelled and controlled. Islam was the language of a serious rival for popular support in the Muslim Brotherhood (as it was of the sheikhs of Al Azhar who had been on the margins during the period of the British and who were identified in part as a force against the development of the society in modern terms.)

Then there were the Sufi Orders, identified often with traditional notables, with 'feudalism', suspected of being used by the landowners and by the British and reactionary forces to bolster 'traditional' attitudes of passivity and hostility to a nationalism which threatened these sections of the colonial order. Furthermore, popular Sufism was seen as an excrescence and an agglomeration of discreditable practices by the new religious movements as well. The latter sought a purified Islam, socially dynamic, active in the world, organised, urban, politically associated with elements of the lower middle and middle classes.

Moreover, the whole notion of tradition was permeated with ambiguities: profoundly authentic on the one hand, all that had to be overcome and was backward, superstitious, ignorant, ossified, inert on the other. Islamic modernism had seemed to come to a halt after the death of sheikh Muhammed Abduh and to have presented no viable ground in the nationalist struggle. The Wafd, the main and most popular party organisation, which had largely defined the political discourse of nationalism for so long, had been secularist and the language of 'progress' and of independence – for many whose ideas were formed at that period – saw no specifically Islamic form which political and economic activity might take.

The relation between the ideology of the nation-state and 'Islam' (however conceived) became tenuous. It was politically made all the more so by the strained relations with the Muslim Brothers which led, in 1954, to the proscription of the movement. The trials that followed had a large impact at the popular and the student-intellectual levels. In the union with Syria in 1958 there was no reference to Islam as the religion of the state. To the pious this strengthened the belief that the government was anti-Islamic. The move into Arab socialism and towards a closer relationship with Russia after 1956 seemed to separate 'Islam' even further from political and economic trends. The socialist laws of 1961, now referred to by many serious Egyptian Muslims as 'the beginning of the Communist period', though they represented rather an attempt of the state to impose further on the economic structures of agriculture and industry without a transformation of the relations of production of a revolutionary kind, confirmed the division of state and religion for many. A second clampdown on the Muslim Brothers in the mid-1960s was announced while the President was in Moscow and it was said that it was Soviet intelligence that had informed him of the assassination attempts that were to be made.

There thus occurred a continuing, phased process of a limited separation of religion from the state. The latter took over ideological space *in toto* as its domain.

In a sense, therefore, this period of the formation and development of the nation state 'cocooned' religion. Organised religious forces seemed to be an obstruction to the kind of social order and institutions of power that the army and the dominant strata came to define as the nature of Egypt. By distancing Islam from the political field the state sought to preserve it in a congregational, educational and private sphere and to block its broader public ideological relationship to the state itself as well as to social experience at the national level. This blockage was at the same time apprehended as *imposed* by the dominant classes of the state and national bourgeoisie upon the subordinated levels of society.

Nasserism and the apparatuses of the nation-state attempted to redefine ideological space altogether rather than merely 'taking over' the ideological functions (whatever they may be!) of religion. Therefore as a set of symbols of collectivity and a language of fundamental, common identity, Islam was too inclusive, total and deep-rooted for the nation-state and the *za'im* either satisfactorily to incorporate or destroy within their own logic of symbolic-ideological totality.

This placing of religion as it were 'beyond' on-going 'national' history, outside the stream of collective national events meant that religion could later be perceived as constant, unchanging, pure, transcendent. These dimensions were crystallised when the historically challenging forces of nationalism and Arab socialism seemed defeated by the history they were supposed to determine and transform. The peripheralisation of Islam was thus to become in time of crisis an additional kind of guarantee of its relevance to a world in which the military and political forces particularly were shaken on their foundation and discredited in all their self-image of historical forward movement and representativeness of the nation, of 'the people'.

The blockage that the institutional depoliticising of the people produced meant that at the moment of trauma Islam seemed re-authenticated: as the eternal, transcendent Word, and as the only total language and mode of apprehending experience that remained that was at the same time not brought into question by that experience. The defeat of 1967 was God's punishment of a political and social order not founded upon Islam. The Canal crossing of 1973 was a proof of the greatness of God, in its own way a vision and a miracle. These perceptions found a ready echo in the post-Nasser regime and fertile soil in many levels of Egyptian society – middle and lower level bureaucracy, white-collar workers, students and teachers, as well as among the urban poor and the different strata of the peasantry.

The collapse of 1967 could be taken to reveal Islam as once again a publicly, concretely, relevant discourse over the widest range of social practice. For the Sadatian regime it was clearly hoped that it would be one of the key cultural-organisational-ideological pillars of the post-Nasserite order, a pillar which the state became most anxious to appropriate for its own foundations. 'Islam' could be a perfect instrument of reaction.

How was such an appropriation to be accomplished and by what modalities, given that so much of the symbolic capital of the nation-state had been exhausted? It is here that ambiguities and contradictions again emerge. For it is by no means an easy matter for the state, even at the formal institutional level which is most amenable to control, to recuperate its ideological structures through Islam. Relations with Al Azhar indicate some of the strains and tensions inherent in attempts to reincorporate in an active dimension the key institutions that relate to legal and cultural 'orthodoxy' and define it.

It was noticeable that the Islamic university emerged into greater prominence in the 1970s, though by no means in a totally unambiguous way. For a start it was no mere pliable and obliging instrument of government policy (and the evidence is not at all strong either that when Nasser attempted to use given sheikhs to put the government line on birth control, for example, that this was at all a spectacularly successful 'manipulation'). It was divided into different, though not always clearly differentiated, factions and tendencies in which the publicly dominant one was until his death in November 1978 that headed by the Rector, Sheikh'Abd el Halim Mahmud. He was often held to be a kind of ideological *pole de relais* for a Saudi interpretation of religion by his critics. But he was also strongly identified with Sufism in its form of an emphasis on teaching and an elite of the illuminated. Some members of this trend were not too far from similar elements in the Muslim Brotherhood. They felt themselves to be in a historical position in which lost ground might be regained, and saw the opportunity of an 'Islamic state' in which they would be the guardians of an expanded realm covered by Islamic legal proscriptions for long subordinated to Western legal models. They looked for a far more influential role in education and public counselling on religious affairs as being integral to state affairs.

This in itself brought tension with the regime, whose 'new rich' supports, technocratic cadres and management, were interested in the prospect of Islamic law being appropriated to the state in a possibly expanded way, but not in a serious extension of influence by the clerical estate who are seen rather as a useful adjunct to the apparatus and ruling strata. It is characteristic at this social level to find a combination of an emphasis on Islamic law *in its punitive and repressive dimensions and interpretations* going hand in hand with:

(a) an ostentatious, luxurious and socially competitive lifestyle; and
(b) disinterest in, or contempt for, sheikhly or Saudi ideological formulations, except where instrumental concerns dictate otherwise.

Furthermore, with regard to the position of the sheikhs themselves as members of Al Azhar, it is interesting to record how many pious Egyptians, even while admiring a particular sheikh, are indifferent to the Azhar or suspicious of the motives and connections of its members as a whole when it comes to political pronouncements. It should never be forgotten that the programme of the Muslim Brothers, not to mention that of other more extreme groups, opposes any special position being given to the sheikhs. The latter are seen merely as advisory, legally skilled specialists and not at all immune to radical criticism. None the less, the Sadat years were clearly a period of relative independence for one stream within the Azhar which emphasised a 'hard' definition of religious imperatives. It did so, with uncertainties and misgivings on the part of the government that encouraged it; that same government which also did the most to ensure at the same time the development of the luxury sector of the consumer economy, the reemergence of old forces that had been eclipsed, the strengthening of new social strata, and increased reliance on Western economic and political relations. A major role in ideological activity was given to the 'conservative' religious forces represented by the late sheikh of Azhar and by much media cultivation of religion. Whether this effectively masked the disjunctions within the society or exacerbated them, we shall consider in a moment.

The very eagerness with which the state courted religion reflects a further point of ideological and political tension. Nasserism, particularly in its 'socialist' forms, was anathema to many of those who were the support base of the state and President Sadat. A whole class-in-formation built on finance and land speculation, construction, brokerage of various kinds, was blocked under Nasser and they felt (as well they might) economically and politically liberated. Yet the calling in question of Nasserism, the reversal of some of its most cherished priorities, and the distance, sometimes clumsily taken, from the figure of the late *za'im* (no newspaper

photographs on the day of his death, a loud omission), put the
state in a quandary with regard to its mass ideological appeal and
legitimation. Nasserism may have been historically profoundly
undermined by external dependency and debt and the increasing
influence of the Western-orientated bourgeoisie as well as the
complex problems posed by the blockages that I have mentioned.
But it generated powerful and continuing structures of relations
and interests (not least in the public sector, the army's position,
the bureaucracy and the whole nature of the nation-state). President Sadat was part of the original Free Officer movement.

It is a familiar and recurring problem – how does one separate
oneself from a system to which one owes the bases of one's position
while in certain vital respects maintaining it? What language is to
be used in this process, when particular dominant symbols have
lost their symbolic power (and, indeed, one has an interest in
finding some reformulation of the discourse of the nation-state
that will exclude them)?

In this ideological partial vacuum, the 'Islamic' dimension is one
alternative source of legitimacy on which the state can try to call,
but which, of course, exists and springs from sources 'outside' it
rather than being generated 'from within'. Moreover, the notion
of an opposition of political power system and religion, not a new
theme in Egyptian history, had been strengthened precisely by the
disaster of 1967.

The state was, therefore, in an ambiguous position. To encourage religious forces of a particular kind that were held to be
anti-left, insistent on punitive law, opposed to Nasserism, respect-
ful of property, pious and concentrating on the moral-legal-
consensual basis of society was important. Yet the state was in the
same process presented with the problem of maintaining a distance
from and control over the religious forces it sought to employ as
ideological instruments for partial purposes directed at very particular and possibly 'unstable' strata: the urban poor, elements of
the petite bourgeoisie, the peasantry in its supposedly 'traditional
minded' forms. For dominant Azharite interpretations and those
of some of the more fundamentalist religious movements do not
reflect the conceptions of the majority of the state's support in the
fractions of the bourgeoisie, the landowners and prosperous 'middle
peasantry', save in very specific and limited areas of personal piety
and in terms of social control.

The logic of this conjunction, as I have schematically indicated it, leads to a position in which the state found itself caught in the incoherencies and contradictory imperatives and those aspects of religious ideology it wished to adopt. It also found that the contradictions between the social and economic processes it had to follow to reproduce and expand its own base necessarily were in opposition to the fundamentalist conceptions of religious groups, and to the class interests, life chances and conceptions of the religious constituency that was to be controlled.

It is thus no paradox that the rise in 'popular religion' (ascetic, puritan, sometimes tinged with millenialism, resentful, activitist) went hand in hand with a period of conspicuous consumption, and *la parade sauvage* of 'Hiltonisation' which is of the essence of establishing those appearances that are essential to the social world of the new rich.

We must not obscure the religious elements that entered into the ideology of the newly dominant social groups. Regarding the post-Nasserite state as salvation and provider of an economic liberation, they also saw themselves as following out patterns of piety in many possible avenues of which I shall only indicate three, using reference to three individual members of the elite of different levels.

Case 1

A university teacher and researcher in his early thirties, brought up in a comfortable middle-class setting, educated in English in a school established by the British (there are French equivalents too). He had to learn Arabic. His entire socialisation of home and school was saturated in 'Western' values and lifestyle. He has been, it is not too much to say, converted to Islam and to a concern with currents of Sufism. In this view the world is essentially that of the interior essence of things. That which is of the exterior, external forms, is totally unimportant and not to be taken as a basis for judging the meaning and significance of the world at all. Only God can judge, only He knows what is behind the veil, that hidden essence of which social forms are but the misleading appearance. Asceticism is a quality of the heart and of the intention, not of economic standing and external way of life. One needs a teacher on the individual way to truth, that truth which is constituted in the individual's self-purification. The individual alone can purify himself.

Society is not problematic therefore. The peasants are happy, one can see it if one can see into their eyes and beyond the merely external signs of poverty. The true task is located not at the social, but at the individual level and in the heart. One can pursue any number of projects and business schemes and connections without contradiction since they are not the inner core of the self and the self's worth. What uncertainties, unsureness or tension there may be is masked in conversation by invocations of the divinity, pious phrases, Qur'anic quotations, the citing of paradigms of right conduct from the *Hadith*, parables of the Sufi masters.

This is by no means an untypical pattern. There has been a resurgence of Sufism in this particular mode at this social level – in the universities, amongst some of those of the bourgeoisie marginalised in the Nasserite period (which they detest), who because of their ages have only a limited personal grasp of the social context out of which came the ideology of nationalism and the nation-state and the nature of the forces it sought to combat. Nasser's rule for them is often seen as despotism and wasteful, frustrating adventurism. They are aligned with the now dominant forces and approve the liberal economic model. But they are not in an economic and social position to participate fully in it and do not share, by and large, the ethic and opportunism of the new rich. They are thus on the periphery still, but in a different sense from before. Their milieu and intellectual formation distance them from a time of speculative opportunity, make them hostile to the apotheosis of the *arriviste*, and *affairisme* is distasteful. Often not 'organically' socialised in an Islamic background through either family or education, such individuals find in Sufism a private source of interpretation of the world. With no inclination whatever for, or social point of contact with, the 'traditional' congregations of the popular Sufi brotherhoods, they meet rather in select, meditative circles round a teacher.

Case 2

This brings me to a second case which illustrates a point made to me by an Egyptian intellectual. He caustically remarked that many people were astonished to find men with doctorates, chemists and scientists and engineers and administrators, supporting the Saudi line on religious law or belonging to the Muslim Brotherhood but having only minimal understanding of the whole Islamic philosophical-poetic-theological-legal tradition. They operate with such a restricted code of religious meaning, in his view, because they come from strata, now part of the intellectual and social elite broadly defined, that are highly educated but not highly cultured.

The attachment to a vigorous and simplistic view of the need for Islamic law to rule society does reflect a kind of *coupure* in their experience. Technocratic, seeing themselves as without ideology, trained in the concept of the neutral quality of scientific knowledge, there are problems to be solved and solutions available. Yet in their own eyes they are constantly hedged around with a society of a singularly unscientific and irrational dimension that resists their worldview. It lacks control. They have risen through a university career themselves. Knowledge for them has been the key to advancement. What now prevents the realisation of what they know should be done for society is the irrational nature of that society itself. It is religious law which can rationalise and order Egypt! It is indeed a necessity of state at this level of development. Is not the reason for the absence of theft and dishonesty in Saudi Arabia today the relentless application of the *sharia*? Society has to be strictly disciplined, loose morals must be fought and the instrument is to hand in the logical and severe precepts of holy law. To them there is *no* contradiction at all in the idea of applying the strict *Hanbali* school of law to Egyptian society (as it is in Saudi Arabia) because after all Saudi Arabia is no longer really different from Egypt. It has made enormous progress, perhaps more. And Islam is a religion of morality and concern for the individual and private property. A leading administrator of Cairo University in discussion saw no contradiction in asserting that religion was a private affair for the individual and at the same time that the corporate state should impose it and use it as an instrument of control over the masses. For he is aware that 'the ignorant people' may pose problems to the new order of which he sees himself as an intellectual representative.

Case 3

Our third case is a judge, now retired, from an old landed family that supported the Wafd party and indeed still does. For him Islam presents an alternative to both capitalism and socialism (a very common theme across many social strata at the current conjuncture). It is against the first because it is opposed to interest and profit which are the source of evil in society. It is against the latter because it is founded on respect for the individual and for private property. Nasser was an ignorant tyrant, the new rich are as ignorant and are vulgar exploiters. The *ancien regime* and the old landed bourgeoisie from which he comes had its faults, but they were nothing compared to the faults of those who succeeded them. Then 'we looked after our peasants, lived with them as one family on the estates', there was none of the class antagonism which has since arisen.

Probity in public affairs and social control would be restored through the Islamic law. This centres, not on the debate about penalties, but on a worked out, logical system in which the role of skilled opinion, judge's discretion and analogy give ample room for adaptation to the modern state. To turn to the law would not be a step backwards, but rather a step towards the rational organisation of society. The sheikhs are ignorant and obscurantist and could not administer the Islamic law in modern circumstances.

Even such brief and sketchy examples show that it is dangerous to talk of *a* dominant religious ideology or shared set of apprehensions at the upper levels of government and society. The picture was, of course, far more complex than I have indicated here. None the less, the Sadatian state did attempt to mantle itself in religion. As part of the means of controlling society it did attempt to make effective what it conceived to be a model of 'traditional' Islam. It evoked the authenticity of the 'traditional' as though that category was 'there', objectively given, something which could, as it were, be applied. What it actually did, in fact, was to *construct* its own version of traditional Islam in ways which reflected the perceptions of the ruling strata, rather than a realisation of the inner religious apprehensions of 'the people' it was taken to express.

Let us take only one example of this attempted ideological imposition. The programme of mosque building illustrated very well the endeavour to construct a model of Islam in space and to witness to the Islamic nature of the ruling order. It had a double aspect. On the one hand, old mosques were preserved while around them urban areas were demolished or 'developed', and they were thus left quasi-isolated in a transformed environment. On the other hand, new mosques were put up in the great public spaces as government mosques. They are of great interest because they reveal how far removed from whatever 'traditional' might be taken to be are the perceptions of religion of the builders. The massive, ostentatious new mosques are built in a totally 'untraditional' spatial and relational universe. They do not articulate space, a social form of which they are a focus, but rather break with old models precisely because they are, as it were, 'just there', isolated, built for their publicness of siting but without relation or making relation to other spaces. They have none of the symbolic-social complexity of mosques in 'traditional' settings but exist to dominate the characteristically open spaces of a modern, capitalist, twentieth-century city. They are placed next to motorways, by the main railway station, on large open sites where they can be *seen*. The conception of an appropriate site obeys this one-dimensional imperative.

Moreover, such mosques are made up of an arbitrary selection of elements of dome, minaret, internal proportions and so forth, which are drawn from quite different historical periods and put together as a kind of *bricolage* which fits better a European view of what a generalised 'mosque' ought to look like – it has a dome, a minaret, and so on – than an indigenous conception. The inner structural relations of such buildings are a kind of patching to-gether, a mixture of elements that does not actually obey the principles of a given period's conceptions of religion but represents a very modern revelation of what the dominant social groups' vision of religion is: a separate category, a cobbling together of elements chosen by superficial and surface criteria rather than springing from some real understanding based on deep appreciation of Islamic culture and practice. The new mosques reveal, therefore, a certain class conception of the nature and public significance of religion and of authentic tradition which can be appropriated by the state.

It is interesting that many people see such mosques as a proof of the *non*-religiousness of the state and as *in*authentic. They are perceived as a kind of ideological rhetoric in stone and one might argue that their political and class nature is evident rather than concealed. They do not clothe the state in a traditionalist mantle, but by traditionalist standards they *reveal* the state to be precisely making a show of religion, an outward form for reasons of secular power, for hypocritical reasons. They are 'external', 'from outside' and do not disguise what the pious regard as the use of religion. The 'spectacular' nature of the mosques, the show with no reality behind it (or not the reality its builders imagine it expresses!), is all too clear.

If the state, therefore, does attempt to identify itself with religious forces without in fact pursuing the kinds of programmes that in ideo-logic such an identification would entail, this increases the consciousness that religion for the state is an artificial language. The sense of break between the class interests and structures that the state in part represents and the discourse within which such interests are formulated for popular consumption, sharpens a feeling of tension upon which other religious forces thrive. The state does not appear to touch the foundations of the society in its public religiosity. It certainly does not thereby pre-empt groups which identify themselves as religious but, if anything, tends to intensify their apprehension of a continuing non-integration of society, a non-integration which can only be transcended by a true remodelling of society on Islamic foundations.

The most extreme of these groups, the now proscribed *takfir wa higra*, showed the ultimate stages to which this conjuncture of religious forces might lead. This links with the Muslim Brotherhood in class and ideological terms were strong. The founder and leader of the group was a disciple of one of the chief intellectuals of the Brotherhood, Sayyid Qutb, and particularly the Sayyid Qutb of the latter part of his career in which he was far more radical and intransigent than before. Prison under Nasser had a profound effect on the young disciple. No *entente* could be possible with the socialists or communists. There was to be no discussion, as among certain elements of the Brotherhood, of the possible benefits of the state sector of the economy or the positive role of the army in society. There was unrelenting hatred for the Nasserite period and everything it represented. The young leader took up the notion that the entire society was a society of unbelievers who should be destroyed. A new, complete, Islamic state based on the Qur'an and the Sunna – the basis of much Brotherhood thinking too – should take its place.

This visionary follower was the son of a provincial notable (an *'umdah* or mayor) and a student at university. This background of the provincial petite bourgeoisie that had migrated to the capital via university and there become socially organised in religious

groups has occured with every greater frequency since the Second
World War in the Islamic movements. There is a sense of exclusion from the nation, of being drawn in and then blocked by
society. Attracted to the cities in thousands, often occupying jobs
in that vast level of the private sector which is made up of one or
two-man establishments, in small trading, ill-paid white-collar
positions they are at the fringes round the centre which dominates
power and services. Dependent, exposed to the ravages of inflation and the uncertain margins of petit bourgeois life and least able
to ensure against them, they are intensely hostile to the practices
of those who dominate the economic order and whose lifestyles
are aggressively luxurious and 'Western'. They have some intellectual attainment, and they are young. There is a strong generational
element with many of the members of this and other less extreme
groups being under thirty and often drawn from families in which
traditional piety is strong.

The defeat of 1967 only confirmed for them the total invalidity
of the entire social, political, economic and ideological order. Yet
it produced no fundamental reformulation. Nasserism was de-
valued but its basic framework appeared to continue. Economic
and social conditions in the cities grew worse in the early 1970s,
strengthening the social pressures to which they were subjected.
They formed, in short, a classic constituency for a radical 'Islamism'.

The leader added to Sayyid Qutb's notion that the society is a
society of unbelievers in the powerful force of *higra*, of going out
from the corrupt society. The two ideas combine in a very powerful symbolic-ideological set: namely, the image of the just community withdrawing from the world, fleeing the domain of the
unjust and hypocrites to take refuge and spiritual discipline in
seclusion and asceticism. This prepares them for the day when
they will return to sweep away the corrupt society and establish the
reign of a pure and original Islam. It will be original in the fullest
sense too, for it recreates the original experience of 'going out' of
the first community of seventh century Arabia. It will go to the
desert, or the mountains of Yemen, and create a kind of 'out of
time, out of history' that will reproduce the conditions under
which Islam emerged. This is a highly charged mimesis. It is
carried to the furthest point at which the leader assumes prophet-
like authority. His word is absolute, he uses the Qur'anic verse
that the earth and all that is on it is God's and takes the earth as

belonging to the group. Those who leave are apostates punishable by death.

Society has no external enemies, as the Nasserite period proclaimed, but *internal* ones. It must be remodelled from within, not directed against the outside. The aim is not to control, but to purge. The blockage of social and economic and political forms produces a move into a chiliastic-totalitarian mode and an extreme formulation of the nature of salvation through action breaking the mould of society. It is the extreme form of the religious critique that will shatter frozen constraints in the dazzling force of symbols of recreation and renaissance.

What for the state is an ambivalent, tentative, heterodox cultivation of religion and the invocation of an (anti-left) Islamic constitution is taken here to the ultimate millenial point from which perspective the state and the society in general appear as sunk in unbelief.

Now this movement, whose leaders were executed following the murder of a former Minister of Religious Endowments in 1977, did *not* represent their religious conceptions of the masses, or of a particular class. But one may see in it the development of certain themes that in a far more limited way are not without resonance in Egyptian society. Religion is being recuperated, it re-emerges from its partial seclusion since the Revolution. As the consolidation of the middle peasantry of the countryside and certain fractions of the professional classes allowed the Wafd to re-form after over twenty years of being apparently not only banned but in actuality no longer a living force, so other groups and movements and tendencies that seem also to 'come from the past' were revealed as possessing new significance.

The strata that formed the original recruitment level for the Muslim Brotherhood – the petite bourgeoisie of the provincial towns and of Cairo itself – are placed under growing strain. Below them in the cities the mass of the urban population copes with a decaying infrastructure of housing and services and, by multiple links of kinship, connections, favours, hammers together a patchwork of occupations, odd jobs, activities in the vast 'informal' sector of the economy which in part services the creaking and ossified structures of the formal economy. *Bricolage* becomes more and more a necessity, even for the state, if spare parts are to be obtained, repairs carried out, services obtained, and if one can know 'how to do it'.

In the 1970s the migration abroad by professionals, skilled and semi-skilled workers and fellahin meant remittances and prosperity for some. Internally, however, migration to the cities (and outside the country) came from the vast, disorganised, peripatetic army of *sans terres* whose only chances of livelihood in the rural areas lay in gang labour sent all over the countryside, or on irregular wage labour for farmers at particular seasons. Their ranks were swelled by those who belonged to the small peasantry (owning less than two feddans) who operated at the economic margins and were being sweated by the government in taxes which were not paid by the wealthy, large, citrus-growers and commercial farmers. The fragmentation of the rural universe, a return to payment in kind, increased pressure on the peasantry through the dismantling of Nasserist legislation intended to protect their position, created indeed a 'traditional' agrarian sector and reinforced the dependency of the peasantry and labourers.

It is not, therefore, surprising that the Muslim Brotherhood re-emerged form the clandestinity into which it was forced, together with the whole ideology of Islamic integrationism. Nor is it surprising that reiteration, repetition of the old discourse in virtually unchanged forms gives one an illusion of timelessness, or of frozen forms whose life has been suspended for twenty years, slowly revivifying. The blockages to which I referred at the beginning of this chapter profoundly affected these religious movements, not only because of the imprisonment of particular groups and individuals and their isolation from social life, but because of the history of the basic social and economic structures of Egyptian society over the past two decades, and the legacy that the Revolution itself had to deal with. The constancy and the unchangingness to which I have referred, the very inflexibility and rigidity of the insistence on the Qur'an and the Sunna, are paradoxically increasingly vital in the current conjuncture as the social world of the masses becomes more and more subject to pressures of many different levels. For the urban lumpenproletariat and the fringes of the working classes, religion is not necessarily in an organised group form at all. It is rather a kind of refusal or challenge in a situation of impotence, as the external dependency of Egypt grows and as internal disarticulation and incoherence once again becomes a present element of everyday life.

The contradictions between the interests of the new rich and groups close to the controlling elements of the state and the broad mass of the people are not grasped analytically in the 'fundamentalist' vocabulary. Equally, religious forces have no monopoly on the different cultural and ideological apprehensions and practices of the people and are not to be seen in some unproblematic way as necessarily the determining force. The practical concerns of everyday life are not structured by 'Islam' but by broad material and cultural factors of increasingly immediate concern. But at the collective level religion is a complex of association, meaning, action that has not been displaced or diminished by the state's controls from above and by the changes imposed from above. Ironically, the state has played an important role in ensuring that religious discourse retains its symbolic power and authenticity which may be turned in many different political and economic directions that the state itself may find difficult or impossible to control.

8 Class and State in the Transformation of Modern Turkey

CAGLAR KEYDER

The origins of the Republican state in Turkey may be traced back to the bureaucratic rebellion against the peripheralisation of the Ottoman Empire. The mechanisms of nineteenth-century integration of the Ottoman economy into capitalist networks, that is trade, debt, and direct investment, had allowed for the rapid expansion of a class that acted as intermediary between the local economy and European capitalism. From a systemic point of view there were two reasons establishing the material basis of a conflict between the traditional bureaucracy and the new class of merchants and bankers. First, these intermediaries were the physical agents of capitalist integration, threatening to change the very principles of the traditional system guarded and defended by state functionaries. It did not require great foresight to comprehend the implications of the replacement of a bureaucratic system by market rationality for the traditional role of the bureaucracy. Secondly, if the bureaucracy attempted to take a more active role in the new world, through effecting a transformation from above of the social system, it risked losing its legitimacy in the eyes of the social groups making up the traditional order. In other words, the social disruption caused by the growth of a new class pushed the bureaucracy towards a dilemma and located them in an ambivalent position *vis-à-vis* displaced social groups of the traditional order.

The existence of potential or actual conflict between a class representing the traditional order and the new class of intermediaries nurtured through the dissolution of that order was due to the mode of peripheralisation of the Empire. In pure colonial situations (such as India) the traditional ruling class had been reduced to being an appendage of the colonial merchant state, precluding a conflict either at the level of surplus appropriation or system definition. Also, in the countries of white settlement, political rule had been established in accordance with the requirements of a merchant, commercial-landowning class. The Ottoman Empire, however, together with a few other cases such as China (and, of course, Japan) had never been colonised, nor had it been an undisputed domain of 'informal empire'. It is not coincidental that the two most prominent examples of non-colonial peripheralisation were similarly inheritors of rich political traditions, and, more importantly, of state officials-cum-ruling classes. Imperial rivalry, an absence of colonisation, and the relative autonomy (*vis-à-vis* imperialist pressure) of the traditional bureaucracy constituted an interdependent set of definitional parameters which guaranteed that the process of peripheralisation would be accompanied by a conflict at the level of the definition of the system. In other words, the social project of the bureaucracy, implicit or declared, whether of a transformationist or a restorationist nature, would necessarily oppose the system definition implied in capitalist integration and mercantile activity.

There was one additional specificity of the Ottoman Empire. It had been a multi-ethnic empire in which a traditional ethnic division of labour had prevailed. During the process of its capitalist integration, however, this ethnic division acquired a new dimension as it was the Christian minorities who predominantly assumed the intermediary role between European capital and the, mostly Muslim, producers. European capitalists found Greeks, Armenians and Levantines more suitable partners in their dealings with the Empire, for understandable reasons. Thus, European economic penetration of the realm was seen and understood by the Muslim bureaucracy to be equivalent to the rise of a Christian *comprador* class. This equation attained greater salience as, throughout the nineteenth century, the Great Powers sought to pry privileges from the Porte for the Christian *millets*, or communities. As a result the bureaucracy came to see their conflict with the minorities in terms of the potential separatism of growing nationalisms – a perspective which gained exclusivity towards the end of the nineteenth century.

Nineteenth-century reformism and the Young Turks

The reformism which characterised most of the nineteenth century
may be seen as derivative and well within the space accorded to
Ottoman bureaucrats in the European inter-state system. The
Young Turk movement towards the end of the century, however,
was of a novel character in breaking away from immediate imperialist impositions.[1] During the last quarter of the nineteenth century new departments within the government and the modernisation of local administrations had served to inflate the numbers of
functionaries associated with the central administration. There
were qualitative changes within the bureaucratic class as well –
that modern and secular component of it which supplied the ranks
of both reformists and revolutionaries grew in size and importance, due in large part to the educational institutions established
to reproduce their cadres. The graduates of imperial schools of
engineering, medicine, and administration, all founded around the
middle of the century, joined the bureaucracy, to serve either in
the military or in the central government.

These 'intellectuals' initiated both the reformist and the revolutionary movement. Their class position, that is, the fact that all
intellectuals belonged to the bureaucratic class – not only in a
genealogical sense, but also in terms of their employment and
location within the surplus-extraction relationship – endowed
them with a state-centred perspective. Hence their primary purpose always remained the reform of the state in order to better
cope with internal conflict and external pressure. This perspective
ensured that they served as the organic intelligentsia of their own
class, formulating its projects and politicising its members whose
interests lay in controlling the transformation of the social structure while safeguarding their privileged position.

Before bureaucratic activism evolved into its revolutionary
version with the Young Turks, it went through several stages.
At first, recentralisation of the Empire was the predominant
concern, following upon the Sultan's centralising initiatives
during the 1820s and 1830s. A conciliatory attitude toward the
West was paramount during this stage, since the central government could only oppose threats with the active support of
European powers. Accordingly, reformism responded to demands by the West to curb the absolutism of the political
authority, and to institute guarantees of citizens' rights and

equality. Reforming bureaucrats went unchallenged not only because they held power over weak sultans, but also because world conditions allowed for a fulfillment of the promises contained in westernising reforms. It seemed, indeed, that the Empire could remain intact, and that its economic integration with Europe would bring immediate benefits as well as long-term prosperity.

During the next stage, official disillusionment with the results of integration into the capitalist system began to reflect the resentment of displaced craftsmen and Muslim merchants. The period had started with the signs of a downturn in the world economy (1873) followed by a disastrous famine in Anatolia in 1874 (whose distant causes could be found in the new orientation of the economy) and was crowned by the bankruptcy of the Porte in 1875. The Russian war of 1877–8 and the 1878 Berlin Treaty following it, served to awaken Ottoman bureaucrats to the external threat of dismemberment of the Empire. It became evident that foreign markets and international funds, and even wars, obeyed an external dynamic against which sincere declarations of the liberal creed and good behaviour in general in Instanbul had no effect. The forcing upon the Porte of the Public Debt Administration (PDA), a form of official financial tutelage, must have emerged as the final demonstration of a capitalist logic to the less suspecting westernisers among the bureaucracy.[2]

During the second stage, the careers of the first generation of westernisers ended as part of the shift of power from the more autonomous civil service in the Porte to the Palace secretariat under Abd-ül Hamid (1876–1909). The new Sultan and a strengthened Palace bureaucracy maintained a certain suspiciousness toward the West: they exercised the old statecraft, of a balancing act, one which had become appropriate in the epoch of intense imperialist rivalry. Such tactics resulted in the constitution of a bureaucratic faction which was avowedly in search of a restorative scheme and which frequently found Islam to be a rallying force extolling the virtues of the traditional order. The restorationist bureaucracy and the Sultan enjoyed an ideological success at the popular level which had been withheld from the administration for at least half a century. Not only had economic transformations disturbed the essentially static order, but the Muslim masses, the peasantry as well as the urban petty bourgeoisie, had found it difficult to accommodate the hastily transplanted tenets of equality and constitutionality – especially since these seemed to serve the immediate needs of mercantile (and non-Muslim) interests. Under such circumstances, conservatism propagated from above, and doused with religious legitimation, must have been reassuring. This probably explains the otherwise difficult to comprehend fact of Abd-ül Hamid's continuing popular appeal to this day.

Westernising intellectuals were excluded from these restorationist schemes. Having fallen out of favour, they experienced a transformation after which they were reincarnated in a more radical version, as Young Turks. Young Turk activism, which defines the third stage, was based on a desire to change the political system and was characterised by its uncompromising opposition to the conservative faction in power. It was, however, also informed by intellectual and political currents in late nineteenth-century Europe, and was, therefore, no longer delimited by an unsuspecting adulation of French republicanism and British parliamentarianism. Its activism derived not from socialism, which was at the time only beginning to attain ideological hegemony among revolutionary intellectuals, but from a radical 'positivism' acquired through contact with French Comtians. Thus, while sharing the social engineering perspective of most intellectual movements in less-developed contexts, their understanding of the Empire and its problems was not based on an analysis of its social structure, nor on a study of the mechanisms of imperialism. Instead, their discourse was primarily anti-absolutist, tinted with an ill-defined resentment of economic dependence. Anti-absolutism was, of course, a platform which could appeal to democrats in Europe: it could even articulate into the official policies of the Great Powers which aspired to establish spheres of influence in a loosely federated Ottoman Empire. This double attraction explains the enormous popularity enjoyed by the Young Turks in European (intellectual and official) public opinion – prior to their coming to power.

There was, however, a second facet to the intellectual constitution of the Young Turk movement, one which supplied its activism with an insufficiently articulated desire to overcome economic backwardness. Since the middle of the century, a neo-mercantilist platform of 'national economic' development had been current among radicals of middle-European and Italian origin. In the case of the Listian doctrine as appropriated in Germany, the idea of a 'national economy' could provide a programme for a bourgeoisie preparing itself for the world stage. Similarly, in Italy, backwardness was seen primarily as a problem of technological catching-up; and it was in terms of industrial development that the Risorgimento had interpreted the idea of 'national economy'. The location of the Young Turks in the social structure was quite different from such proponents of Listian doctrines in Germany or Italy; rather than constituting a group within the society whose immediate interests would be served through the establishment of a protected domestic market, and who would seek to influence the political structure, the Young Turks were part of the administrative cadre. They lacked precisely what their European counterparts possessed: there was, as yet, no manufacturing bourgeoisie in the Ottoman Empire whose interests could be served through the construction of a national economy. On the contrary, the trading bourgeoisie would be against any such attempt. Since, however, it was the state mechanism which was aimed at by the Young Turks, this all-powerful position could be used to create a client group which would serve as a surrogate bourgeoisie. It was primarily important to take over and defend the state in order to safeguard its privileged status in the social structure: if the state mechanism lost its structural dominance the bureaucracy would no longer be in a position to save the Empire or nurture a bourgeoisie; nor would they be able to protect their own class interest.

The Young Turks came to power in the form of the Committee of Union and Progress (CUP) in 1909, following the adoption of a Parliament and a Constitution in 1908. It is important to recognise that the initial purpose of saving the state was cloaked in various principles of cohesion between 1908 and the defeat of 1918. The Young Turks were initially considered, by themselves and others, as Ottomanists whose struggle aimed at equality and federation among the various ethnic and religious groups of the realm. Upon having to confront the reality of secessionism supported by European intervention, the naïve version of Ottomanism soon ceased to exist. Implementation of policies which attempted to establish uniform practices in the Empire, for example in the field of education and language of instruction, were prevented by European embassies through invoking the Capitulations and late nineteenth century treaties. Administrative reform, although carried out to a certain degree, was impeded by the insufficiency of state revenue; an insufficiency due to an inability to raise customs duties and to tax foreigners, and the necessity of ceding close to one-third of the revenue to the PDA. All of these obstacles began to appear to the bureaucracy as extensions of the ethnic heterogeneity of the Empire, or as the consequences of co-existence with Christian minorities. Their attempts at constructing a political entity based on the European model of the nation-state were opposed by the same statesmen they were trying to emulate.

The Balkan Wars constituted a turning point in relations between the CUP and the Greeks and Armenians. After 1912, Armenian political parties reneged on their support for the CUP, and were convinced of the necessity of internationalising the Armenian problem; Greeks were becoming 'Venizelist' – followers of Venizelos, who advocated a summary solution to the Ottoman problem through annexation of Christian-populated regions by Greece. It was in this political context that the CUP leaders veered rapidly towards a policy of Turkish nationalism.

Without delving into the intellectual background of Turkish nationalism, we can mention briefly that a majority of the proponents of this ideology had recently arrived from outlying Turkic areas of the Empire, and had received their nationalist schooling mostly in Europe. The CUP leaders themselves knew next to nothing about Anatolia, the supposed motherland. It was, however, becoming apparent that Muslim Turks constituted not only the largest ethnic group, but also, by default, the most loyal. If the state were to be saved, such a loyal group was a necessary prerequisite even if it had so far remained silent. It did not take long for the CUP to advance from this diagnosis to an active policy of nationalist cultivation, one which excluded Christian minorities. In the process of cultivating the Muslim Turkish element, the CUP enjoyed a particular freedom during the war years due to the absence of inner-state constraints on bureaucratic policy-making. When the principal imperialist powers controlling the Empire became active enemies, the CUP leaders had the occasion to pursue their ideological design freely. The alliance with Germany not only provided the autonomous space they needed, but also actively supported the nationalist goal.

It might have been possible for the bureaucracy to recreate its hegemony in the social structure through the establishment of political control over the economy, had it not been the case that

their class struggle with the bourgeoisie was displaced ideologically on to a level of ethnic and religious conflict. The Greek and
Armenian minorities were seen not only as carriers of the logic
of the market and agents of a social system which would eventually dispense with the traditional ruling class, but also as the
internal support of an imperialism preventing the bureaucracy
from reconstituting traditional class balances. When the First
World War started, the bureaucracy felt two simultaneous needs;
to neutralise the minorities in order to prevent a resurgence of
imperialist imposition; and to find for itself a client group in the
economy without running the risk of this group becoming another
internal support mechanism for external pressure. Therefore the
economic actors subject to political control by the bureaucracy
could not be the Greek or Armenian bourgeoisies: they had to
originate from ethnic groups which did not pose any threat to the
integrity of the state.

It was through such a process that the organisation of a war
economy came to depend on the promotion of Muslim merchants
and businessmen. These aspiring entrepreneurs were brought
together under the aegis of the CUP party organisation, usually in
co-operative schemes, to found 'national' companies for the
financing and carrying out of trade. These companies replaced to
some extent the minority merchants who had until then monopolised both internal and external trade; the war period witnessed a
move towards the fulfilment of the Ottoman bureaucratic ideal of
total political control over the economy.[3]

The constitution of a Muslim merchant class during the First
World War, although important as a reflection of Young Turk
nationalism, could not entirely replace the overwhelming economic dominance of Greeks and Armenians whose numbers and
networks embodied quite a different order of strength. In other
words, in carrying out its economic policy the bureaucracy, even if
it could establish political domination over the realm of the
market, still had to confront a distrusted Christian bourgeoisie.
This situation was resolved with the expulsion of the Christian
minorities during and after the war. Armenians were driven out of
Anatolia in 1915 and when the Greek army occupied western
Anatolia in 1919, a state of active belligerence ensued. Most of the
Greek population of the Empire rallied to the Hellenistic idea,
forcing them to emigrate when the Turkish army recaptured the

occupied lands. When the war ended, a massive exchange of populations with Greece was agreed upon.[4] As a result of the First World War, 1.2 million Greeks had escaped or were expelled to Greece. Thus the neutralisation of the minorities which began during the war was completed in 1924, the first post-war year in Anatolia. In less than a decade, about 3 million Greeks and Armenians had perished, departed or been expelled from what became Turkey. This number was equivalent to one-quarter of the remaining Muslim population, and probably contained 90 per cent of the Ottoman bourgeoisie. Thus did the bureaucracy win the war.

The state of the new republic

Through the period of its retreat, the Ottoman Empire had been carved into nation-states: its final demise arrived with the protracted war that ended in 1922. In 1923 what remained of the old Empire was a potentially viable unit where Muslims represented some 97 per cent of the population, and Turks were by far the dominant ethnic group. Irridentist threats dispelled, the fashioning of a nation-state had become possible. The upheaval of the war period had, however, greatly altered the social structure and the class balances within what remained of the Empire. The actors who were to be involved in the attempt to impose their projects on the social system as a whole had changed greatly due to geographical and demographic dynamics. The class conflict between the bureaucracy and the merchant bourgeoisie, whose outcome, under a more orderly historical evolution, would be expected to determine the social structure of the new political unit, had found its *denouement* through displacement and annihilation.

An alternative scenario to what ensued could have been a 'middle-class' rebellion by the commercial bourgeoisie – akin to some Latin American trajectories. This scenario was excluded, however, for two reasons. First, the 'middle class' in Latin America often included a section of the landed oligarchy who had themselves diversified into industrial production. The rebellion, therefore, had an aspect of intra-class struggle, where the political authority representing the oligarchy was not totally opposed to the new challenge. In the Ottoman case, however, such a landed commercial class was lacking; besides the bureaucracy derived their *raison d'être* from peasants and petty producers, that is, the stratum whose existence would be most threatened under capitalist development. The bureaucrats' attitudes toward capitalist development were, therefore, highly ambivalent. This was unlike the situation in which political authority was linked to large commercial landholdings – precisely the economic form whose defeat would have been required for the further development of the urban classes. Secondly, and more importantly, the commercial classes, like the bureaucracy, suffered the same ideological dislocation of their class conflict, in seeing their principal problem in religious and ethnic terms. For that reason the Christian bourgeoisie attempted to stage their struggle in the inter-state theatre, not principally through social demands designed to favour their access to political authority, but through demands of ethnic and religious autonomy. From this point of view, the Christian commercial bourgeoisie never entertained the option of becoming a class for itself through exercising influence over the state. Especially during the later period, rather than looking at the Porte as a political authority to be swayed in the direction of its economic interests, they had rejected the Ottoman state as a legitimate field to be conquered and utilised. Christian merchants, by opposing the legitimacy of the Ottoman state in favour of its dismantling, also relinquished the possibility of a bid for political struggle and primacy through a 'middle-class' revolution. More than any other single factor, this reluctance and inability of the Ottoman bourgeoisie to claim political power decided the subsequent development of the state and ruling classes in Turkey.

In summary, it was the peculiar status of the bureaucracy as a ruling class, which implied the absence of a land-owning commercial oligarchy, and the ethnic differentiation which occluded the class struggle, that prevented Ottoman social development from embarking upon any of the well-known trajectories seen elsewhere. At the end of the war, a balance emerged which pitted a strong bureaucracy without a clear social project against weak commercial interests who were, as yet, in no position to entertain the possibility of class rule.

The principal determinant of this balance was the fact that during the war years Turkey had lost most of its Christian commercial class. Whatever remained of the bourgeoisie was too weak to constitute a class with an autonomous stance against the bureaucracy.[5] Furthermore, the surviving commercial class was concentrated – to a greater degree than before – in the two cities of Istanbul and Izmir, now pale reflections of their former glory. The provincial cities, where economic change and cultural awakening could be observed at the end of the nineteenth century, had lost most of this momentum and reverted to their sleepy incarnations as administrative centres. The beginnings of a civil society had thus been suffocated before their fruition: once again the rule of the state threatened to become compact and supreme.

It was as a result of an arduous struggle that the Turkish Republic was established in 1923, with its capital in Ankara, but with essentially the same bureaucratic cadres which had governed the Empire in Istanbul. The 1920s were a period of 'modernisation from above' or superstructural reformism, carried out by an increasingly authoritarian regime. The Kemalist faction within the bureaucracy behaved in an exclusionary manner in an attempt to isolate and eradicate the better-known CUP cadres, and in forcing Kemal's potential rivals into a passive positions. By 1929, the process of forming a single-party dictatorship had also been largely completed. There was an assembly to which deputies were appointed, through a process euphemistically known as 'elections'. But an electorate was lacking: a system of two-degree elections amounted to the designation of a group of men who then ratified the names sent to them from Ankara. There was not much need for the deputies to function in any legislative capacity, since the government neither felt accountable to the Parliament, nor seemed to be in need of legislative initiative. Although the rank and file of the administrative apparatus were imported directly from the imperial bureaucracy of the Porte, the government which came to enjoy unchallenged power represented one particular faction within the bureaucratic class. This was a result achieved after years of intra-elite struggle, with waves of purges which left a uniform cadre in Ankara professing total obedience to Kemal.[6]

The ruling faction was concerned not only with eradicating all rival elites but also with achieving a formal appearance of uniformity among the populace, supposedly reflecting the individual bereft of any local affiliation. Thus all associations of popular Islam in the form of sects, orders and *tekkes* (Dervish groups) were banned while, at the same time, the traditional head-dress and clothing were outlawed. In rejecting communal structures of cohesion, the bureaucracy sought to delocalise and departicularise. This rejection reflected the desire that universal associative principles should apply to all individuals and from such association should follow the reproduction of the society. Since, however, they could not embrace the market as an organising principle, the bureaucrats would have liked to ensure cohesion by fashioning novel links between the state and society. Like their predecessors, however, they could not successfully conceive of the form and the nature of such links. Instead, they redoubled their militancy to combat what they thought of as rival principles. Only towards the end of the 1920s, with the Italian and Soviet examples in sight, did it become possible to envisage alternative linkages with society while safeguarding the status of the bureaucratic mechanism. As a result, the 1920s witnessed a recourse to the characteristic authoritarian equation: a politically strengthened centre combating rival principles of social cohesion, while reluctantly permitting the development of the market and its implicit organisational forms.

Statist authoritarianism

By 1929 the bureaucratic faction in power had emerged victorious from the intra-class struggle, while the frantic pace of reformism had subsided with the potential and actual rivals of the leadership dead or exiled. It seemed that the forthcoming task of the bureaucracy would be to prepare the ground for transforming the economic system in such a way that their own position within it would conform to that envisioned in the Young Turk project. A new trade regime with specific duties was instituted at the end of 1929, and the coincidence of this with the world crisis allowed the government to embark on a restrictive trade policy. It was fortuitous that political developments and the economic cycle were mutually reinforcing, thus allowing the attention of the bureaucracy to be concentrated on economic matters. In fact, 1930 and 1931 were periods of feverish economic innovation; perforce they became years of major transformation in the political regime as well. A new state form (the range of state functions and the nature of the relationship between the political power and the economy), together with the set of measures originally formulated to combat the crisis, resulted in a regime which embodied the culmination of bureaucratic reformism. In its basic dimensions this regime, and consequently the bureaucracy–bourgeoisie balance, remained in force until the end of the Second World War.

Various official and para-governmental organisations were established in the early 1930s, in order to guide the economy and the population toward a statist scheme of self-sufficiency. One significant aspect of these undertakings was the emerging propensity of government activity to colonise society: not only directly, but also through the formation of strictly ideological apparatuses which were *de facto* under the control of the central authority. The 1931 Congress of the Republican People's Party and subsequent government action aimed at banning all existing organisations with any kind of autonomy, confirmed this course. It also became clear that the Turkish republicans had discovered the organisational innovations brought to the European scene by Italian fascism. This was most apparent in the self-conception of the party and its place in society. The 1931 Congress defined the political order as a single-party regime where the party assumed the responsibility of ruling in the name of the nation. In doing so the party would abide by 'populist' principles, being vigilant against special privileges that sought to divide the population. In fact, 'a main principle' was to consider the 'people of the Turkish Republic not as composed of separate classes but divided into members of various occupations for the purpose of individual and social life'. Hence the Party would aim at 'establishing social order and solidarity instead of class struggle'. This solidarity would be immediately instrumental in 'involving the State directly in activities required by the general and supreme interest of the nation – especially in the economic field'.[7]

The combined administrative and economic policy innovations indicated that the bureaucracy had succeeded in unifying itself around the principle of politically-led social change. This goal required both a defensive and an active stance: the first led to the elimination of all societal autonomy while the second invited attempts at economic planning and ideological conformity. Within the defensive rubric proscriptions arrived rapidly. In 1931 the Turkish Hearts, a legacy of Young Turk nationalism, were closed down. Again in 1931, a new press law gave the government the right to close newspapers and magazines for publishing anything that 'conflicted with the general policies of the country'. In 1933 a university 'reform' expelled two-thirds of the 150 teaching staff at the only institution of higher learning, Istanbul University. In 1935 freemasonry was outlawed despite its roster of former and actual dignitaries; shortly after, the Turkish Women's Association was closed. During this entire period party hacks exaltedly wrote about the requirements of the revolution, the need to be unified, the necessity to sacrifice. Of greater interest was their penchant for analogy: examples were drawn indiscriminately from Italy, the Soviet Union, and, later, Germany. The point was repeatedly made that in these countries the necessity of the press, or the university, to be aligned with government policy was recognised and requisite measures were taken. These three countries were seen as paving the way for a new social system (as a revolution out of a defunct liberalism).

By 1933, and definitely by 1935, the authoritarian nature of the government had been well established, leaving no channels of dissent remaining. The crowning touch, but really a pronouncement after the fact, came in 1936 when Ismet Inonu, the prime minister, in his capacity as acting secretary general of the Republican People's Party, declared full congruency between state administration and party organisation. With this declaration, all state officials in the administrative branch became loyal party officials. With the hindsight provided by Third-World nationalist development schemes in the 1960s and 1970s, the Turkish experience emerges as one of the first examples of what was to become a fairly common pattern. Under the guise of a novel social system, a political elite and a nascent bourgeoisie joined forces to isolate a national economic space for themselves in which heavy oppression of the working class and exploitation of the agricultural sector would allow for rapid accumulation. All this was to be achieved under a more or less xenophobic ideology of national solidarity, one denying the existence of conflicting class interests in favour of a corporatist model of society.

During the 1930s a measure of industrial development had created opportunities for the bourgeoisie, but wartime shortages led to favourites and profiteering, resulting in bitter divisions. One significant instance of the developing rift between the bureaucracy and the bourgeoisie was the 1942 Wealth Levy. Ostensibly instituted to tax extraordinary earnings, its burden fell mainly on

minority merchants. Rather than coalescing the Muslim bourgeoisie with the bureaucracy, however, this levy seriously damaged business confidence. Once extraordinary conditions
passed, the seriousness of the damage became apparent, with
politicians repudiating the experience and bureaucrats rushing to
condemn it. The damage had been done, however, to the previously unassailable alliance between the bureaucracy and the
bourgeoisie.[8]

The last years of the war exhibited further instances of alienation between the bureaucracy and the bourgeoisie. A more radical
wing of state managers had attempted to speculate about the
post-war world, believing there would be an independent niche for
Turkey between the two emerging world orders. Expanding upon
the left version of étatist ideology, they planned for a bureaucrati-
cally controlled post-war reconstruction. However, neither internal class balances, nor the ill-diagnosed state of the world, would
allow such bids at autonomous solutions. The final effect of such a
bureaucratic endeavour was to convince the bourgeoisie of the
necessity of ending the pre-1945 political balance and declaring
unambiguously Turkey's position in the world system. Immediately after the war, when the *casus belli* of the Cold War was being
discovered, a Soviet demand concerning territorial concessions by
Turkey came to their aid, convincing the US Government of
Turkey's need for economic and military aid. Simultaneously, and
in rather direct response to various American critics who expressed their hesitation with regard to Turkey's previous pro-
German attitude, to the Wealth Levy, and to the single-party
regime, the Turkish government announced that there was a
pressing need for an opposition party in the Parliament and that
elections would be held in 1946.

It seems that the bureaucratic ranks in power greatly underesti-
mated both the strength attained by the bourgeoisie and the
distance which now separated business circles from the statist
policies of the previous period. What was hoped for was a party of
loyal opposition that would work with the bureaucracy in order to
evolve a negotiated set of policies to suit the new world situation.
The political regime would remain essentially the same even if the
economy gained some autonomy and some of the statist administrative apparatus were dismantled. Elections in 1946 provided a
rude awakening for the bureaucracy: the opposition party (the

Democrat Party) had gained surprising strength after only a brief period of organisation. With extensive allegations of fraud, the single party returned to power and the main opposition party remained a minority in the Parliament. From 1946 until the new elections in 1950 accomodation and appeasement were the principal tenets of government behaviour. All public criticism was recuperated in the form of new policies and new appointments; American experts were allowed to draw up the new economic programmes. Concessions were given in the realm of religion, tainting a previously pristine record of militant secularism. The field of opposition that was conceded, however, had irreversibly created a public space in which all classes joined to participate in the impending anti-authoritarian revolution. Agreements among the elite on the proper management of the economy would no longer be sufficient to contain the anti-absolutist current. A political solution to the débâcle was inevitable.

The ideology of the 1950 Revolution

Until the 1950 elections, politics had been the business of the elite, with power being transferred within the bureaucracy, or shared with a bourgeoisie who were few enough to permit face-to-face negotiation. With the decision to introduce a multi-party parliament in 1946, however, universal suffrage and electoral politics arrived together to articulate the split in the ruling coalition. Parliament was transformed into a forum of debate. The two pillars of the opposition platform were economic and religious freedom: these upheld the market against statist intervention, and local traditions over the political oppression and ideological onslaught of the centre. This platform, which was a necessarily transformed, but readily recognisable, version of the first bourgeois revolution succeeded in mobilising a following of truly mass proportions.

The sudden discovery of the market was, of course, primarily due to the bourgeoisie's disenchantment with bureaucratic control over the economy. Having gained sufficient strength through politically mediated accumulation, they had reinforced their ranks with profiteering under wartime policies. Now, they could differentiate themselves from the bureaucracy at the level of ideology as well. Against a corporatist solidarism which employed the 'national good' as a categorical imperative, they reached out to the tenets of market liberalism. Individuals were promised freedom from controlled prices, from various arbitrary restrictions and from a state whose principal concern remained the collection of taxes. The market would bring with it a field opportunity where economic accomplishment could be pursued independently of the structure of state-granted privilege. The promise of an autonomous economy carried with it the image of producers freely competing in the market without the interference of bureaucratic control. For the bourgeoisie who felt themselves to have come of age, this would be a desirable state of affairs. It must be remembered, however, that the population which could be characterised as living within capitalist relations of production remained and extremely small minority. In 1950, out of a population of 20 million, 80 per cent lived in the countryside – the great majority being small producers. Self-employment was the rule in urban retail trade and in services as well. Even in manufacturing, 37 per cent of the workers were self – or family – employed, while around 400 000 wage-earners worked for employers. These figures indicate that the overwhelming majority of the population were petty producers who might well be expected to subscribe to the ideals of a 'simple market society'. In other words, the market ideal did enjoy an objective correlate in the Turkish political arithmetic, and did not remain a purely ideological construct mystifying capitalist relations of production.

Together with the market, religion constituted the second focus of opposition during the 1946–50 period. The reformist current during the 1920s had aimed at eroding autonomous community traditions, especially religious ones, thereby seeking to replace such cohesive principles with centrally propagated rules of conduct. The ruling faction of the bureaucracy, consistent with the reformist project, had sought to implement a programme whereby the state-society linkage would be grounded in the novel status of the state, which would be exclusively secular. While the state would still dominate society, the bureaucracy could no longer be legitimated through recourse to official religion. Instead legitimation would spring from behaviour in harmony with principles associated with modernity. The ruling faction was adamant in its understanding of these principles as entailing militant secularism.

For this reason it came into conflict with a variety of local and popular traditions, its excessive zeal in laïcisation often inciting reaction against the regime.

It was by no means the case that the religious establishment, representing official Islam had opposed the idea of reformism. The Ottoman *ulama* were part of the bureaucratic class, and during the latter half of the nineteenth century, the higher *ulama* had been instrumental in providing ideological justification for the reforms. It was mentioned above that Abd-ül Hamid's restorationism which succeeded in combining official and popular Islam at one level, had found wide support among the common people. Later, at the beginning of CUP rule, an important rebellion had expressed discontent with the new constitutional regime in exclusively religious terms. At that time, as was also to be the case during the Republic, the rallying call was the presumed loss of the *sharia* – the Islamic legal code – meaning that the reforms were infringing upon the established order, and, more importantly, on the life-world of the groups rebelling. Islam emerged as the binding principle of that life-world, that sphere of existence which had not been penetrated by political society. For the peasantry and the urban petty bourgeoisie above all, Islam became a banner of defence against the political centre whose guiding principle was believed to be militant reformism. Accordingly, the type of Islamic faith and organisation employed under this banner was not of the orthodox-official variety: it was a version easily articulated with local traditions, and with accounts of the exploits of legendary heroes and mystical sects.[9]

The Young Turks had acted to separate the political establishment from its religious legitimation by secularising all Islamic courts, schools, and foundations; Kemalists had followed by abolishing the Caliphate and adopting a state policy of strict laïcism. This divorce, however, amounted to an amputation of the principal ideological apparatus of the state, with the important consequence of leading to a separation between a secular state and a society for which Islam, in providing rules of conduct at individual and communal levels, continued for some time to be the popular cohesive principle. The bureaucracy was forced to cope with this separation not only to legitimate themselves at the popular level, but also to pre-empt uncontrolled ideologies from filling the vacuum created by the divorce of ruling and popular belief systems.

On the other hand, with the rejection of religious orthodoxy as a pillar of state authority, a more popular Islam had a chance to solidify around an increasingly unitary basis in society. It may therefore be argued that the reformist zeal of the bureaucracy was uniquely instrumental in coalescing the various elements of popular culture into an 'Islamic reaction'.

The economic crisis of the 1930s had seen attempts at arousing a nationalist consciousness in response to the failure of an economic society organised through the market mechanism. Nationalism, however, remained an elite ideology, employed more effectively as an instrument of control than as a mobilising platform. The centre itself never attained an economic and social dynamic to carry the urban petty bourgeoisie and the peasantry out of their tradition-bound world. As a result, popular forms of social transaction continued to be those of the imperial past, and this apparent conservatism came to define the ideological confrontation with the centre. When the centre became more oppressive in its ideological intrusion, the peasantry and the petty bourgeoisie of small towns took refuge more resolutely in tradition, inviting the bureaucracy conveniently to label their behaviour as obscurantist reaction.

The creation of a modern society according to Western norms had been an avowed goal of all reformers since the nineteenth century. What this project amounted to in context was the eradication of parochial and particularistic allegiances in favour of the constitution of a *Gesellschaft* whose functioning was presumed to assure the cohesion of isolated but rational individuals. The target, then, was not religion *per se*, but those traditions, customs and rules of daily conduct which were claimed to be grounded in, and legitimated by, the maxims of Islam. Islam in its Turkish version is not a particularly otherwordly religion; its lack of a separate religious institution is perhaps an indication that its realm is primarily that of the caesar. It seeks to define and provide meaning to a social universe: its believers thus identify as Islamic the meaning and the structure behind their entire lived relation with the socio-political sphere. It is curious that Ottoman-Turkish reforms identified their task negatively, as unseating, rather than constructing an alternative to, community-based social life. In other words, they had to accept violence at the symbolic level as the desirable course of action. The notion that a particularly intolerant attitude toward the symbols of traditional society – such as clothing, or daily religious observances – would entail lasting and substantive changes at the level of practice was, perhaps, nowhere as fervently pursued as in Turkey. With Kemalism, not only was religion repudiated as the basis of the political and ideological authority of the centre, but popular Islam also lost all its institutional foundation through the banning of the *tarikats*, or Islamic brotherhoods; the closing down of sacred tombs; and the proscription of traditional dress. The Kemalist government created various departments within the bureaucracy designed to control from the centre all aspects of religious life. Thus, secularism came to signify political control over religious life by bureaucrats, rather than, as the term usually implies, separation of church and state.

A corollary to such an understanding of the relationship between religion and the state was that any oppositional mobilisation protesting the oppressive political authority could claim to be acting to restore the social status of Islam. In the absence of an entrenched political tradition, resentment of the reformism of the state was expressed in the vocabulary of religious conservatism – the only language commonly accessible to the majority of the people.

The opposition's political contestation in the 1950 elections was a declaredly populist one: 'the people' had been politically dominated, socially oppressed, and economically exploited by the bureaucrat-bourgeois bloc. The two dimensions of the opposition platform reflected this antagonism in appealing to universal principles of economic and religious freedom, the ideological content of which did not readily reveal a class bias. It was, of course, a former component of the power bloc, the maturing bourgeoisie, which acted as the mobilising elite, and probably stood to gain the most from a populist victory. Nevertheless, against the absolutist authority of the bureaucracy, resistance based on universal principles potentially unified all social classes, whether or not they had become aware of their particularist class interests. Even the illegal communist party supported the Democrat Party in the 1950 elections. What is historically curious is that the organising principle of Latin American populisms was an anti-liberalism, seeking to replace the rule of the market with political mediation of economic outcomes. The 1950 movement in Turkey took on the character of a latter day liberal resistance to absolutist rule, except that a much larger proportion of the population (compared to, for example, seventeenth-century England) was mobilised to form a common front with the bourgeoisie. In the following three decades the elements of this 1950 populist mobilisation remained important dimensions of Turkish politics even when class-based interests came to be much more fully articulated.

The demise of liberal populism

By any measure, the Democrat Party's accession to power in 1950 constituted a fundamental break in Turkish history. For the first time, a popular electorate expressed its political choice and voted against the statist tradition of several centuries. Paternalism, control from the centre, and reformism from above decisively rejected while the market (and capitalism) were given free rein. Of course, the large majority of the population was as yet ignorant of the implications of an unbridled market economy. None the less, its immediate benefits appeared tangible, and the unknown seemed far more desirable than what was recently experienced. The bourgeoisie, however, was politically the most conscious party in the populist mobilisation. It was aware that the new era heralded its political and ideological domination at the expense of the bureaucracy and its awkward attempts to propagate a statist system with a nationalist ideology. It must certainly not be forgotten that the bourgeoisie had engaged in a relatively easy battle, as the war had already been fought on the world scale and won (as far as Turkey was concerned) by the proponents of free enterprise and the market. Nevertheless, it was this battle which signalled the transition from a capitalism under bureaucratic tutelage to a capitalism based much more solidly on the market mechanism.

The bureaucracy's (or the Republican People's Party's) defeat in electoral politics, assured its subordination to the bourgeoisie during the subsequent phase of Turkish political-economic development. The bureaucracy lost its status as a social class with its own project and individual bureaucrats became state managers whose autonomy (and the degree of it) would depend on the nature of the accumulation process and intra-bourgeois balances. Despite the rich historical heritage of a state tradition, after 1950 political power remained in the hands of the bourgeoisie.

The unleashing of the forces of the market after 1950 was accompanied by rapid economic development, social and geographical mobility and the formation of a bourgeoisie and a working class. Peasants migrated to urban areas. The cities were transformed from seats of the elite to poles of economic activity. The anti-bureaucratic sentiments of the previous period were gradually reincarnated into a populist agenda which aimed at incorporating a new population into the capitalist sector as workers and consumers.

Between 1950 and 1960 the population of the four largest cities increased by 75 per cent and the urban population (settlements of 10 000 or more) from 19 per cent to 26 per cent of the total. This meant the arrival of 1.5 million immigrants into urban areas and of 600 000 into the four largest cities (net of natural growth). In other words, one out of every ten villagers migrated to an urban area in the 1950s. Such geographical mobility was truly the beginning of national integration, eradicating physical distances and bringing into brutal confrontation peripheral and central cultures. Until the 1960s the city retained enough of its elite heritage to intimidate the newcomers. Immigrants who now lived in shantytowns reacted by staying apart and reproducing their village culture in the *faubourgs*. During the 1970s, however, the culture of the city was totally absorbed into that of the suburbs. With the resulting homogenisation, political behaviour more consonant with the class model became prevalent. By this time second-generation immigrants who had not readily experienced material improvements in their lives had become the dominant urban group.

Despite frequent accusations of catering to religious obscurantism, the Democrat Party had managed – through its economic programme – to transpose the terms of the ideological debate to an essentially secular domain. The principal confrontation of the 1950s was that between the proponents of unbridled market freedom and of a politically directed economic development. On the necessity of rapid economic change the parties did not differ. Yet the implications of economic growth were fervently, but mostly implicitly, debated. The inheritors of the elite tradition, the bureaucracy and the intelligentsia, resented the new alignment of social classes which seemed to leave out of the equation the role to be played by an as yet unchartered cultural capital. This resentment surfaced in the form of nationalism and a crude version of the dependency perspective whose prescription was economic planning by the intelligentsia in the service of the nation.

In fact, the demise of the Democrat Party in power was precisely due to the failure of the market model in assuring the continuation of the economic prosperity that had characterised the early 1950s. It was then that arguments favouring a degree of political management of the economy gained force. Bolstered by international concern over an increasingly haphazard economic policy which did not respect the exigencies of the world market, the opposition platform succeeded in driving a wedge between the government and an aspiring industrial bourgeoisie. The military *coup d'état* of 1960 which responded to the discontent was supported by the intelligentsia, the bureaucracy, and the industrialists, who were increasingly wary of the wasteful populism of the ruling Democrat Party. The regime which followed was a synthesis of the two ideological positions prevalent in the 1950s, that is, market liberalism and planning for capitalist development. With this successful synthesis the conflict between the elite tradition and market promotion lost its importance. Capitalist differentiation had allowed for the evolution of a significant industrial bourgeoisie that was in need of an efficient administrative mechanism to manage the external and internal aspects of economic policy. Institutional innovations following the 1960 *coup* established just that.

Politics and ideology of import-substituting industrialisation

The post-1960 political synthesis was based on an agreement concerning the desirability of constituting and strengthening an internal market.[10] A 'national' capitalism would be pursued through protectionism to devise the means of rapid accumulation for the industrial bourgeoisie. Rapid accumulation, of course, involved an accelerated pace of economic growth and social relocation. In Turkey the years of import-substituting industrialisation witnessed a sustained economic growth rate of around 7 per cent per annum, bringing with it opportunities for urbanisation and rising expectations. As long as growth could be maintained, social dislocation was contained within the bargaining channels sanctioned by the system. When economic growth slackened during the second half of the 1970s, however, all the implicit conflicts rose to the surface and the permitted field of ideological competition was no longer sufficient to respond to all the needs.

Regardless of party affiliation, governments of the period pursued the goal of industrial development with political management of the economy. The largest right liberal party (the Justice Party, which replaced the Democrat Party banned in 1960) naturally emphasised the market component of the ideology, while the old bureaucratic party (the Republican People's Party) now in opposition embraced the managerial aspects. Both, however, espoused an incorporationist rhetoric which exhibited strong populist elements. Economic and social transformation were celebrated and the 'people' were promised a share in newly available material wealth. At this level of appeal to popular groups not much difference could be found between the two major parties: independent producers in agriculture and newly urbanised shantytowners as well as the working class were equally courted within electoral contest. Around this shared core the right-wing Justice Party utilised a large dose of nationalist symbolism, while the bureaucratic party upheld universalism and an aspiration to European standards of human rights. The prevailing economic model and its policy requirements, however, prevented either party from appearing conservative or defending losing social groups, a fact which invited other political movements to fill the gap.

Material progress and economic amelioration came to represent, in this atmosphere, the unquestioned goal. This goal, however, was not grounded in a belief in the autonomous individual and his freedom of action, as it had been during its initial formulation. Instead, individuals still regarded the state as the paternalist source of fair rewards. This was especially true in as much as the state assumed the role of guarantor of an equitable distribution of income. The 1961 constitution, in setting up the institutions of the new era, had stipulated that the state would assume all the functions required by social justice. A precocious welfare model of entitlements had been formulated which was also consistent with an economic model based on the expansion of the internal market. The state was intimately involved in all aspects of distribution through legislating various components of the social wage and producers' prices.[11] One of the significant dimensions of the period was precisely this politicisation of all distributional problems. Due to this political dimension being so visibly present in the economy all debate on the distribution of income was conducted at the level of the state. Political parties campaigned explicitly on issues of distribution and the chimera of an autonomous economy never took hold. Under conditions of economic growth bargaining over distribution took place at the political level, but the accountability of the state was especially highlighted during economic failure. In other words, while economic growth served to legitimate the political system, economic difficulty immediately resulted in a questioning of the state's legitimacy.

The two characteristics which have been mentioned here provide clues toward an understanding of the crisis at the end of the period, that distributional problems had come to the forefront and that the two major parties could not respond to the needs of the losing groups. Hence the rapidity of economic transformation both required a split and polarisation within the core ideology – due to growing distributional problems – and strengthened marginal ideological currents seeking to respond to the demands of neglected groups.

The ideological crisis depended closely on the nature of the economic transformation. It was already mentioned that the economic model privileged the construction of an internal market through protection of the industrial bourgeoisie. This protection and the high profits received through it allowed for the creation of a unionised working class which fought for and received high wages. The success of collective bargaining together with a relatively tight labour market led to considerable union strength which, in turn, gained its own momentum. The Republican People's Party saw this potential as the necessary ingredient of its transformation into a social democratic party. Thus, in the early 1970s a separation between the two main currents of the ideological platform began along the traditional (European) lines of right-wing liberalism and social democracy. What prevented the transformation of the RPP into a social democratic party was the limited weight of organised labour within the working class, and the small proportion of the working class within the total population. Non-union workers tended to be either less proletarianised or much worse paid – prone to other ideologies than social democracy in both cases. Petty producers and traders, including the peasantry, felt naturally closer to the conservative flank behind a market ideology. Thus, it was not politically expedient to opt for a strictly social democratic social base. However, as capital became less willing to accommodate labour's demands during the second half of the 1970s, industrial conflict became prevalent and the two centre parties – the RPP and the Justice Party – were forced to define themselves in strictly pro-capital and pro-labour terms. This effectively eroded the common ground of populist appeal.

Long before this erosion, this very concern for covering the middle had allowed for a proliferation of political platforms falling outside the sanctioned field of contest and which were thus labelled 'extremist'. The search for a stronger ideology than populist developmentalism started earlier on the right, mostly because the resentments of the neglected groups could articulate more readily into the more particularistic versions of past ideologies. The goal of constructing modern industry had necessarily meant a rapid destruction of the old order. Not only was traditional small capital gradually driven off the market, but the entire balance of social forces, especially in small provincial towns, suffered an upheaval. As new growth poles developed in the north-west and the south, these drew the rest of the country under their influence and violated the previously insular nature of small town Anatolia. There was no restructuration for these towns: they lost their standing and became subordinate to the new pattern of domination emanating from the seat of modern industry. Agencies of new corporations were set up and their representatives gained a new status which now evaded small capital of local origin. A similar dynamic could be observed in larger towns, with the traditional petty bourgeoisie, formerly of 'middle-class' status, rapidly losing their relative position even if not succumbing to proletarianisation. The recently urbanised shantytown population contributed another element whose resentment in the face of declining opportunities would lead to a disenchantment with populist rhetoric.

As long as economic growth persisted, the 'costs' of industrial development were covered through the opening up of new investment and employment opportunites. Once the slack appeared, however, the populist-developmentalist rhetoric of the political core lost its appeal. The development of modern industry appeared only in its destructive mode, without any redemption through the creation of new employment. Resentment built up at the lopsidedly incorporationist ideology of development which had depended strictly on economic growth for its fulfilment. It was this gap that right-wing political currents successfully filled. Their appeal ranged over a large spectrum from the unemployed informal sector of the big cities to traditional, small town businessmen in relative decline. What connected this loose tissue was the explicit rejection of economic ends as final goals. In an appeal either to the spiritual values of religion or to a transcendentally defined nationalism, immediate material gains were relativised. At the same time the left was blamed for the excessively 'materialist' preoccupation which was held responsible for the spiritual bankruptcy of the country. In both these currents – nationalistic and religious – new platforms were built upon elements derived from the dominant and contesting ideologies of former periods. In the case of the religious party, for instance, the discourse consciously evolved out of the reaction against the militant secularism discussed above. The constituency targeted by the new religious party was necessarily more limited compared to the populist mobilisation of 1950, consisting of social groups which felt ready to abandon hope for material salvation under the existing regime. This constituency was attracted to the National Salvation Party's electoral platform which advocated a national development strategy as well as a programme to stabilise the losses of the small town petty bourgeoisie. Yet their numbers remained small, confined to social groups remaining outside the axial class formation.

A similar judgement may be passed on the nationalist movement although its discourse enjoyed a very different articulation. In the 1930s in particular official ideology propagated from above had briefly appropriated some of the more extreme themes of pan-Turkism. This racist reading of history derived from an exclusively intellectual heritage with scarcely any resonance in popular culture. During the Republican period a sensitive balance between the official ideology of nationalism and its more militant versions attaining popularity among university students, with the latter tending to be instrumentalised against the left. The post-1970 evolution of the nationalist movement was partly due to the concurrent strength of the socialist movement, but it also enjoyed a seemingly autonomous popular appeal. Once again, in terms of electoral performance the political party representing this movement (the Nationalist Action Party) did not even attain 10 per cent of the votes, yet it did succeed in forging a fascist social movement which ruled the streets, especially in the periphery of urban centres and in small towns. The organisational model of fascism allowed the nationalist current to transform itself from its former elitism to a movement aiming at the same social base as the religious movement. The differences in constituency between the two right-wing currents were probably due to age and temperament rather than to any discernible sociological stratification, which also explains their intense rivalry during the 1970–80 period. However, the fascist movement made much more significant inroads into the administrative mechanism due to the attraction of its activism to technical cadres in state employment holding disappointing jobs. During two periods in the 1970s when the Nationalist Action Party was part of the government in coalition with the Justice Party, its cadres virtually controlled certain state agencies, and were able to use this control toward the recruitment of militants.

In the face of economic crisis during the late 1970s, not only did the argument over distribution become more acute, but also the neglected social strata came to suffer more immediately the results of a truncated transformation. Organised labour could protect some of its gains but unions succumbed to lower real wages after 1977; non-union labour and the informal sector suffered more abrupt reversals together with unemployment. At the same time as the capital-labour struggle intensified, divisions within the working class also became significant.[12] In provincial towns outside the growth poles of modern industry, the costs of progress became tangible as the economic boom of mid-1970s came to an abrupt end. The landscape was dotted with unfinished construction projects and empty factory buildings. On one axis, then, the two major parties veered toward the polar ends of the formerly shared legitimating ideology; while on the other axis various articulations of resentment competed for primacy. The crucial new development was the disappearing of the middle in the ideological spectrum and the concomitant de-legitimation of the state. The state could no longer perform its institutional role of distribution; its economic agencies were more and more privatised; its ideological apparatus was divided up among the more radical political currents. In this explosion of a previously compact ideological discourse, the state lost all of its legitimate authority, and existing political movements were too polarised in their commitments to attempt a joint rescue mission.

Epilogue

During the last sixty years Turkish history has traversed two distinct periods. The first, which lasted until 1950, was characterised by militant secularism and the creation of a capitalist nucleus. In 1950, an alienated communal tradition was mobilised by the new bourgeoisie through an appeal to anti-authoritarian economic liberalism and religious freedom, to replace the republican bureaucrats. Islam served, in this juncture, to represent all in the old social order that had been threatened. In the second stage, from 1950 to 1980, what transpired could more readily be interpreted through the normal evolution of capitalism. The principal axis of confrontation shifted from an elite-masses problematic to a class one, where certain alliances prevailed as a function of the economic model. Religion, together with secular nationalism, was now relegated to the role of a vocabulary of protest. The dominant discourse gradually became class based.

For a brief period in the 1960s and the 1970s it looked as if Turkey would experience a transformation similar to those of southern European countries, with a strong social democratic movement defending democracy and civil rights, maintaining a check against the renascence of traditionalist and chauvinist reactions and able to secure a relatively even distribution of economic gains. The civilising impact of social dissolution and economic growth, the integration of multitudes into the urban world and the gradual marketisation of agricultural petty producers seemed to augur a bright future within the folds of an expanding Europe. By contrast, the prognoses of the late 1970s were uniformly pessimistic: it became evident that whatever feeble social contract had earlier emerged did not penetrate deep into the consciousness, nor could faltering economic growth provide a sufficient gravitation. The state, which appeared to have completed its transformation into a capitalist one, was marred by the unsettled political spectrum giving way to privatisation and internal conflict. In addition to being unable to fulfil its functions toward the industrial bourgeoisie, it rapidly lost its legitimation first in the eyes of the social groups excluded from the populist equation, and eventually – parallel to its privatisation – for the vast majority of the population. It was a classic case of social disintegration which might have led to civil war had the political sides been more clearly defined or polarisation more universal. As it was, the vestiges of legitimacy that the military enjoyed once again came on the agenda and the state's monopoly of violence was re-asserted. The process of this assertion demonstated incontrovertibly the exclusion of Turkey from any European trajectory; instead the pattern of populism–crisis–*coup* suggested a path more similar to Latin-American examples. If indeed such an assimilation has occurred, the beleaguered democratisation process observable since 1983 may yet come into its own.

Notes and references

1. For the history of Ottoman reform movements, see R. Davison, *Reform in the Ottoman Empire, 1856–1876* (Princeton, 1963); S. J. Shaw and E. K. Shaw, *History of the Ottoman Empire and Modern Turkey*, vol. II : *Reform, Revolution and Republic* (Cambridge, 1977). For the Young Turks see E. E. Ramsaur, *The Young Turks: Prelude to the Revolution of 1908* (Princeton, 1957), and F. Ahmad, 'Vanguard of a nascent bourgeoisie: The social and economic policy of the Young Turks, 1908–1918', in O. Okyar and H. Inalcik (eds), *Social and Economic History of Turkey* (Ankara, 1980).
2. On the Public Debt Administration see D. C. Blaisdell, *European Financial Control in the Ottoman Empire* (New York, 1929).
3. Ahmad, 'Vanguard of a nascent bourgeoisie'; and Z. Toprak, *Türkiye'de 'Milli Iktisat'* (*'National Economics' in Turkey*) (Ankara, 1982).
4. This exchange was compulsory for Greeks living in all parts of Turkey except in Istanbul, and for Muslims in Greece except those living in Western Thrace. See D. Pentzopoulos, *The Balkan Exchange of Minorities and Its Impact on Greece* (Mouton, 1962).
5. For the economic situation in the 1920s, see my *Definition of a Peripheral Economy: Turkey 1923–29* (Cambridge, 1981).
6. The best account of the politics of this period is in M. Tunçay, *Türkiye Cumhuriyetinde Tek Parti Yönetiminin Kurulmasi (1923–1931)* (*The Establishment of Single-Party Government in the Turkish Republic*) (Ankara, 1981).
7. Ç. Yetkin, *Türkiye'de Tek Parti Yönetimi, 1930–1945* (Single-Party Government in Turkey) (Istanbul, 1983), p. 98.
8. On the Wealth Levy, see E. C. Clark, 'The Turkish Varlik Vergisi reconsidered', *Middle Eastern Studies* (May 1972).
9. Ş. Mardin, 'Religion and secularism in Turkey', in A. Kazancigil and E. Özbudun (eds), *Atatürk, Founder of a Modern State* (London, 1981); and B. Toprak, *Islam and Political Development in Turkey* (Brill, 1981).
10. A useful collection of essays on the so-called 'planned' period in

Turkish economy is O. Türel (ed), *Two Decades of Planned Development in Turkey* (1981 Special Issue, *METU Studies in Development*).
11. See the essays in E. Özbudun and A. Ulusan (eds), *The Political Economy of Income Distribution in Turkey* (New York, 1980).
12. For the more economic aspects of the crisis see K. Boratav, Ç. Keyder, Ş. Pamuk, *Krizin Gelişimi ve Türkiye'nin Alternatif Sorunu* (The Evolution of the Crisis and the Problem of Alternatives for Turkey) (Istanbul, 1984).

9 The Zionisms of Israel

TEODOR SHANIN[1]

'Until a people confronts its own past, it has no future.'

(E. Genovese)

'Hic Rhodus, hic salta.'

Zionism and Zionisms: the road to Israel

Let us begin with a paradox: social complexity is often best presented and grasped in this way. At the heart of the questions of Zionism lie two seemingly contradictory sets of facts, and a question, 'Why?'. To the broad lay public of outsiders with liberal or socialist sympathies, Zionism is the guiding ideology of Israel. This state emerged some decades ago as the Middle East's chief bully, an oppressor of Arabs and a global ally of most reactionary regimes. The 1982 bombing of Beirut and other conduct sustain this image. But then, how does one fit into it the Tel Aviv demonstration of 400 000 who shouted their fury against the Lebanese war and blocked its further unfolding? What about the 2000 Israelis who pledged to go to military prison rather than serve in the army of occupation? After all, the mass of them were Zionists by self-definition, and indeed believed themselves to be defying their government *because* of Zionism.

To those who know more of the history of Zionism or who have lived it, another related contradiction presents itself. Both as an ideology and as a political movement, Zionism has displayed a heterogeneity of direction and purpose. Within this heterogeneity two trends appeared whose opponents disagreed violently; a fundamentalist wing of extreme nationalism ('monistic', that is, undiluted in self-definition) and a moderate (in its nationalism) liberal and socialist tendency. During the initial seventy years of the history of Zionism, the political organisation professing moderate Zionism consistently had the upper hand in numbers, resources, votes and, at a later stage, in the control of the state machinery of Israel. This majority harshly fought its weaker adversaries and yet, in the last resort, retreated before them and adopted their aims.

The question 'why?' must begin with a review of the nature of Zionism. Zionism represented a multiplicity of concepts, values, emotions, strategies and tactics, closely interlinked with powerful networks or organisation. Yet, two, or possibly three, long-term political goals formed the hard core of the Zionist declaration of faith and definition of purpose, as well as Zionism's self-applied measure of ultimate success. It is these which distinguish Zionism as an ideological entity.[2]

In order of importance, the most crucial of these aims was defined at the first Zionist congress in 1897 as the creation of a *legally recognised Jewish national home in Palestine*. This was formally ratified by the 1917 Balfour Declaration and facilitated by the mandate subsequently granted to Great Britain by the League of Nations. After decades of doubts, changing interpretations and political vicissitudes concerning the advisability and possibility of statehood, it took final shape in the so-called 'Biltmore Declaration' of 1942, in which the Zionist leadership unequivocally interpreted this aim as the creation of a *Jewish State* in the land of Israel. The main engineer and spokesman of the Biltmore Declaration was David Ben Gurion, by 1948 the first Prime Minister of the state of Israel.

The second aim of Zionism was the *concentration* of the Jewish people from all around the world in the National Home/State of Israel. While the general aim was accepted by the whole of the movement, the measure of concentration deemed advisable or necessary, varied from an elite, which would form the culturally unifying centre of world Jewry (the Achad Ha'am view), to the 'in-gathering' in Palestine of every single Jew in the world. The explanations and/or rationalisations of this aim varied once again: the building of a new better society away from the old ghetto-world, the wish to counter ethnic assimilation, the experience or fear of anti-Semitic persecutions.

The third aim, that of 'productivisation', was somewhat less commonly accepted and traditionally associated with the socialist wing of the Zionist movement. Indeed, it formed the specific contribution of this wing but, for a time, permeated the whole of the movement. Initiated by the Russian radical Zionists, it called for a transformation of the social structure of the Jews from being a 'pyramid standing on its top', with numerous merchants and intellectuals and few workers and farmers, to the like-that-of-the-other-people position, where this situation is reversed. The creation of a National Home and the concentration of Jews was to provide the necessary preconditions for such a transformation, leading to a 'healthier society' or even to Tolstoian pacifist communalism expounded by the writings and followers of A. G. Gordon. To the Poalei-Zion supporters of Borochov, this transformation entailed the proletarianisation necessary for the subsequent proletarian revolution.[3]

The roots of our paradoxes lie in the fact that this widespread Zionist political goal was underlaid and informed by two dramatically different and contradictory *Weltanschauungen*, one fundamentalist, the other universalist.

The thought world of fundamentalist Zionism resembles that of nineteenth-century European romanticism. Man is a wolf to other men, yet he is not alone, for he is born into a nation. National exclusivity is the basic unity of men. The world is divided into nations – supreme, natural and eternal collectivities locked in a constant struggle, which constitutes the crux of history. Social organisation, fully expressed in the modern state, must serve the main purposes of the nation, that is, to secure its maximum strength and unity against external foes. True morality consists in transcending personal interests for the sake of the national community and the state. To do otherwise is treason. Realism consists in grasping all this to the full. A powerful mystical link relates the exclusive symbols of nationhood, a territory, a language, and so on. To the initiated, history often appears as a Manichean vision of poetic grandeur as, for example, in Jabotinsky's poem-dream of the future, in which 'From blood and sweat/A race will emerge/ strong, generous and cruel.' Powerful emotions link feelings of collective grievance toward outsiders with ambivalent love/hate relations toward one's own people, who never measure up to what is seen to be their manifest capacity and destiny. In the Jewish/ Zionist context, the main issue in such a world outlook is that of the weakness of the Jewish nation. The aim is to overcome this weakness, resulting mainly from the dispersion, and to make the nation and its state all-powerful. Zionism is the political and organisational expression of the Jewish claimant-combatant in the eternal worldwide power-struggle between nations.

The second world-outlook underlying Zionism has been very much the opposite of nationalist fundamentalism. It has its roots in the universalism and anthropocentrism of the Renaissance and in the evolutionary rationalism of the nineteenth century, providing the point of departure for both liberal and socialist movements and for most of the European social sciences. Man as such is the supreme value and the primary unit of analysis. The supra-human entities: nation, religion, state, class, and so on, are historical and relative; the attitude adopted toward them must depend on the extent to which they (or their abolishments) would serve the maximum self-realisation of the greatest number of individuals. Man equals man or, in formal political symbols, vote equals vote at an election. It is in the unrestrictedly equal relation to the racial, national or religious outsiders that universalism and humanism are best measured. True morality consists in transcending personal and group egoism and securing universal and equal suffrage for all. Realism consists in demystifying the supra-human and laughing out of court eternal national claims. History is the progression from barbarism toward the society of man – rational, tolerant, peaceful, co-operative and equal. The alternative was spelled out with an uncomfortable predictive force by an Austrian writer, Grillparzer, at the end of the nineteenth century: 'From humanity, through nationality, to bestiality.'

The liberal-socialist wing of Zionism adopted the universalist world outlook, while at the same time accepting the strategic supremacy of exclusively Jewish interests, aims and organisations. (These have been expressed in the World Zionist Organisation and, with respect to Palestine, by the demand for an exclusive use of Jewish labour.) Logical, ideological and political inconsistencies resulted. Those were conceptually bridged by a more or less sophisticated theory of temporary suspension of aims – a 'theory of stages'. Universalist aims and ethics were adopted in principle, but temporarily and exceptionally suspended to ensure realisation of basic national aims – an essential preliminary stage. The creation of an independent state, or a Jewish majority or else an Arab–

Jewish parity in Palestine, were treated as the point at which the dispensation ends, a dividing line beyond which the farther parts of the political programme would be put into operation. To be sure, even before 'the farther stage' is reached, some political measures of a universalist nature should be introduced, the right mixture of 'national' and universal to be defined pragmatically. In any case, the faster one goes, the faster the end of the nationalist stage would be reached: this would then leave the movement and its members free to expose fully their true universalist and humanist selves, liberal or socialist as the case might be.

The history of Zionism in the period 1917–48 was dominated by the confrontation between the coalition of the 'moderate' Zionists led by Weizman and of fundamentalists who eventually formed the Revisionist party led by Jabotinsky.[4] The main carrier of the 'moderate' universalist world outlook in the Palestinian Zionist context and the major political force within Weizmann's coalition has been the Zionist labour movement, which dominated the Palestinian Jewish political arena.

The period commenced with the Balfour Declaration, which committed Britain to the establishment of a Jewish National Home in Palestine, while British troops marched into the country where they were to stay for the next thirty years. The euphoria within the Zionist movement was quickly quelled by the events which followed. Arab political and armed struggle in 1920/1, the British White Paper of 1922 (introducing formal limitations on Jewish immigration), and the 1923 British suggestion for establishing an Arab Agency in Palestine on par with the Jewish one, all acted as a forceful reminder of the political realities of the 'Middle East'. The country was not simply an empty property which could be given away, the Arabs of Palestine could not be simply written off. The new British rulers, and even their Jewish first High Commissioner, were British first and foremost and pursued interests which were primarily those of Great Britain. Nor was there any overwhelming wish within the Jewish Diaspora to avail itself of the new opportunities. Even among the 4500 volunteers – soldiers of the Jewish Legion who reached Palestine with the British army – only 260 decided to settle there.[5] The so-called Third Immigration (1920–4) never exceeded 9000 per annum, and many left within a short time. The Jewish population of Palestine in 1922 was 83 000 out of a total of 725 000, that is, 11 per cent in all.[6] Hopes for massive financial help from wealthy Jews around the world did not materialise either.

The reappraisal of the political scene which followed defined the outlook of the Zionist movement between the two world wars and emphasised its fundamental divisions. Attitudes toward statehood, relationships with the Palestinian Arabs, British rule and the 'class issue' provided the crucial dividing line. From 1925 onwards, the newly-established Revisionist Party demanded the immediate creation of a Jewish state which would then solve the problem of immigration and settlement by a worldwide 'evacuation of Jews into Palestine'. This conception of Zionism, expressed by Jabotinsky, held also that the decisive political factors are military in nature. To this end the Zionist movement should concentrate on the creation of Legions – a professional military force. Arab objections would be inevitable and were to be met by an 'iron wall' until they submitted. Class division in Palestine weakened national unity and was anyway bogus because 'there are no classes in Israel, only pioneers'. Compulsory national arbitration was to settle any dispute concerning Jewish wages, while Arab/Jewish trade union action of other forms of inter-ethnic co-operation were to be totally opposed as treasonable.[7]

As to the Zionist majority, their interpretations of the term 'National Home' varied over time. In 1917, Weizmann as well as Balfour aimed at a fully fledged statehood using a synonym for reasons of tactical expedience. Yet before too long statehood as an aim receded into the indeterminate future or else disappeared altogether, while 'National Home' came increasingly to mean freedom of immigration, the social advance of Palestinian Jewry and its self-autonomy under friendly rule. By 1930, Weizmann could declare that 'The context of Zionism is to create a number of material foundations on which an autonomous, compact and productive community can be built. . . . Palestine could become a Jewish state if it were an uninhabited country. But it is not an uninhabited country.' This statement (described by a contemporary historian as 'not a tactical device' but 'a deep and genuine reaction to the political cul-de-sac') was powerfully supported on behalf of the Zionist Labour party by its leaders Katzenelson, Ben Gurion, Tabenkin and others.[8] The organisation of settlements and construction was presented as the only way to 'do' Zionism and to confront sucessfully British rule and Arab nationalism. The

Zionist socialists and liberals declared their commitment to live on equal terms with the Arabs. (Their long-term programmes varied from a Jewish state with the right of an Arab minority secured, via a confederation of ethnic 'cantons', and as far as a Jewish–Arab state of two equal nations in the whole of Palestine – *the Brit Shalom* and *Hashomer Hatzair* view.) This approach found its fullest political expression in the tactics of *Havlaga* (self-restraint), when in the 1930s the Jewish armed units of *Haganah* were ordered not to retaliate over and above strict self-defence, for 'we shall have to live together in the future'.[9] Policies of co-operation with the British Government were also adopted, although to a decreasing extent as the British restricted Jewish immigration and settlement. Inter-class compulsory arbitration and class peace were vehemently opposed by the Zionist Labour movement. Struggle for social justice was to proceed on a par with that aimed 'national goals'.

The historical development of the 1930s – Hitler's rise to power, anti-Jewish policies elsewhere in the world (especially in Poland and Rumania), the resulting wave of Jewish emigration to Palestine, the military struggle of Palestinian Arabs in 1936/39 and finally the Second World War – resulted in a general heightening of Jewish nationalist feelings. The Jewish population of Palestine was growing numerically as well as in its economic and political strength and confidence. All this was closely linked with changes within the Zionist movement. A shift of power occurred toward the Palestine-based Zionist labour movement, which since 1933 came to represent about 40 per cent of the delegates to the Zionist World Congresses. A major political shock hit them in 1938. The British Government declared its intention to limit Jewish immigration immediately, to stop it altogether within five years and to turn Palestine into an independent Arab state thereafter. In what followed, the majority of the Zionist moderate leaders were rapidly converted to the idea of immediate Jewish statehood: Ben Gurion in 1939, Katzenelson in 1941, Weizmann in 1942.[10]

Despite those developments, the main ideological dividing line within Zionism remained. In the political competition for the support of Jewry in Palestine and on a world scale, it was the moderates who dominated Zionism, for decades winning every election and forming the majority in every one of the executive bodies. The Revisionist opposition increased its representation within the Zionist Congress to 15 per cent in 1929 and, at the peak of its influence in 1931, had about 23 per cent of the delegates. By 1933 their support among the electorate was back to 14 per cent, after which the Revisionist Party left the Zionist Congresses to reappear in 1946 with only 11 per cent of delegates.[11] They did not fare any better inside Palestine.

The superiority of the moderate wing of Zionism over the fundamentalists was rooted in the social characteristics of Palestinian Jewry before 1948. It came mainly from the Jewish-European secularised middle classes, especially its idealist student spearhead. They brought with them the powerful impact of a universalist, often socialist, outlook. In the countries (and universities) which they had left behind, they encountered radical and socialist movements with which they were often closely linked as natural allies in battles against anti-Semitism. In Palestine they found themselves struggling for minimal wages in an erratic labour market, facing grasping Jewish farmers who preferred cheap Arab labour. Many left the country. Others built trade unions and co-operatives, crystallising the political self-consciousness of a militant labour movement. Labour militancy was 'anti-boss' but also 'anti' the ethnically defined competitors in the labour market (a situation only too common in the rest of the world). The labour movement, and especially the General Confederation of Unions (the *Histadrut*), rapidly grew into the most important power organisation of the Palestinian Jewry, dominating the political, economic and cultural scene and reinforcing in turn its own mass support. Israeli-born *sabras* – still few in number – took their cues from their elders. To all these, the extreme nationalist declarations, military tactics, forms and salutes and the loud unity-of-the-nation anti-socialism of the Revisionists conjured up memories of the anti-democratic and anti-semitic forces of Europe. The Revisionists could count on massive support only in some of the poor quarters of Oriental Jewry, less orientated towards Europe, less universalist, less working-class conscious and more anti-Arab.[12] But these Oriental Jews were relatively few in number before the creation of the state of Israel.

Relations between the two wings of Zionism in Palestine were characterised by severe infighting, mutual recriminations and, at times, ruthless use of force. The Revisionists castigated the Zionist majority as opportunist, if not downright treasonable in its universalist/nationalist ambivalence and in its anti-militarist stand. They attempted to build up an alternative Zionist world organisation. Revisionist trade unions were organised, calling for co-operation with the Jewish employers, breaking up strikes and fighting socialist symbols. A Revisionist military underground (*Irgun Tzvai Leumi*) was set up, challenging the supremacy of the *Haganah* – the mainstream Zionist organisation's military arm.

The Zionist majority reacted in kind. The ideas of the Revisionists were rejected as Fascist and their similarity to those of Mussolini repeatedly stressed. The Clausewitzian doctrine of a world of constantly fighting nation-states was declared to be a self-fulfilling prophecy, especially when related to territorial demands of a kingdom-of-David size state: it was a way to entangle Israeli Jews in a war which would never end. Slogans of national unity were said to serve and conceal class exploitation and social injustice. Most importantly, chauvinist rejection of universalism was treated as dangerous as much to the suppressors as to the suppressed, since 'a people oppressing another people cannot itself be free'.

The stand of the Zionist majority was backed vigorously by all the force of the main Jewish organisations in Israel: the Jewish Agency, the *Haganah*, and *Histadrut*. The minority position of the Revisionists was turned against them as powerful emotions were mobilised against the 'splinterers of national unity'. The Revisionists fought back. On both sides militants were slandered, dismissed and physically assaulted in meetings, pickets and street fights. In 1928, when the Revisionists celebrated Jabotinsky's arrival in Palestine with a military parade through the streets of Tel-Aviv, their own historian noted that: 'the route was jammed by a dense and violently antagonistic crowd shouting "Militarists!", "Generals!"'[13] The political and physical confrontation peaked in 1933 and again in the 1940s when a virtual civil war developed (the so-called 'Season' operation of the *Haganah* in which adversaries were kidnapped, beaten up and even handed over to the British police[14]). The battle lines were unequally drawn, the relatively weaker Revisionists getting, on the whole, the worst of the fighting.

The creation of the state of Israel and the war which followed did not lead to reconciliation within the Zionist movement. If anything, the controversies over the character of the new state acted as a new divisive force. The stakes were higher, both politically and personally. The new political context re-established both the pre-state dividing lines and the decisive superiority of the moderate Zionists. The Revisionists were kept out of the Provisional Government. The various military undergrounds, now legal, became part of the newly created Israeli army but maintained autonomy and jostled for power and prestige. In April 1948, the Irgun (the Revisionist military arm) and its allies captured the village of Deir Yasin near Jerusalem and slaughtered its population, while the Revisionist leadership later defined this action as a necessary and justified strategem to put the Arab population to flight. The anger and revulsion with which this news was received by the Zionist majority emphasised sharply the underlying divisions in general outlook, in political stance and in their emotional/moral underpinnings.[15] In June 1948, with the Arab armies still only ten miles from Tel-Aviv, a head-on clash came in the '*Altalena* affair.' The Irgun refused to hand over the arms on this ship despite an order to do so by the Provisional Government. A short but furious civil war was fought as a result, lasting only a couple of days but leaving sixteen killed on both sides and hundreds disarmed and arrested. The Irgun military structure was smashed, Begin and the rest of its leadership was put under temporary arrest and their particular military units dispersed.

The political finale of this stage was reached in the first parliamentary election in January 1949. The Herut Movement campaigned as the main fundamentalist group. It called for support for the Irgun activists, commanded by Begin, invoked the martyrdom of the movement in the anti-British struggle, and demanded that war be waged until the whole of Palestine was conquered. In the election the Herut came in a poor fourth with 11.5 per cent of the vote and, to the surprise of commentators, took an even lesser share of the vote within the army units still at war. By the second election, in 1951, Herut's support was down to 6.6 per cent of the total. The two main Zionist labour parties, Mapai and Mapam, collected more than half the total vote in both these elections, with the remainder going chiefly to other Zionist moderates. Non-Zionist electees were few. By the early 1950s the Jewish state (and its Jewish majority) was an undeniable political reality: Mapai dominated the government, Mapam provided the major opposition.

De jure belli and by the will of an overwhelming majority, the
stage was set for the realisation of the moderate Zionist programme and its universalist perspective within the state of Israel.

The jump which was not: 1949–67

In Greek mythology there is a story of a notorious braggart who
boasted continually of an exceptionally long jump he once made
on the far-distant island of Rhodes. Greek mythology has immor-
talised the answer of a local wit to those claims. The response, as
much a joke as a basic law of verification, was *Hic Rhodus, hic
salta* ('Here is Rhodes, jump!'). When all is said and done, deeds
are the best test of declarations of intent, even if one does not
accept for political life the simplicities of moral fables.

One cannot and should not write a history of the state of Israel
in a few pages. But one can highlight in this way the essential
trends and basic evidence relevant to the matter at hand. The
history of Israel is the history of an increasing sliding towards
fundamentalist policies, of national self-centredness disregarding
rights of the 'others' and of the acceptance of power as self-
legitimating – all these enmeshed with extreme self-righteousness.
The universalist commitment to total equality of rights for the
non-Jews in Israel in the Manifesto of Independence 1948, was
closely followed by the Law of Return, 1950, which gave immediate citizen's rights to every Jewish immigrant. Simultaneously, a
set of laws concerning 'absentees' (*nifkadim*) made every locally
born Arab who was outside the territory of Israel, at a given date,
a foreigner subject to expropriation.[16] A Jew from the Bronx by
the very fact of his Jewishness acquired legal rights within Israel
while most of the Arabs born in Haifa had lost it. A consequent
legal debate, over 'Who is a Jew?' specified that the Jewishness of
a Jew is valid only if she/he is of true Jewish stock by the orthodox
standards, that is, either born of a Jewish mother or else religiously converted. It was also ruled that a Jew who converted to
Christianity loses the legal rights which go with Jewishness (the
case of the brother Daniel, 1962). The logical and legal contradictions between the Manifesto of Independence and these laws were
simply disregarded.

As to the 'absentees', the 1948/9 war created hundreds of

thousands of Arab refugees, creating a sight as disturbing as it was familiar to those who had symbolised the problem of refugees in Europe five years earlier. Furthermore, with the refugees in camps, attempts at peace negotiations were checkmated. An offer by the Israeli government to negotiate on the basis of a proposal to allow back 100 000 refugees and to participate in the resettlement of others was made in the early days of July 1949 – very much a nationalist/universalist compromise within the moderate Zionist frame of reference. It was rejected by the Arab governments, furiously condemned as treason by the Zionist fundamentalists, promptly dropped, and never heard of again. Nobody bothered to ask the Palestinians. The non-negotiability of the return of the refugees has since become the formal stand of the Israeli government.

An even more poignant test of the *de facto* rules of the game according to which Israel was being run arose over the fundamental issue of property. In the public mind of the Israelis the issues of residence and citizenship were often interlinked with, and clouded by, the genuine enough problems of military security. Issues of personal ownership would not qualify as easily for such a criterion. The main non-Jewish group on the territory of Israel was the Arab peasantry. The main non-Jewish property was land. Right at the very beginning the Israeli government took over both government lands and the landed properties of the 'absentees'. Within twelve months, additional lands were taken over by the state, including property belonging to those Arabs who still resided in Israel but were in a different village at the doomsday date, and that belonging to those who were ordered out 'temporarily' by the Israeli army and to those whose lands were handed over to Israel by agreement. A new, grotesque term – 'A resident absentee' – was coined for the non-Jews (and only non-Jews) manipulated out of their property. In the 1950s and 1960s the creeping process of expropriation of Arab lands continued. For example, in 1961/2 an area in Galilee was closed for unspecified 'security reasons', then given over to build the township of Karmiel, in which Arabs were formally barred from residing. (In official sources, the campaign was explicitly referred to as the 'Judaisation' of Galilee). At the same time, Arab agriculture has had its economic viability severely curtailed by being excluded as such (that is, as Arab) from a variety of extension services and improvement measures.[17] By

1967 two-thirds of the Arab lands as of 1948 were in Jewish hands. Most of this land was now owned by the KKL national foundations and was rented out on long-term leases to Jewish farmers under conditions explicitly barring sub-letting to Arab peasants.[18]

There is a long list of examples of aspects of discrimination, formal and informal, along ethnic lines within Israel. Military rule was established territorially in some districts of the country, but the consequent administrative limitations, such as the necessity to ask for a military permit to leave the area, or subjection to the proceedings of military courts, were used only against the Arab residents of those districts. Equal voting rights existed, but the only attempt to create an autonomous Arab political movement, with a programme of moderate nationalism very much resembling the Zionist one (*al-Ard*), was banned by the courts in 1964 and its leaders detained.[19] (It was declared illegal despite the fact that it was never claimed any illegal action had been attempted by it.) There were practically no Arabs in the main sections of the civil service, especially in its top grades. Arabs were formally barred from joining most of the political parties, and so on.

It was clear, that after Independence the moderate Zionist government was implementing the basic assumptions of the earlier 'theory of stages'; Independence did not lead to policies and perspectives of ethnic equality. These contradictions between the universalist outlook and brazenly nationalist practices did not go utterly unchallenged. Within the 'moderate' camp, the internal opposition to the aggressive nationalism pursued by the government found symbolic expression in the confrontation between Ben Gurion and Sharett, Israel's first and second Prime Ministers. With most of the political parties of Israel too weak to play a substantial role and the Zionist-socialist Mapam immobilised by a factional split, the duel was fought mainly within the leadership of Mapai, the ruling party.

Typically, the confrontation focused on foreign/military policies, even though a much broader set of issues was clearly at stake. Again typically, Ben Gurion had chosen for himself the Ministry of Defence in the government, while Sharett took the Foreign Office. Sharett and his friends demanded 'policies of negotiations' and objected to many of the 'retaliatory actions' by the military. They were opposed primarily by Ben Gurion, his 'young men' and army commanders. In the resulting conflict, Mapai's moderates showed weaknesses which were to reappear time and time again in similar situations (for example, when the relatively moderate Prime Minister Eshkol faced the war pressures of 1967). Compromises were achieved and hailed as a victory for moderation. Ben Gurion came under increasing pressure and eventually resigned after the Israeli raid on the Jordanian village of Khibya in 1953, with Sharett taking over the Prime Minister's office. But, this led to the unleashing of powerful anti-Sharett political pressures. Every border clash (often following Israeli initial attacks, as reported in Sharett's memoirs) led to an immediate clamour for retaliation from the army command and from the press. Gossip campaigns were launched attacking the 'soft' Prime Minister for failing in his defence duties, and every attempt to cool things down was sabotaged by Ben Gurion's men in the army – especially by its Commander-in-Chief, Dayan. After numerous defence scandals and party rows, having authorised 'retaliation actions' time after time against his better judgement, Sharett finally resigned in 1955 and Ben Gurion returned triumphantly to power.[20] Nearly at once, in 1956, came the war against Egypt in alliance with Britain and France. The humiliation of retreat under barely concealed US orders, the lack of any tangible political results, and the bitter feeling of many that a big opportunity to come to terms with the reforming Egypt of Nasser had been lost, did not lead to a reversal of the hard-line policies. It did not even lead to a return to Sharett's policies of ambivalence. After 1956, the Ben Gurion 'hard line' was irreversibly 'in', in terms both of institutionalised power and of popular support. It promoted a further slide towards nationalism.

The failure to realise universalist goals by a government of the moderate Zionist majority was by no means merely a trick of a small group of legislators and politicians. If anything, the 'masses' of Israeli Jews often expressed themselves in a more fundamentalist fashion than their leaders. The anti-Arab mass hysteria which preceded and followed the 1956 war bears clear testimony on that score. However, the character and direction of how views and feelings developed can best be grasped by watching those explicitly committed to the internationalist brotherhood of man. The kibbutz Gan-Shmuel was for years one of the most left-wing communities of the *Hashomer Hatzair* brand of left Zionism – a symbolic hotbed of treason in the eyes of the Israeli fundamentalists.

In the 1960s a girl born in the kibbutz fell in love with an Arab neighbour. They married and the husband applied for membership in the wife's commune. In a secret ballot the majority of the members of Gan-Shmuel refused to accept him despite the outcry of its radicals. The questions 'Would you share your neighbourhood with a Negro?' or 'Would you let your daughter marry a Jew?' are a fair test of the actual norms of human relations all over the world.

On a less personal level, the expropriation of Arab land was tacitly or explicitly accepted by the majority of Israelis, who considered such behaviour elsewhere to be criminal. What is more, the group directly involved was the elite of the Zionist labour movement – the kibbutzim settlers. Once again it was the kibbutz movement of *Hashomer Hatzair* (as we may recall, the former supporters of a programme for a dualist, Jewish–Arab, state) which took over the lands of the village of Bir Im. (This was an exceptionally sordid story of a Christian Arab village which had shown particular friendship to Israelis in the 1948–9 war. Its inhabitants were later asked to evacuate their houses for a week and then brazenly refused permission to return. They were later to see their houses dynamited by the army while an appeal was still pending in the courts. The case became the symbol of Israeli disregard for Arab minority rights, of the stubborn insistence of its people to go back and of the moral unease of Israeli intellectuals, including some Establishment figures.)

The 1967 war as a moment of truth

To moderate Zionists, the main legitimation of nationalist policies, and of the ever delayed end to the 'suspension' of universalist principles, was fear for the existence of Israel. Since 1948, Israel has lived in a state of uneasy truce with its neighbours: with no formal mutual peace treaty, with mutual military infiltrations and clashes, an arms race, and so forth. Fear of 'showing weakness' in the face of an enemy, who was numerically superior and was calling for the destruction of the newly created state, was deliberately mingled with memories of the European slaughter of 1942–5. There was no military opposition from the 13 per cent Arab minority in Israel, but they could still be regarded with alarm as the 'fifth column' of the Arab states. Relative weakness was felt to justify, at least partly, nationalist policies and reactions 'as long as the conditions are what they are'.

This explains why the 1967 war marked not only a turning point in the history of Israel, but also a moment of truth in the political history of moderate Zionism. The military defeat of the Arabs created occupied territories with a mass of 'additional' Palestinian Arabs living there. The manifest military superiority of Israel over its neighbours undercut any justification for the perpetual delay in the realisation of universalist principles. The exchange of the occupied territories for peace, a Palestinian 'national home', and a reversal of the process of escalation with the neighbouring countries, seemed distinct possibilities. A sense of the unlimited power of Israeli arms swept the Middle East while an economic boom added to the optimism of the Israelis. After a short *intermezzo* the government was once again completely in the hands of self-professed Zionist moderates. In the eyes of its citizens, Israel finally seemed powerful enough to choose. 'Here is Rhodes – jump!'

Within a short time the Israeli government of Golda Meir made its post-1967 policies clear. In spite of an explicit declaration to the contrary (in the speech of the Minister of Defence on the day the war began), a policy of territorial aggrandisement was adopted. The only problem within the government was how much of the occupied territories to hold on to. Once again, 'public opinion' – organised and spontaneous – was, if anything, even more extreme. A 'not one step back' stance was forcefully advanced by the neo-fundamentalist 'Greater Israel Movement', which for once united Herut, the religious factions and numerous Labour Party members of extreme nationalist persuasion. That was not the end of the demands, for within a few years, an editorial comment of *Davar* – the Israeli Labour Party mouthpiece – could declare that, 'our current outlook which regards the River Jordan as a "security border", may have to be revised and moved further on in view of the delivery of American aircraft to Saudi Arabia.'

While at its beginnings the occupation was kept sensibly flexible ('liberal' on the West Bank, much harsher in Gaza, where the resistance was stronger), the political self-organisation of the Palestinians was banned and potential or actual leaders detained, exiled or dismissed from public functions. The existence of the

Palestinians as a distinct entity was rejected. The declaration of
the Israeli Minister of Defence, that the Palestinians do not exist
because they missed the boat by not claiming self-emancipation in
1948, was supported for a time by many liberals, including,
Haaretz, the leading daily paper in Israel.[21] (It sounded like a
macabre joke – a notice 'Further applications for nationhood will
not be considered, by Authority', hung on a locked door by a
second-generation immigrant.) As usual, on both sides of the
nationalist Jewish/Arab fence, the denial of existence of an ethnic
group was used to justify disregard of its legal rights. The policy of
expropriation of Arab lands proceeded and was intensified. In
Rafah, Akraba, and so on, Arab farmers were ordered out, Jewish
farmers settled, often employing the expropriated Arab farmers as
wage labourers.[22] The protests inside Israel were answered by
Ben-Porat (a journalist who often acted as a mouthpiece for the
Ministry of Defence) with a demand 'to rip aside the veil of
hypocrisy' and to remember that in the present as in the past 'there
is no Zionism, no settlement of land, no Jewish state, without the
removal of Arabs, without confiscations'.[23] By 1973 the so-called
Galili protocol became the official government policy, supported
by the most powerful trio of Labourite ministers: Meir, Dayan and
Galili. It made explicit and official the 'Judaisation' and stage-by-
stage, *de facto* annexation of the occupied territories.[24]

Post-1967 military policy seemed to be at pains to prove Isaac
Deutscher's remark that Israel was turning into the 'Prussia of the
Middle East'. It was characterised by a constant brandishing of
power, by disregard of non-military considerations and by a
sweeping arrogance along the lines of 'we are above everybody,
everybody all over the world'.[25] The February 1973 shooting down
of a Libyan civilian aircraft on the personal order of Israel's
Commander-in-Chief, resulting in the death of 100 civilians, and
the flashy commando raids on Beirut, were typically linked with
the manifest decrease in competence of the army command and in
the unchecked spread of corruption within its supply and organisation networks. Reports about torture of prisoners were increasingly heard. Internationally, Israel found itself in alliances with
some of the most reactionary and corrupt of the world's politicians
and regimes: with South Africa, Somoza of Nicaragua, and Amin
of Uganda.

This expansionist, militarist and reactionary image of post-1967 Israel, increasingly devoid of the former justification of military weakness, shocked the more conscientious moderate Zionists. This was not the Zionism they believed they had been realising. Many of them condemned 'the infamy of Bir Im' and 'the crude slander . . . which maintains that Zionism was founded upon expropriation and exploitation'. Bar Nir, a Mapam MP and one of the pioneers' generation, angrily answered Ben-Porat that he would never have come to Palestine if he had thought that Zionism was to be founded on Arab expropriation. Writers, artists, professors and political militants of a moderate Zionist background spoke, petitioned and demonstrated against the fundamentalist policies of the Israeli government. In spite of vicious hostility in the mass media and 'public opinion', waves of protest arose in 1968, 1970, and 1972. The petitions were rejected, the demonstrations met by police force, the direction of political developments did not change. The heterogeneous protest movements proved no match for the consistent and ruthless pressure from 'the machine' of the state and the mass media.

As against the increasing hawkishness of the dominant policies, some voices of 'dovish' moderate opposition could also be heard within the Labour Party and government circles. The Minister of Finance complained about the costs of the occupation. The Minister of Foreign Affairs talked about the moral dangers of power. The head of the Confederation of Labour declared that the utilisation of Arab labour was defeating the Zionist aim of productivisation, since by now it was Arabs who are building Tel-Aviv. A Labour Party general secretary even demanded the recognition of the Palestinians and negotiation with them. Yet, notwithstanding these cases of non-conformity at the top, invariably followed by a public witch-hunt of the offenders by the press and right-wing politicians, the direction of Israeli politics did not change. Of these politicians who challenged the hawkish avalanche (Sapir, Eban, Ben Aharon, and Eliav), the first died while the others rapidly became ex-Ministers and ex-Secretaries. The government of what used to be called the moderate Zionist proceeded to execute fundamentalist Zionist policies with the support of a 'moderate Zionist' electorate. Within one generation and without dictatorship, concentration camps, executions or a one-party state, a massive liberal and socialist force in Israel was democratically deradicalised – an outstanding example of political thought-reform.

The next war, that of 1973 with Egypt, tore down the veil of post-1967 self-congratulatory euphoria. The surprise was over-whelming. The 1967 war was not 'the end of it'. Arabs could fight, conquer and kill. Israeli generals could be stupid, and were. The Israeli army could be and was ill-prepared. The help of the United States was essential and already needed on the third day of the war. The majority of the Israelis felt bitterly cheated and unjustly punished. So they had been, in terms of the government promises of 1967–73, even though the war was not in the end a defeat, nor was the country in any danger of destruction. The defeat was mainly in the mind: in the feeling that the many extra dead could not be accounted for in terms of unambivalent 'success' and that the deeply believed 1967 promise of final victory turned out not to be true. Each war seemed only to lead to another. In terms of the Zionist debate in the 1930s and 1950s, and the moderate Zionists' premises of old, the time had clearly come to look at the political balance sheet and to consider a new strategy. But those were not the old days. Israeli society had changed. The creature of mod-erate Zionism was displaying a momentum of its own.

Shadows of the 1973 war hung heavily over the Israeli political scene; recriminations and resignations were followed by a political realignment. A group of ex-Labourite, ex-generals and some others in the 'middle generation' (the 'youngsters' of Ben Gurion days) established a new party of the 'middle ground' – the DMC. Some of them, like Sharon, 'went all the way' and joined the Herut. The DMC was breaking Labourite hegemony over the state apparatus, the professional soldiers and the senior police. In the same period the pent-up resentment of the Oriental Jews, supporters of Herut, was now politically allied with the Confedera-tion of Industry Owners' representation, the party of General Zionists. The resulting Likud party coalition overtook the Align-ment of Mapai and Mapam in the May 1977 election.

The new government of Begin was the first to give the fun-damentalist Zionists state power in Israel. Its junior partners were the DMC and the smaller religious parties. The change in the political arena was, in fact, even deeper. The whole party scene shifted toward the fundamentalists. Within a few years the heterogeneity and careerism of the DMC leaders made it disintegrate with very little of its electoral support going back to Labour. The religious parties not only joined the Likud government but also moved sharply to the right. The leader of Herut was in full control of the government coalition. The smaller factions of the Zionist left proceeded to decline. Most importantly, the Likud's main alternative, the Alignment, was now led by Peres – another of Ben Gurion's 'young men' of the 1950s and someone on the right wing of the Labourite spectrum.

Likud government policies – the 'heavy hand' toward the occupied territories, monetarism and a free market economy, the first invasion of Lebanon, and so forth, contained little surprise. They did what they said they would. The peace treaty with Egypt and the inflationary boom gave it all the appearances of success. New elections strengthened Begin's personal prestige and Herut's party hold. In their view, to suppress the political will of the Palestinians, a few more steps were needed, of which the destruction of the PLO in Beirut came first. It looked like a simple military matter: the loyal support of Israelis for their army and government seemed assured. But the explosion of dissent among the Israeli middle classes, and among their sons in the officer ranks and crack units of the army, came as a nightmare to Begin and his men. In the Israeli context, it meant that the Lebanon war had to stop fast. The report implicating Sharon in a massacre and his departure from the Ministry of Defence, the inability of the Israeli army effectively to control southern Lebanon and the army's mounting losses, were quickly followed by Begin's resignation in 1983. A Chile-like crisis of a Friedman-like economic strategy led to further disarray. The close correlation of European/middle-class dissent and Oriental/plebeian loyalty added a particularly brutal and racist dimension to the political conflict.

This historical, thumb-nail sketch of Zionism and Israel brings us to the heart of the paradoxes named above to the question 'Why?' It was moderate Zionism that lay at the origins of Israel but showed little ability to turn its own ideological promise into a viable political strategy for the government it controlled. It gave way to most of the fundamentalists' demands. It eventually gave way to a fundamentalist government. But then, the resilience of some of its deeper premises came as a shock to the fundamentalists and to the cynics alike. The dreams of the 1930s and 1940s were down, but not out. The younger generation of army-educated Israelis was not immune to the universalist message and was well able to turn moderate Zionism overnight into a banner of defiance. Its strength clearly lay outside the party organisations and manipulations – the reserve officers who led the Peace Now movement, were mostly 'non-party' with strong 'moderate Zionist' leanings. Many thousands were ready to march at their summons, to protest and to refuse. For many decades the 'moderate' lady has been riding a tiger of chauvinism, unable to climb down or to control its charge. It seems now that the tiger is unable to get rid of its rider either.

The simple answers

There are two quick and easy answers to the question as to why a quarter of a century of moderate Zionist rule produced results at such variance with its formal goals. They are popular with the nationalist theoreticians of both sides. On the Arab side it is the everlasting falsehood of the Zionists; on the Israeli side the pathological anti-Israeli hostility of the Arabs. Both are sustained by a grain of truth. Both are false when used as *the* complete explanation of the question at issue.

There is little doubt that within the ranks of the moderate Zionists there were those who preached lofty humanism while never actually meaning what they said. Others simply followed the most powerful leaders. Yet, the bitterness and bloodshed in the intra-Zionist struggle before the 1950s cannot be simply dismissed as personal, or as a factional settling of scores. It reflected the force of the liberal-socialist stand within the leadership and the rank-and-file of the Zionist majority. Even a two-faced declaration would be indicative here, for, as the English say, hypocrisy is a bow to morality; it shows what people believe to be right. It is the true ambivalence of thought (not window dressing but genuine intellectual confusion) which seems particularly relevant here. Too many of the old guard of trusted Zionist supporters and those who followed them have displayed a deep emotional outrage and political opposition since 1967 to have been simply reacting to an essentially known and accepted 'white lie'.

There is little doubt, on the other hand, that the undifferentiated hostility of the Arabs and their fiery rhetoric hampered the compromise-prone or internationalist tendencies in Israel. While constantly cheering and quoting the Israeli critics of Israel, the Arab side could hardly show any ideological equivalents. And what can arouse more suspicion of nationalist double-talk than such double standards? The hostility of the defeated after 1948, and especially the hostility of the Palestinian refugees could be, and at times was, understood by many within Israel. However, in contrast to the consistently nationalist policy, an internationalist or even moderately 'dovish' policy needs a partner. One cannot practise it fully on one's own any more than one can make love singly. For many years not one small Arab group operating in any Arab country was explicitly and consistently universalist in its attitude toward the Israeli Jews, that is, genuinely ready to grant them all that it assumed for itself in terms of national self-expression.[26] Israeli fundamentalists and the mass media have never missed an opportunity to rub this in, together with daily quotations from the destruction-of-Israel rhetoric of the Arab press and Arab leadership. As Brecht once remarked, one becomes a nationalist for a moment by the very fact of meeting a nationalist of the opposite side: stupidity makes those it meets stupid.

Nevertheless, to attribute the nationalist degeneration of Israel mainly to Arab hostility, or Arab chauvinism simply to Zionist cruelty and falsehood, was usually but another means of escape towards the infectious stupidity that Brecht talked about, an only-too-easy moral indignation against the shortcomings of *others*. Nor is it satisfactory simply to point to the 'objectivity' of the vicious circles of nationalist hostility, since behind such supra-human concepts stand people and leaders who decide, choose and act. It was the lack of a consistent and powerful attempt to quell the nationalism of both 'us' and 'them' by the political action of the Zionist 'moderates' which has to be explained. Jewish and Arab chauvinisms have contributed handsomely to the existing situation, but the strength of nationalism and its capacity to impose its positions on the moderates need further analysis. The issue of Arab and Palestinian nationalism and where it leads should be discussed elsewhere and by another person. Here I shall pursue the question 'why?' as it concerns the Israelis, by looking at its elements: Israel's classes, parties, international connections and ideological determination.

Before attempting this, a reference should be made to a mode of analysis which, while in no sense definable as an 'easy answer', shares with such explanations an essential determinism of approach. This mode of analysis assumes that it was inevitable that the very fact of the acceptance of a *Jewish* state (that is, a state 'of' an ethnically defined nation and not simply of its residents and citizens) produced nationalist and repressive policies and predetermined the history of Israel. The point is taken, but as a complete analysis it seems unsatisfactory because of the historical experience. Ethnically defined states (for example, the USA) have been oppressive, but origins marked by extreme nationalism have not necessarily blocked later developments toward universalism. And it is the *direction* of development which is at issue.

The new rulers and the new proles

The degeneration into a fundamentalist world-outlook cannot be explained purely in terms of political ideologies. Thought does not float in the air but is linked with the social structure of power relations. Israel is a new political society and a new state; its class divisions and elites came into being within the last two generations. It is the development and character of the Israeli power elite, its classes and its ethno-classes, that have relegated to the margin some of the basic principles of moderate Zionism, especially its socialist component.

First, there has been the role of the army, its senior officers and defence-related new capitalists. The sudden emergence of explicit and public pressure by army generals and their allies in 1967, their capacity to impose 'their own' Minister of Defence and to force the hand of the Prime Minister as far as war was concerned, was the first time that the previously politically tame military leadership had openly shown its teeth in Israel. The seven-fold increase in value of the production of the defence industries in 1967–73 (inflation made later figures less meaningful) has meant the rapid growth of classes and groups to whom militarisation and occupation were excellent business. The Israeli-wrought changes to the economy of Israel and of the occupied territories and the 'deluxe colonisation' financed by the authorities and increasingly based on Arab labour, have had similar effects. There has been a rapid growth of local millionaires while at the same time well-to-do non-Israeli Jews have increasingly invested capital, stimulated as much by the high profits as by national sentiments and plans for retirement.[27]

In the Israel of pre-Independence and early post-Independence days there was a deep division between the power elite of 'those who serve' and the entrepreneurial top of the middle class – 'those who make money'. By now, the business elite, rapidly increasing its wealth, has acquired a significant social bridge to the political leadership. The linkage is via the increasing number of retired senior army officers taking up management posts in private and public industries, or else moving into politics. By the mid-1970s the numbers of colonels and generals in the reserve reached in all about 3000, of whom about 20 per cent 'went into politics' the others mostly 'accepting posts' or going into business.[28] By now the number would have doubled. The army officers turned politicians or business managers are steeped in military experience, linked by a common past, very Israeli in their appeal to the locally born *sabras* and indeed representative of many of them. This new caucus of 'men of action', rapidly growing into the main establishment 'cadre', has been 'pragmatic' in the sense of sneering at lofty principles and egoistic in its personal and public outlook. To these 'new men' the universalist, and often socialist, principles of moderate Zionism are empty phrases, a rhetoric to be shed painlessly if need be. Their group intuitions are either fundamentalist or opportunist. In the context of post 1967 Israel, both have meant the perpetuation of the existing reality.

With moderate Zionism increasingly turning into a rhetorical mask at the top of the politico-economic pyramid, some have looked for its defence to the 'lower classes' in Israel. The socialist tendency within moderate Zionism could be, and at times was, used as a unifying banner in the fight for social equality, within Israeli Jewry. Yet, such chances became slim as a result of the violent nationalism of the overwhelming majority of the Jewish/ oriental plebian ethno-class, created by the very success of the Zionist enterprise. Arab workers in Israel are excluded as far as any 'unity of the deprived' is concerned, because of the hostility and reluctance of these Jewish proles to make common cause with 'ethnic enemies'. The tens of thousands of Arabs coming daily to work in Israel from the occupied territories, deprived of citizen

rights, underpaid and under the heavy surveillance of the security
service, provide an atomised stratum at the very bottom. Above
both Arab strata, those from Israel and those from the territories,
stand Jewish labourers and small entrepreneurs originating from
Oriental Jewry. While limited in their life-chances, Oriental Jews
are prone (in a manner reminiscent of the poor whites of the South
in the USA and South Africa) to express anti-government opposition through 'rightist' slogans and to define their own identity
through violent anti-Arabism. The few attempts to organise
Oriental Jews on their own and around the issues of socio-
economic inferiority (especially the so-called Black Panthers
movement of the 1970s initiated by children of immigrants from
Morocco) scared the Establishment badly but were contained and
dissipated by small reforms and 'large' nationalist slogans. The
demographic change within Israeli Jewry (with the 'Orientals'
increasing from less than 10 per cent to more than 50 per cent of
the population) has been one of the major reasons for the increase
in the power of the political 'right'. The old-comers who once
organised socialist unions have by now retired or else have been
promoted out of the working class by the influx of new immigrants
or Arabs. They know that they are 'part of it all', even though
often feeling ambivalent towards post-1967 Israel. (It is this constituency, and their families, which provides a major part of the
middle-class non-conformist vote.) Strikes continued, but there
was no related increase in consciousness of the need to relate these
to the moderate Zionist dream, or, for that matter, to any other
programme of structural social change.

Political parties and Trojan horses

The life of political parties of Israel has displayed some specific
characteristics which were of relevance to the issue at hand. These
political parties were never simply voluntary organisations of the
supporters of some particular views. To use the Dutch/Indonesian
term, these have been *aliranes*: vertical organisations which, in
addition to orientating political action, also attempt to satisfy the
institutional needs of their members, through the party bank,
party housing schemes, party contacts and controls in schools,
labour exchange, medical care, and so forth. To belong to a party

involved a reciprocal relationship embracing a range of social and political benefits paid for by an unconditional political loyalty to the party leadership. This was true in particular of the religious Zionist movement and of rural communities. Political constituencies held captive by the party system facilitated the control of non-conformist ideas and doubts. With the process of deradicalisation of the Left, these captive electorates were often led wherever their leaders wanted them to go.[29] It is not accidental that it is the urban middle-class areas of North Tel-Aviv and Jerusalem's Rechavia – that is, the residential areas of the secular and economically more independent better-offs – where most of the liberal and socialist non-conformism survived best.

Also significant has been the characteristics of 'the top' of the political parties, that is, the stratum of professional politicians. The origins of the parties/*aliran* meant that many members joined up for reasons which had little to do with ideology. In the period of statehood, the parties increasingly became coalitions of vocational, ethnic, and other interest groups, led by people to whom politics was just another way to go after personal gain – a line of business. De-ideologisation of the political parties and the barrage from the nationalist news media have weakened the defenders of universalist causes more than their xenophobic counterparts. An important role in the defeat of moderate Zionism was played by the internal take-overs of the Labour parties by their right-wing factions, led by alleged pragmatists, but actual cynics. It was matched by the phenomenon of Trojan horses – Labour leaders breaking ranks and forming more nationalist and careerist parties of little consistency which however, 'opened the gates' of the Zionist Labour camp to its enemies. Peres and Dayan symbolised these two trends and there were many more Pereses and Dayans, large and small.

Israel and the external connections

The life of Israel has been particularly closely related to that of the world at large. Ideologically, the Zionist movement has seen itself as the vanguard of Jews all over the world. As time went by the meaning of the Jewry/Israel connection shifted but its significance remained strong. To American Jews, unconditional support of

Israel (referred to, quite wrongly, as 'Zionism') became a central communalist ideology related to emotions of guilt or anxiety as much as symbols of identity and 'machismo', reinforced by ostracism against any 'internal' offenders of the new faith. To Israel, the financial and political support of American Jewry became increasingly important for the balancing of its defence budgets and for the lobbying support of Israeli foreign policy in the face of its growing international unpopularity. The major change in Israel, felt particularly strongly since 1967, was the shift to the US diaspora from the initial political orientation towards Europe and European Jews, or towards the Third World. It meant new cross-currents which were more conservative and came to assert the duty of Jewish outsiders 'to put their money where their mouth is', rather than to put their lives and careers on the line as in the older days of the European-bound Zionist movement. In addition, Israel's small size, military needs, international ambitions and hostile neighbours made alliances with world powers particularly important. Those self-defined needs of Israeli policy-makers merged with the US post-Vietnam attempt to hand over regional police functions to suitable allies. This 'opening' tied Israelis into the growing significance of US Jewry in US politics and its deepening hostility towards the USSR. The Soviet Union was blamed for supporting 'the Arabs' as much as for the repression inside its own territories of Jewish ethnic identity, itself often Zionist in form. Many of the exploits of the Israeli army and intelligence services in the 1970s carried the unmistakeable characteristic of 'playing to the gallery' of present and future patrons. The problem of autonomy of Jewish and Israeli interests as against those of the global powers was increasingly coming to the fore. So did the possible diversity of goals between Israeli policies, that of its patrons, and those of local Jewish communities. The discovery that the anti-semitic junta of Argentina (supported by the US) was supplied by Israeli weaponry, while Israeli diplomats kept strangely silent about anti-Jewish attacks there, exemplify those tensions.

Concepts, emotions and controls

While governing, moderate Zionism has performed most ineffectually in conditions of major international crisis. To take an example: the 'dovish' Mapam opposed on principle military 'retaliation policies' and territorial aggrandisement; in the decision taken to begin the 1956 war its cabinet ministers were simply side-stepped. Yet, in the following week Mapam declared the war necessary and even managed to put in its bid against retreating from the freshly occupied territories. Many of the other Zionist moderates have done likewise, then and since. Such about-turns were often followed by a shamefaced return to the initial 'moderate' positions at times paradoxically strengthened (for example Uri Avneri and his *Haolam Haze* journal in the 1956 war and after). The impression left was that of people simply swept off their feet. Accepting the strength of the institutional pressures for 'national unity,' an additional major factor appeared within the very idelogical structure of moderate Zionism. When, in the days of upheaval, a *Weltanschauung* of strict overall consistency and easily propagandised simplicity, like that of the extremist Zionist 'monism', confronts an eclectic outlook with contradictory principles and suspending clauses, the simpler outlook proves superior in impact. In particular, it wins with those less versed in and less inclined towards conceptual speculations and ambivalence: farmers and workers, petty clerks and petty politicians, soldiers and generals. Like patches on a fabric, political ambivalence and doubtful ideological bridges, dispensations and somersaults are the first to fail under conditions of high pressure. The 'theory of stages' has been the focus of these ambivalences.

Extreme nationalist solutions have found powerful support in Israel in the institutions of socialisation. These have operated at two levels. The daily schooling in national symbols and national emotions, the spread and partial imposition of religious education and mores, the educational experience of military service – all have deepened and perpetuated nationalist views. The results were evident in the swing to the right of many in politically active youth in Israel.[30] However, to understand the full force of the 'ordinary' socialisation on an otherwise critical population, one must consider a second type of ideological control. For two decades, Israel has been repeatedly swept by emotional upheavals of nationalist hysteria – public rectification campaigns one can say, unleashed by the political leadership, the army command and the mass media. Frequent wars have often, but not exclusively, provided the pretext. Fear of destruction; Jewish blood spilt; Gentiles' eternal hate; only power can secure existence; national unity – these messages have been hammered mercilessly home, conceptually and emotionally. When such a therapeutic brain-storm subsided, the mind was left a neurotic desert of drained emotions. With this went the compulsively repetitive talk about 'politics', the compulsion to switch on the radio every hour to hear the latest news and the hate of symbolic enemies and traitors. And each time this happened a few more of those who previously doubted the pure nationalist gospel and who questioned military solutions, gave in, at least for a time. Some retreated, others hid, still others were fully absorbed into the nationalist fold.

The paradoxes and the future

Our tale began with a double paradox and is to end with a few more of them. It has been said that paradoxes, once recognised, improve vision. One should add that unresolved social paradoxes do not disappear with time but rather become part of a new crop of super-paradoxes and make them harsher. Also, by uncovering contradictions, paradoxes throw light on possible dynamics and on alternative outcomes.

Moderate Zionism, combining a universalist perspective with the nationalist 'suspension' of parts of it, has for generations acted as the dominant ideological formula, self-image and legitimation of Israeli Jewry. After the Second World War, and even more so since 1948, it has also been accepted by Jewish communities around the world. Over the years it gradually lost its initial humanist and radical stimulus. It was not dead and exercised its influence by making some political solutions more acceptable, while limiting and blocking others, and keeping under its spell, consciously or unconsciously, thousands of political activists of undoubted political vigour. All the same, the kernel of genuine moderate Zionism, often unrealistic but sincere, shrunk. The signs of 'the end of ideology', as regards moderate Zionism were strong. Not for nothing, did Israeli youth use the idiom 'to flog Zionism' (*lehárbits tsionut*) to signify the contrast between mumbled preaching and reality. The preferable alternative became a brisk command by the state authority.

Israelis, old and young, who grew up within the norms and

values of moderate Zionism, gradually learned to follow any governmental authority, responding to the ever-repeated call for national unity against the ever-hostile world. Faced with the defeat of an ideology they had lived by, some, especially the elder ones, simply hid from the horrors of a recognition, negating a life span. Others, especially those who went through the social education of the Israeli school and army, 'dropped their dreams', and became 'pragmatic' in the sense of do-your-job-efficiently, look-after-your-family-and-to-hell-with-them, any 'them'. Thoughts about emigration to a softer spot of the world often followed – there are many of them now around the world. At the same time, explicit and outspoken fundamentalism proceeds to make new converts.

Since 1967, the occupation has accentuated it all, reproducing the vicious circles of anti-Palestinian repression, ethnic clashes and chauvinistic self-justifications. Combined with the social and ethnic processes in Israel it resulted, by 1977, in Begin's Government, and in the perspective of fundamental Zionism ruling Israel for generations through the democratic consent of its majority. A chain of local wars against disobedient neighbours was to supplement the internal chauvinism-producing cycle of ideological hegemony. Lebanon was its beginning.

But then, something went wrong with the scenario. The paradoxes of the past within the present caught up with Israel in a moment of strife. At least temporarily, it shifted the political scene and immobilised those who had seen themselves as its new directors and script-writers. It appeared as a set of new super-paradoxes of the future.

First, the leaders of fundamentalist Zionism treated their advance to power and the victories of Israeli arms as a law of nature. Jews were bound to produce victories. The fury of many 'good Jews' over Beirut and the sharp decline in the effectiveness of the army and its further losses staggered them. Severe social, economic and military crises followed a war which was neither lost nor won. Moderate Zionism was back in the running. Spiritless in the government and party opposition, it has shown its teeth in a spontaneous swell of dissenting public opinion – a major blocking force to the government's will. It could not simply be disregarded – too many of its adherents were Israel's best officers, most effective commandos, ablest writers, and most prominent professionals. The fundamentalists came to face the paradox of the Israeli democracy-for-the-Jews. Its universalist ingredient cannot be reduced democratically, at least not for a time. One has to live with it or substitute it with a military dictatorship confronting (and thereby alienating) much of the country's intellectual elite and source of strength. It would also mean, for once, to repress Jews, something at which some of the extreme nationalists would balk.

Second, the parallel paradox of moderate Zionism is that of their own social constructions and analytical inadequacies. It was their policies which shaped Israeli society as it is today: the resentment of Oriental Jews turned underclass in a society of alleged social democracy, the enhancement of religious bigotry, the wars, and the 'vicious circle' of the occupation. Begin's war infuriated and remobilised many of them, enhancing their ability to oppose some of the policies they objected to. But they have little to offer except a return to positions which produced the situation they are fighting. The rise of the moderate Zionist masses checked the war in the north. A moderate Zionist government would change but little.

Those few Israelis who have thought it through, face a third paradox, linked to the others. The only force capable of changing Israel from the inside, and doing so democratically, are the moderate Zionists. It is on them also that the defence of parliamentarianism in Israel and the defence of the Palestinians from a new forced exodus has to depend in the future. Yet the whole history of moderate Zionism's rule and decline shows their weakness. Jewish anti-Zionism tried to drop this baggage of ideological inconsistencies, but it failed time and time again to construct a real political force. In a nationalist perspective, Jewish and Arab nationalism produce each other, blocking internationalism as a view acceptable to large majorities. The broad international perspective in which extra-Israeli forces play their role – the USA, the USSR, Arab states, American Jews, and so on, does not internationalise Middle Eastern cognition. On the contrary, it makes nationalism and particularism harsher and more convincing.

There are only two possible general approaches for those who search for an alternative 'from the inside' to the Israeli status quo. One is to call an end to the 'dispensation', that is, to the theory-of-stages suspension of principles which led moderate Zionism right into the ideological and political house of its fundamentalist adversaries. This would mean trying once more to purify what was universalist and humanist in Zionism and to reclaim the Zionist banner from the hands of the overwhelmingly Zionist majority of today. The chances for this alternative do not look good. A basic problem remains within any honest and thus mericiless self-analysis of the type required. What would prevent such an opposition from sliding into nationalism in the same way that its left-Zionist predecessors did? That second possibility is to cut loose from an ideology which facilitated moderate Zionism's surrender of its long-term programme and to build up a consistent world outlook(s) and political programme(s) and movement(s) based on universalist principles, to face on equal ground the ideological and political consistency of extremist nationalism. The moral collapse of Soviet communism, its Great Power politics, has blocked for the Israeli majority and especially its youth the simple solution of turning in this direction for the answer (as was often enough done before the 1960s). A non-Zionist solution for Israeli Jewry, capable of laying foundations for 'a new majority', will have to be more original. This perspective is again not very promising. Any attempts to challenge the nationalism which now reigns supreme will encounter the high suppressive efficiency of the Israeli establishment, which can count on the massive support of the majority in Israel. An anti-nationalist challenge will have to face the vicious circles in which outbursts of Jewish and Palestinian nationalism again and again reinforce each other. It will be as short of people and resources as of concepts and ideas.

What happens when political and social paradoxes coalesce into situations where all alternatives seem no longer realistic? In the first place – nothing happens. The status quo proceeds, its contradictions may worsen, but its powers of compulsion and corruption are sufficient to keep it going all the same. Of those who oppose it, large numbers retreat into private worlds. In the longer term, slow, deep and implicit processes proceed and eventually break the surface, and then the unexpected takes its turn. The fundamental rules of the game change, shaping new worlds and opening up possibilities of new solutions. But these new scenes are built out existing human and ideological materials and understandings. In that sense, the nature of Zionism and the fundamental division in it – the entrenched collective cognition of Israeli Jews – will be central to those futures.

254   *The Zionisms of Israel*

Notes and References

1. This chapter is based on an early version published as 'The Price of
   Suspension', in U. Davis, A. Mack and N. Yuval-Davis, *Israel and the
   Palestinians* (London: Ithaca Press, 1975). The considerable changes
   introduced represent another decade of experience, and some new
   conclusions.
2. The relevant sources are too numerous to be quoted in full. To name
   a few of the most significant (all of which will be of importance insofar
   as the next paragraph is concerned): W. Laqueur, *A History of
   Zionism* (London, 1972); I. Cohen, *A Short History of Zionism*
   (London, 1951); N. Lucas, *The Modern History of Israel* (London
   1974); S. Avineri, *The Making of Modern Zionism* (New York, 1982).
   And more critical of Zionism, M. Selzer, *Zionism Reconsidered* (New
   York, 1950); A. Buber, *The Other Israel* (New York, 1972); I. Ilam,
   Introduction to a Different History of Zionism (Hebrew) (Ramat Gan,
   1973); N. Chomsky, *Peace in the Middle East* (New York, 1974).
3. Laqueur, *History of Zionism*, ch. 6; Lucas, *Modern History of Israel*,
   ch. 3; Avineri, *Making of Modern Zionism* pts 13, 14, 15. Also P.
   Merchav, *A Short History of the Israeli Labour Movement* (Hebrew)
   (Marchavia, 1967), chs B, C and D.
4. Laqueur, *History of Zionism* chs 5 to 9; Ilam, *Introduction to a
   Different History*; Chomsky, *Peace in the Middle East* Introduction.
   Also J. B. Schachtman *et al.*, *History of the Revisionist Movement*
   (Tel-Aviv, 1970).
5. Laqueur, *History of Zionism*, p. 447.
6. Cohen, *Short History of Zionism*, pp. 254–9.
7. Schachtman *et al.*, *Revisionist Movement*, especially pp. 18, 39–41,
   220–3; Laqueur, *History of Zionism*, ch. 7.
8. Ilam, *Introduction to a Different History*, p. 99; Laqueur, *History of
   Zionism*, pp. 356, 515; Schatman *et al.*, *Revisionist Movement*,
   p. 281. To quote a declaration by Ben Gurion at the time: 'We do not
   want the Arabs to sacrifice Eretz Israel. The Arabs of Eretz Israel will
   not be victims of Zionist fulfillment. To our understanding of what
   Zionism is about we do not want and we cannot build here our life on
   account of the Arabs' (Ilam, *Introduction to a Different History*,
   p. 63).
9. S. H. Sankovsky, *A Short History of Zionism* (New York, 1947), pp.
   153–9; E. Luttwak *et al.*, *The Israeli Army* (London, 1975), pp. 12 and
   13; T. Lamm, *Zionism's Path from Realism to Autism* (Jerusalem,
   1974); Lucas, *Modern History of Israel*, p. 178.
10. Laqueur, *History of Zionism*, pp. 530–47; Ilam, *Introduction to a
    Different History*, pp. 136, 149.
11. Cohen, *Short History of Zionism*, p. 262.
12. For example, Schachtman *et al.*, *Revisionist Movement*, p. 331.
13. Ibid., p. 184, Also pp. 182, 212–14, 329.
14. Lucas, *Modern History of Israel* pp. 214–21.

15. J. de Raynier, *A Jerusalem Un Drapeau Flottait sur la Ligne de Feu* (Neuchatal, 1950), pp. 69–74. Also a declaration of the Haganah commander of Jerusalem in *Davar*, 12.4.48. For the *Altalena* affair, see Luttwak, *The Israeli Army*, p. 38.
16. Introduced as emergency regulation 1949 and made law in March 1950, see S. Jiryis, *Arabs in Israel* (Hebrew) (Tel-Aviv, 1966), ch. 2, especially pp. 62–7.
17. Ibid. pp. 67–80, especially section 125 of the mandatory Emergency Regulation (Defence) 1945.
18. *Reports on the Legal Structure, Activities, Assets, Income and Liabilities of the Keren Kaiemet Leisrael* (Jerusalem, 1973), pp. 6, 18, 49, 56–7. For exemplification, see the legal proceedings against the Jewish farmers subletting land to the Arab peasant, for example, *Haaretz* 5.11.71 (see also n. 30).
19. Jiryis, *Arabs in Israel*, pp. 117–21.
20. See Sharett's diaries for 1955, *Maariv* of 14.6.74, 28.6.74, 5.7.74, 12.7.74, especially the records of 11.4.55 and 7.8.55. For a short political history of the moderate trend from Weizmann via Sharett to Eshkol, see Lamm, *Zionism's Path*.
21. *Haaretz* editorial on 8.7.73.
22. The Israeli press had documented it all (for example, ibid. 10.3.75 and 13.8.73 for takeover of the Rafah lands and the use of the labour and its ex-owners by the new settlers).
23. *Yediot Ahronot*, 20.6.72.
24. Ibid., 16.9.1973. In view of the highly propagandised, in Europe, declarations of moderation by the Labour Party leaders those facts should be kept in mind.
25. See his excellent description and critique of the spirit of the military elation in 'The Non-Jewish Jew', Selzer, op. cit. pp. 73–86.
26. The one such case since the 1950s seemed to come in the 1970s in the declaration of the Palestinian Community Party. Quoted after *Bemaavak*, February 1974.
27. See 'The Secret of Polak', *Haaretz*, 21 June 1974, as exemplifying the success story of an entreprenuer who left Chile because of the 'Reds' and now makes high profits in Israel employing under-paid Arab labour from the occupied territories. Also a PhD thesis by J. Yatziv at the Department of Sociology, Hebrew University, discussing the land deals at the occupied territories and so on.
28. A. Kapeliuk, 'Generals in Demand', *Le Monde/Guardian Weekly*, 6 November 1973.
29. See P.Y. Medding, *Mapai in Israel* (Cambridge 1972) who related depoliticisation of the Labour Party membership to its social characteristics.
30. Lamm, op. cit.; Chomsky, op. cit.

Index

257